Dual-Career Families

*Contemporary Organizational
and Counseling Issues*

Uma Sekaran

Dual-Career Families

Jossey-Bass Publishers

San Francisco   •   London   •   1986

DUAL-CAREER FAMILIES
Contemporary Organizational and Counseling Issues
   by Uma Sekaran

Copyright © 1986 by: Jossey-Bass Inc., Publishers
                       433 California Street
                       San Francisco, California 94104
                              &
                       Jossey-Bass Limited
                       28 Banner Street
                       London EC1Y 8QE

Library of Congress Cataloging-in-Publication Data

Sekaran, Uma.
   Dual-career families.

   (A Joint publication in the Jossey-Bass social and
behavioral science series and the Jossey-Bass management
series)
   Bibliography: p. 227
   Includes index.
   1. Dual-career families—United States. 2. Married
people—Employment—United States. 3. Work and family—
United States. I. Title. II. Series: Jossey-Bass social
and behavioral science series. III. Series: Jossey-Bass
management series.
HQ536.S42   1986   306.8'7   86-15206
ISBN 1-55542-005-2

Manufactured in the United States of America

The paper in this book meets the guidelines for
permanence and durability of the Committee on
Production Guidelines for Book Longevity of the
Council on Library Resources.

JACKET DESIGN BY WILLI BAUM

FIRST EDITION

Code 8629

A joint publication in
The Jossey-Bass
Social and Behavioral Science Series
and
The Jossey-Bass Management Series

To Usha and Ramesh —
the exemplary dual-career couple

Preface

Dual-career families: For some, this recent societal phenomenon conjures up the image of couples rolling in wealth, wielding power, experiencing glory, and leading a life of happiness beyond the wildest dreams of the vast majority of the working population. For others, the concept evokes the dismal picture of a society in which stable marriages are relatively rare, the number of children abysmally dwindling, and organizational performance compromised due to the absence of nurturant full-time homemakers who provide emotional support and rejuvenation for the weary professionals after a day's hard work. Neither vision captures the reality of the dynamics in dual-career families. Dual-career couples currently remain an enigma not only to society but also to organizations.

The number of dual-career couples has increased from 900 thousand in 1960 to 3.3 million in 1983 (Conference Board, 1985)—an increase of 267 percent over a twenty-three-year period (averaging an increase of 11.6 percent of the 1960 count each year). The rate of increase can be expected to be much greater in the near future because of the numbers of women currently preparing themselves for professional careers in the various universities and training centers across the country. The dual-career phenomenon is here to stay, and the sooner top management, organization development consultants, personnel directors, and the shapers of organizations at all levels come to grips with it, the easier the adjustment process will be.

My research and that of several other scholars is helping to form a comprehensive portrait of this emerging sector of the work force, a portrait whose value to organizations, counselors, and researchers is steadily increasing. *Dual-Career Families* describes the critical, practical and emotional dilemmas that couples face and discusses the nature of tensions and stresses that they experience in an attempt to provide a kaleidoscopic perspective for managers and counselors and to focus on ways of maximizing benefits for all sectors of society. With a clear understanding of the dilemmas and problems that dual-career couples experience, institutions can design innovative organizational systems that will accommodate the changing work force and help organizational members be more productive. Such innovation now will avoid future financial losses from high rates of employee turnover, absenteeism, work alienation, increased training costs, and lost opportunities to take advantage of technological gains because of a work force constantly in flux. Dual-career couples will enjoy working for organizations that understand and can respond to their needs and concerns. The quality of life in our society will be enhanced if the family system can be preserved intact even as individual family members increase their ability to avail themselves of opportunities for self-actualization.

Dual-Career Families: Contemporary Organizational and Counseling Issues has, as its title suggests, the twin major objectives of (1) alerting organizations to the dangers of ignoring the phenomenal growth of dual-career spouses in the workplace and proposing a proactive course of action to be initiated by them at this stage, and (2) providing counselors with a systemic perspective on the intricacies and complexities involved when two spouses attempt to prioritize, balance, and maintain the integrity of two careers and a family. Though focused mainly on dual-career families, many of the issues and concerns discussed here are common to all nontraditional families, and hence, many of the recommendations made in the book would also benefit most nontraditional family members.

Two other audiences will also be interested in the book—

dual-career spouses themselves and researchers. No doubt, there will be a major overlap in the audiences for this book, since a large proportion of managers, counselors, and researchers are themselves members of dual-career families.

That counselors are increasingly sought after by dual-career spouses is dramatized by Toufexis (1985a) in the *Time* magazine article titled "The Perils of Dual-Careers: Married Couples Who Work Are Crowding Therapists' Offices." Counselors can effectively help spouses only if they fully understand the whole range of issues faced by the couples and are thus able to adopt a systemic approach to therapy. Counselors both inside and outside organizations can enhance their effectiveness by being sensitive to the comprehensive range of issues confronting dual-career couples. Organizational and societal architects can also be encouraged to create facilitating social structures for these couples only when they know what structural and procedural changes will help dual-career members. This book aims at clarifying these issues. Finally, since findings from several hundred published studies have been integrated into this book and fruitful directions for further research are discussed in the last chapter, I expect that researchers will be stimulated to advance investigations in this important area.

Overview of the Contents

The first three chapters focus primarily on the nonwork aspects of dual-career couples' lives, highlighting the stresses as well as the rewards that the spouses experience. In the first chapter, I define the term *dual-career families,* draw distinctions between dual-career and dual-earner families, and present a profile of the current generation of dual-career husbands and wives. The five major dilemmas of role overload, role cycling, identity establishment, social network, and environmental sanctions that all dual-career couples experience to one extent or another and the stresses these engender are then discussed. Chapter Two explores the work, family, and personal worlds of the spouses and the overlaps among these three facets of their lives. Asymmetries in the spillovers from the work sphere to the family sphere for the husband and the wife are explored, and the effects of these on the unequal division of household work and parenting responsibilities and the resultant feelings of competition and frustration experienced by the spouses are examined. Useful stress management techniques are then described. In Chapter Three, I discuss the quality of life in dual-career families using the results of my empirical research. Based on the central life interest and sex-role orientations of the two partners, I develop a typology of couples that illustrates which couples are most likely to experience a very high and which a very low quality of life. I use this typology to speculate on the reasons for possible inconsistencies in some previous research findings. An important message in this chapter is the critical need for families to define what success means to them individually and as a family.

Chapter Four focuses on the issues of primary concern to dual-career spouses during their five life-cycle stages: the prelaunching stage, the young married stage, young parenthood, mature parenthood, and the preretirement stage. For each stage, I offer suggestions for mitigating the experienced stresses through various problem-solving techniques that provide options for enhancing the quality of life.

To a certain extent, dual-career spouses have to bear a direct responsibility for their chosen life-style, but the environment in which they operate has to be friendly if they are to be productive at work. Since work is a significant part of dual-career family members' lives, the next three chapters focus on what organizations can do to improve the work environment for these families and how these improvements will benefit the organizations by increasing organizational effectiveness. Chapter Five emphasizes the need for organizations to proactively deal with the changing composition of the work force—especially the surging numbers of dual-career spouses—and with the challenges this phenomenon poses for management. Using a cost-benefit analysis, I explain the advantages of utilizing dual-career professionals' talents and the price that organizations pay for ignoring their special needs. This chapter also explores other reasons for organizations to modify their structure and processes. These reasons include the changing values of organizational members, the expanded definition of careers, the different ways in which excellence is conceptualized, the shifting attitudes toward upward mobility, sex-role tensions at the workplace, obsolete hiring practices, as well as the new dimension of corporate responsibility—preserving the family as a viable social unit.

In Chapter Six, I use an input-throughput-output model to examine organizational effectiveness and describe current organizational hiring practices. I then discuss the changes that would be necessary in the advertising and interviewing procedures for organizations to attract and retain the most productive members from among the increasing number of dual-career members entering the labor market. Chapter Seven discusses the six steps in the throughput stage: socializing members, creating alternative work patterns, training and mentoring, developing parenting policies, designing career paths, and counseling. I discuss current organizational practices, recommend changes, and evaluate what organizations have accomplished so far. I highlight the need for enlarging the scope of current employee-assistance and counseling programs in organizations.

Some issues and problems emanating from the dual-career life-style may require counseling outside the work setting. The next two chapters are particularly addressed to counselors and provide a framework for holistic counseling. In Chapter Eight, I discuss the counseling needs of dual-career families at all five stages of their lives. The issues examined in Chapter Four are here explored from a counselor's perspective. Chapter Nine addresses the undercurrents in the family from a systemic perspective using the five major dilemmas as the basic framework. The counseling techniques used by therapists are cited and a note of caution concerning counselors' own sex-role biases is made.

In Chapter Ten I discuss the future of dual-career families; trace the likely trends in value shifts in the family system, organizations, and society as they relate to the dual-career family phenomenon; and indicate directions for future research on dual-career families.

Acknowledgments

Writing this book has been a pleasure and a challenge. My most sincere thanks go to each and every one of the dual-career spouses who voluntarily participated in my survey. But without the many graduate assistants who procured references, collected data, and tabulated the results of my ongoing analysis during the last seven years, my work would have been extremely difficult. I wish to particularly recognize and sincerely thank Julie Garrett, William Brand, Catherine Pierson, Pattie Veech, Usha Sekar, and Rukmani Das for helping me extensively in data collection. Lynne Jones, the mother of two small children, cheerfully worked on the computer from her home, subjecting the data to extensive analyses and tabulating the results. Sara Jayaram and Claire Mullins prepared summaries of several studies that were used in my research and are referenced in this book.

Words are inadequate to express my special appreciation to my excellent colleague and dear friend Coral R. Snodgrass for patiently reviewing the first and second drafts of the manuscripts for this book and offering plentiful suggestions that substantially improved its organization. Vicki Krantz, a senior vice-president of Central Savings and Loan, offered critical comments that helped to substantially improve the content of this book. I most sincerely and deeply acknowledge her help. The bibliography was typed by Donna Reynolds, who painstakingly corrected and updated it from time to time without a murmur of complaint. To such a pleasant helper and friend goes my deep appreciation.

I could not have ventured into this area of investigation without the initial grant provided by Southern Illinois University at Carbondale to print questionnaires, make periodic trips to Saint Louis to negotiate with organizations and collect data, and secure the aid of two graduate assistants. To this institution I owe a debt of gratitude. Finally, I am privileged to be in a marriage in which both my husband and I can be whatever we want to be. This book is in no small measure an outcome of the healthy facilitating processes that operate in our marriage.

I would be remiss if I did not publicly acknowledge the

very professional way in which the staff of Jossey-Bass Publishers interacted with me from the time I submitted the book proposal until the time of its publication. Prompt attention, quick responses, and helpful comments and suggestions from the editors added immensely to my joy in writing this book.

Carbondale, Illinois   Uma Sekaran
August 1986

Contents

The Author

Uma Sekaran is professor and chairperson of the department of management at Southern Illinois University in Carbondale. She received her M.B.A. degree from the University of Connecticut at Storrs (1974) and her Ph.D. degree in management with an emphasis in the behavioral sciences from the University of California at Los Angeles (1977).

Sekaran conducts research primarily in the areas of international management and dual-career families and their implications for organizations. The National Academy of Management has honored her with Best Paper Awards for her work. She is the author of two textbooks, *Research Methods for Managers: A Skill-Building Approach* (1984) and *Managing Organizational Behavior for Effective Performance* (in press). She is coeditor of *Leadership: Beyond Establishment Views,* with Jerry Hunt and Chester Schriesheim. Sekaran was invited to be a member of the Focus Session of the Commission on Work and Family Linkages at the American Association for Counseling and Development Convention in Los Angeles in April 1986.

Sekaran has been a visiting professor at the Indian Institute of Technology in Madras, India, and was a part-time lecturer at the Staff Training College for Bankers in Bombay. Prior to coming to the United States, Sekaran was a banker in India for nineteen years and brings extensive business and banking experience to her teaching and research.

Dual-Career Families

*Contemporary Organizational
and Counseling Issues*

ONE

Portrait of the Dual-Career Family

Dual-career couples and the concept of the dual-career family evoke powerful responses in a wide cross section of the population in this country. This is understandable, since dual careers have far-reaching implications not only for the members of such families but also for the organizations that employ them, the counselors who advise them within and outside the workplace, and the society in which they live. Dual-career couples, most of whom are proud of their life-styles, still constantly seek and hungrily look for innovative techniques to cope with the exciting but highly demanding and tension-provoking facets of their lives. Their employing organizations watch the development and growth of this phenomenon and its possible influence on business and industry, wondering how they themselves might be affected in the future by the increasing number of dual-career family members in the work force. As of now, however, most organizations do not even know how many of their staff are from dual-career families, and so they are scarcely prepared to cope with the unique problems of such employees. However, organizations are beginning to recognize that they should have a better understanding of the dual-career phenomenon and hence are eager to learn more about dual-career family professionals.

Counselors, whether entering into helping relationships within an organizational setting or outside of it as family therapists, marriage counselors, or vocational guidance specialists, now have a new range of issues to deal with as the number of nontraditional families increases. Indeed, they must sometimes find themselves at a loss to help dual-career spouses who have

1

voluntarily chosen to lead a complex life-style but find themselves confronted with a bewildering and unmanageable array of problems at the mental, physical, and emotional levels. Our society is also left wondering about the short-run effects and long-range implications of dual-career families. Increasing numbers of articles appear in national newspapers, journals, and magazines about the various problems and prospects that face the dual-career family. Even the television networks air programs that highlight the major issues central to the life-styles of dual-career families. Perhaps no other single social change since the industrial revolution has touched such a vibrant chord in so many sectors of society as the dual-career family phenomenon has!

What are currently referred to as nontraditional families —that is, families in which both husbands and wives are gainfully employed outside of the home—will cease to be viewed as nontraditional a decade from now as increasing numbers of families become two-paycheck households. It has been conjectured that families in which the mother is a full-time homemaker, the father is the single provider, and the children in the family are at school will constitute as low as 7 percent of all American families by the end of the 1980s (Young, 1980). It is an undisputed fact that the number of dual-career families is steadily increasing and will rise dramatically in the near future, given the vast number of prospective dual-career family members who are currently undergoing professional training in colleges, universities, and other training centers all over the United States.

In pursuing their life-style, dual-career spouses experience many frustrations. Most of these frustrations stem from conflicts with the culturally normed, traditional patterns of behavior followed by organizations and the persons they employ. Numerous problems, dilemmas, and stresses are experienced by nontraditional couples as they desperately try to shape their lives into meaningful patterns. Their attempts to balance two careers and a family are sometimes unsuccessful, and the marriages of these couples often end in separation or divorce. The divorce rate in families in which wives have had five years or more of college education is greater than that in families in which wives are not so highly educated (Houseknecht and Spanier, 1980). Likewise, it has been shown that the divorce rate in families where the wife is a professional is higher than in the general population (Berman, Sacks, and Lief, 1975). My own research indicates that many dual-career couples do not give any thought to the important issue of what success means to them. Since they do not have clear goals, they have difficulty in purposefully channeling their energies and often become frustrated by their lack of progress.

Nontraditional Families

The term *dual-career family* was coined by Rapoport and Rapoport (1969, 1971a), pioneers and founding architects of dual-career family research, to denote the type of family structure in which the husband and wife pursue active careers and a family life simultaneously. Dual-career families are a subset of nontraditional families, that is, families in which both spouses individually pursue work roles for monetary gain while simultaneously maintaining a family life. Such a life-style is in contrast to that of traditional families in which the husband is the sole breadwinner and the wife is the homemaker.

Several types of nontraditional families exist in our society. For instance, gays, lesbians, and unmarried heterosexual partners working and living together constitute nontraditional couples. However, the two basic variant patterns of nontraditional families that I will consider are dual-career couples and dual-earner couples; the primary focus of this book is the dual-career couple.

The distinction between these two kinds of families lies in their approach to the work situation. In the former, both spouses pursue careers (as opposed to jobs). In the latter, one or both partners have jobs that, unlike careers, do not demand a high degree of individual commitment to the work role or constant updating of professional knowledge. Thus, while those who are committed to a career must keep in touch with developments in their professional fields and usually expect to be upwardly or laterally mobile, jobholders do not necessarily have the same built-in goals and opportunities with respect to their work life.

Again, those who pursue careers are likely to ascribe different meanings and values to work and set different goals for pursuing their vocation than those who are jobholders (Lamb, 1982). Rapoport and Rapoport (1976), for instance, stated that while dual-career families tend to emphasize occupation as a primary source of personal fulfillment, dual-earner families may look elsewhere for satisfaction. Others have suggested that those pursuing careers are intent on self-actualization in their work role and those who pursue jobs are more interested in the income that the job brings. Of course, some jobholders may feel committed to their work and dedicate themselves to it, and some who pursue a career may do so purely for the income, status, and recognition that it brings them. Also, despite the importance they place on their careers, many professional wives may not be able to dedicate themselves to their careers because of family and child-rearing responsibilities. A small minority of professional husbands also chooses to prioritize family over career.

The distinction between dual-career families and dual-earner families also gets blurred when spouses currently holding jobs are preparing themselves both educationally and technically to move up in their organizations. For instance, many women and men who are currently pursuing careers entered the job market as jobholders in the sixties and seventies and worked their way up. Thus, a dual-earner family may become transformed into a dual-career family over a period of time.

Various terms are used to refer to dual-earner families: dual-worker families, two-paycheck families, dual-income families, two-job families, and so on. Spouses in dual-earner families may both hold jobs, or one of the partners may hold a job while the other pursues a career.

Members of dual-career families also exhibit variations in their employment patterns. Both spouses may pursue careers in the same or different fields or occupations and in the same or different organizations, or they may even singly or jointly operate their own family enterprise. The term *coordinated couples* refers to families in which the spouses work in allied fields in the same or different organizations (Butler and Paisley, 1980). On the one hand, such families may experience "institutional coordination"; that is, the couple may work for the same organization but in different task areas. On the other hand, they may have "speciality coordination," meaning that they work in the same field but not in the same institution. An example of the former would be a design engineer and a marketing manager who work for the same manufacturing company, and an example of the latter would be two computer technologists, one working for IBM and the other for Apple. Further, there are complementary couples who, though specialized in different areas, complement each other. An example would be an organizational psychologist and a statistician who is researching employee behavioral problems. A coordinated couple could either work together, closely coordinating their professional activities, or they could each work independently and go in different directions. Of course, there are other dual-career families in which the spouses are in totally different fields that are not coordinated in any way. An example would be a gynecologist and a civil engineer.

Five Major Dilemmas

Pursuing a nontraditional life-style may provide its own rewards, but all nontraditional family members experience several dilemmas as they go about their daily lives. Most nontraditional family members must face such problems as finding two jobs in the same area, deciding whether and when to have children, and handling the demands of their jobs, children, parents, house, and friends all at the same time.

To fully understand the dynamics in nontraditional families, we must examine the five major dilemmas faced by all nontraditional couples (Rapoport and Rapoport, 1976; Moen, 1982): (1) the role overload dilemma that results from the several roles taken on by the couple as spouses, parents, jobholders, friends, relatives, and so on; (2) the identity dilemma that is triggered by confusion between acculturated roles and acquired roles; (3) the role-cycling dilemma that marital partners face when they want to have both a family and careers, which may receive different priorities at different stages of life; (4) the social network dilemmas that arise because of the limited free time that the spouses have to interact with others; and (5) the normative dilemmas experienced as a result of environmental sanctions.

Since most of the tensions experienced by spouses are a function of the dilemmas they face, we will be better able to understand what goes on in nontraditional families—especially the dynamics of interactions between dual-career partners—if we can identify the source of their stress. This will offer us ideas on how couples can deal with their problems or be helped to reduce their tensions.

Role Overload Dilemmas. Spouses in nontraditional families have to attend to two major roles—doing their jobs at the workplace and keeping the home in order. Since both spouses work outside of the home, they have to share the responsibility for housework, child care, and so forth. Even if hired domestic help reduces the burden of household chores and child care to some extent, it will not completely eliminate all the family responsibilities and cares of the spouses. A considerable amount of planning, organizing, training, directing, and supervising still has to be handled by the spouses. In families with children, the offspring need a great deal of parental care, love, and emotional support. As the spouses attend to these home duties and responsibilities before and after a day's work outside the home, they experience physical exhaustion and mental stress. More often than not, such excessive strains are more acutely felt by the wives since they take on the major burden of household and child-care responsibilities, as typified in a couple's response to my interview survey (details of the survey are provided in Appendix B). The wife had this to say:

> There don't seem to be enough hours in the day. I am constantly worried about how to complete the project at work within the due date, and carry my work home. But then, when I enter the house, there are several other things waiting for

me. I need to spend some time with the children, make sure that they have their supper, and get them off to bed. Then I have to get things ready for the next day—children's dress, what they need to carry for lunch, and such things. By the time all these get done and the house is quiet, I am too tired to work on my office papers. I go to bed thinking of all the things that remain to be accomplished!

When his turn came, the husband described their household arrangements in this way:

With the two of us working, I pitch in and try to help my wife as much as possible with the housework. Of course, I attend to all the chores outside the house, such as taking care of the yard when it needs to be mowed and cleaning the car. I also help my wife to bathe the kids and wash the dishes. Unless both of us do these things, the work will never get done, and I do not like to walk around a dirty house. I do as much as I can and then relax with a can of beer.

Identity Dilemmas. Spouses in nontraditional families frequently experience internal conflict trying to establish who they are and what they are becoming. The gender-based roles and values internalized by them early in life conflict with the nontraditional roles they are now trying to establish and often create role and identity confusion. For example, a husband who shares household and child-care responsibilities could, at times, doubt his manliness. A wife could similarly agonize over the fact that she is not a good wife and a good mother since she is away from home for the major part of her waking time. This dilemma is captured by what a woman manager said during my interview with her:

I enjoy my work and am really doing very well in my job. Actually, I am expecting to get pro-

moted next year. My only unhappiness is that I
cannot be more with my children and be a "good"
mother to them. I sometimes wonder if the job is
worth sacrificing time with the kids. Once they
grow up, I can never get back these moments and
experiences again.

Role-Cycling Dilemmas. Spouses have to make decisions
about various issues that arise at different stages of their life
cycle. Chief among these are decisions regarding the ideal time
to start a family, how many children to have, and how to space
them. If the spouses want to make progress on the job as well as
raise a family, the timing of the children becomes important. If
they wait too long, the wife might be past the childbearing age
or face health complications; but if they begin raising a family
soon after their marriage, the wife may not be able to return to
her job or career. Even if she can, she may often lose many of
the benefits she has already gained at the workplace, including
the possibility of advancement.

The following thoughts of one middle-aged professional
wife nicely describe the dilemmas of role cycling:

After much discussion, my husband and I finally decided not to have children. When we married fourteen years ago, we thought that I should
first complete my education and get my master's
degree. Then I got a job and was thrilled about it.
At that time, we thought that we should postpone
having a child for five years. We constantly went
back and forth on it because I was already twenty-
six when I started working and I would be thirty-
one by the time I had my first child. But we agreed
that waiting would help us to get established in our
careers and in the family. But then, I got promoted
before the end of the fourth year on my job, and
the new responsibilities involved traveling—I had to
be out of town at least six days in the month.
There is no point trying to raise a child under these

circumstances. The options were either to reject the new assignment or decide not to raise a family. We decided we would adopt a child when we are ready.

Thus dilemmas arise as to when work should take precedence over the family and when the family should take precedence over work. Couples invariably experience stress in trying to arrive at rational answers to these questions.

Social Network Dilemmas. The time available for socializing is extremely limited for nontraditional couples. Such couples have to make conscious and deliberate choices as to who will be included in, and who will be excluded from, their network of close social contacts. Most social interactions tend to be couple based, and the boundaries of the social network tend to include only those with whom the couple interact on a professional basis. Lack of time may force the couple to exclude others to whom either or both of the partners would like to be close, including their relatives. One doctor, asked about her social life, remarked:

> I have very little time for social life. I haven't even visited my cousin who recently had her first baby. At one time we were very close, but now I don't have the time to see her or spend any time with her at all. It feels terrible, and I don't know if she understands how busy I am. I talk to her over the phone sometimes, and that seems to be the best that I am able to do.

Making decisions about who is to be excluded from the family's social circle can be painful, and the aftermath of guilt feelings and internal conflict provoked by the forced choices, along with the anger and resentment of the excluded people, can produce considerable stress and pain for the couple.

Normative Dilemmas or Environmental Sanctions. Although attitudes may now be changing, society in general does not look with favor on nontraditional families and, in fact, sometimes views them with alarm. For instance, society frowns on families that choose not to have children, and this puts pressure on nontraditional families to opt to have children. But then the nontraditional wife gets caught in a bind. When there are children in the family, the wife is expected to personally take on the responsibility for their good behavior, growth, and development, and this means that she will have to subordinate her work role to her family role. If she does not do this, she is not considered to be a good mother. But if she does, she is likely to find it difficult to progress in her career. Moreover, if she does not pursue a work role, she denies herself the chance for self-validation through the kinds of rewards that are derived primarily from the workplace (Davis, 1982).

Thus, the discrepancies that exist between the life-styles that nontraditional spouses would personally prefer and the normative behaviors that are prescribed by society cause dilemmas and psychological stresses for nontraditional families. What one free-lance photographer said in this connection is interesting:

> We are lucky that we live in California and nobody here bothers much about what we do or how we live. My house is always a mess, and I sometimes come home too tired to cook and feed the family. So, we just jump into the car and go out for dinner three or four times a week. My mother sure would not approve of it, but so long as she is in Cleveland and I am here I am safe.

Additional Stresses

In dual-career families, each of the spouses aspires to get actively involved in professional careers that demand intense ego involvement, long hours of work, much stamina, perseverance, tolerance for ambiguity, and psychic energy. Such couples experience acute pressures in trying to manage their work lives and family lives, simultaneously. It is not easy to balance both sets of activities, given the time and energy constraints that the couples face. Moreover, this balancing act calls for a reordering of roles, priorities, and schedules that runs counter to the traditional pattern of gender-based behaviors inculcated in us since birth. When children are born, juggling the activities poses an even more formidable challenge to the spouses as they anxiously aspire to give their best to their careers, their children, and their marriage.

Moreover, since both spouses in dual-career families usually want to advance in their careers, competition and conflict between the spouses arise frequently in these homes. For example, a recent article in *Glamour* magazine (Doudna, 1985) describes the roller-coaster relationship of actress JoBeth Williams with theatrical director John Pasquin. Both were highly competitive professionals. When Williams was offered a role in *Stir Crazy*, however, she began to feel guilty about her success, since Pasquin was fumbling in his career. At the same time, however, she was resentful that she could not enjoy her success. John felt angry and frustrated with his own situation and also felt guilty because he made her feel bad. The early days of her success are said to have been characterized by angry phone calls and tremendous resentment when she went away on location. The situation did not improve until he went into therapy.

In effect, the opportunities, demands, and constraints faced by dual-career couples take on added dimensions of complexity since both spouses are deeply committed to two distinct facets of their lives—a full-time, demanding career to which each is personally and professionally committed, and a wholesome and happy family life to which both are emotionally, psychologically, and perhaps spiritually committed. Added to this are the unique problematic situations encountered by dual-career families with young children, when both spouses have to travel on official duty, when one or both are transferred, or either or both have to be out of town for long periods of time to participate in training programs or for other reasons. Managing both aspects of life to optimize the satisfactions at work and in the home becomes a formidably challenging task. Some families cope with their dual roles fairly well on their own, but most need help and counseling.

Rewards of Dual-Career Couples

One might wonder why families opt for dual-career life-styles given the many stresses and strains the couples face. The fact is that this life-style, despite its agonies, offers numerous rewards as well. The excitement and challenge in this type of marital arrangement generally appear to outweigh the exhaustion, time limitations, and diminished social interactions that the couples experience (Rice, 1979). Despite the dilemmas they face, the couples derive intellectual and psychological benefits from their life-style. In other words, the rewards of being a dual-career family more than compensate for the stresses experienced by the spouses. The compensations and gains come in the form of heightened expressiveness and self-worth, collegial partnership, a sense of competence acquired through successfully solving the challenging problems that arise in families from time to time, and other psychologically enriching experiences.

Expressiveness and Self-Worth. Careers provide opportunities for accomplishment and creativity and offer an avenue for individuals to achieve self-actualization. Career wives in particular experience enhanced self-esteem and self-worth and gain a greater sense of importance and power in the family as they become involved in making family and other financial decisions (Burke and Weir, 1976a; Rapoport and Rapoport, 1976). The husbands in such families feel "special" because they have adopted an unconventional, liberated life-style. Indeed, husbands who do not feel they have lost status because of their reduced importance as the sole provider of income for the family or because of their having to share some of the domestic burdens come to savor the excitement of their life-style and to experience a great amount of life satisfaction. In my interviews with a couple who had been pursuing careers for about eight years, the husband said:

> I am glad my wife has a career. She is a happy woman doing what she wants to do, and I am proud of her. We do a lot of things together, and it

is exciting. I cannot imagine coming home to a
wife who is cooped up all day and does nothing
but nag when I come home from work.

Collegiality. Both husbands and wives in dual-career
families experience a sense of collegiality. Marriage to a professional colleague entails fertile intellectual interactions that make
life exhilarating and provides opportunities for each partner to
play a part in the successful development of the other's career.
It is also quite possible that the quality of the spouses' interactions with each other may rub off on their children, who are exposed to an intellectual, problem-solving environment from
early on in their lives. Collegiality is thus likely to make both
marriage and family interactions stimulating.

Sense of Competence. In dual-career families, spouses
face new challenges from time to time. Resourcefully countering
them gives the partners a feeling of confidence in their own
competence. This sense of competence provides them with even
greater energy and motivation to face the further challenges
that will inevitably come their way. Thus, a revitalizing mecha-
nism is built into these family structures. A professor describing
his experiences said:

> There is never a dull moment in our lives. No
> sooner do we take care of one problem than an-
> other situation arises waiting to be resolved. "If
> things can go wrong, they will." But we seem to be
> able to handle the problems without too much dis-
> location in the family.

Other benefits include greater potential for meaningful
communication between dual-career spouses and a greater sense
of purpose (Epstein, 1971; Hopkins and White, 1978). Marital
satisfaction is also greatly enhanced in families where the wives
pursue careers out of choice and not merely due to economic
necessity (Orden and Bradburn, 1968). There is also evidence to
show that children in such families exhibit pride, independence,
and creativity that enhance their growth and development (Gap-

pa, O'Barr, and St. John-Parsons, 1980; Johnson and Johnson, 1977).

It now becomes understandable why couples choose to lead dual-career family life-styles. Obviously, the spouses view the many psychological rewards and the numerous tangible benefits—a higher standard of living and greater status and prestige—of a two-career family as more than compensating for the exhaustion, time pressures, emotional strains, and diminished social interactions that nontraditional family life entails. The large number of dual-career families who have opted for this life-style are eager to experiment with a way of living that does not offer any guarantees for success but is challenging and adds new dimensions to the couple's life.

Benefits and Stresses of Different Types of Couples

Having discussed some of the stresses and benefits of dual-career couples, let us now compare the experiences of different types of couples. When both partners work in the same area of expertise, they tend to integrate their activities both at the workplace and at home. These coordinated couples also maintain an extensive network of professional contacts. However, such couples also face difficulties. For example, both spouses may not be able to find jobs in the same location, they may not have opportunities to move together if one or both want to move, and each may not be individually recognized for work produced as a couple (Butler and Paisley, 1980; Bryson and Bryson, 1980). Working in different areas of specialization and in different organizations has the advantage of intellectual exchange between the partners in two different areas of expertise, while at the same time minimizing the risk of arousing competitive feelings.

In professional pairs of university professors, the productivity of the husbands has been found to be much greater than that of their wives and that of husbands who are not dual-career family members. The professional wives contributed to the professional as well as the family needs of their husbands, subordinating their own career needs. Not surprisingly, they expressed dissatisfaction with their rate of professional advancement, the amount of interaction they had with their colleagues, the degree of freedom they had to pursue long-term goals, and the differential achievements of the spouses. The wives also stated that they took major responsibility for home management and did not have enough time for professional, avocational, or other domestic activities. However, most of these wives did not indicate that they were necessarily dissatisfied with the current allocation of the home tasks (Bryson and Bryson, 1980; Heckman, Bryson, and Bryson, 1977). Differences in income between the husbands and wives in the university professional pairs were significantly related to the number of children in the home and to the number of responsibilities shared by the husband at home.

Earlier research by Epstein (1971), who studied the lives of professional pairs who were law partners as well as marital partners, indicated that these joint partnerships did not evidence the ideal of equality since the wives played subordinate roles in the law firms. Their work role was only one of the roles they played and came second to their family role in importance. Thus, as law "partners," husbands and wives were not partners in the true sense of the term. The wives, however, had flexible time schedules and did not have to worry about job security, nor did they suffer the indignity of unequal pay for equal work. Thus, they enjoyed some privileges and some drawbacks by being dual-career partners.

We can thus see that there are several advantages and some tensions experienced by professional couples, especially the wives. Members in different types of professional families seem to pattern their structural arrangements and psychologically adjust in different ways. Despite some trade-offs in their careers and the consequent tensions experienced, the spouses still seem to be keen on pursuing the two-career life-style.

A Profile of Dual-Career Family Members

Is it possible to draw a portrait of a dual-career couple? Is one profile emerging or are several different profiles emerging as more and more of the population become part of the two-career phenomenon? Surveys conducted between 1972 and

1985 offer some hints about what the profile has been and how it is changing. Before proceeding further with our discussion of dual-career families, therefore, let us examine the backgrounds from which typical dual-career family spouses come and what attributes successfully established nontraditional family members possess. Such a description will also enable future researchers to trace longitudinal differences in profiles of subsequent generations of dual-career families.

Wives in dual-career families who are by now well established in their careers usually had fathers who were well educated and held managerial or other prestigious jobs; their mothers were educated and had themselves perhaps worked. The wives were also close to their parents. They were usually the eldest or only child of the parents, did not have older brothers, and, if they had siblings, there was a big age gap between them and their siblings. These women were encouraged by their parents, especially by their mothers, to pursue a career. Bebbington (1973), however, found that some dual-career wives had tense relationships with their fathers and that some had been separated from their parents for a long period of time during childhood or had experienced other difficult situations.

According to an article in the *Wall Street Journal,* the father-daughter relationship seems to have changed significantly in the 1980s, and many executive fathers are now actively preparing their daughters for corporate life (Watkins, 1985). They teach their daughters how to analyze company reports, help them plan careers, and recommend sports activities so that the daughters can learn to be competitive and will be exposed to "team dynamics." Some fathers are even urging their daughters to sit in on company meetings. In effect, executive fathers are now grooming their daughters to become executives. Twenty-five years ago, says Rebecca Stafford, president of Chatham College, a women's college in Pittsburgh, many executives sent their daughters to college "so we could talk to our future husbands" (p. 21). James Kemp, an industrial psychologist, notes that the difference in attitudes between now and a generation ago is like the difference between "black and white": "Twenty-five years ago, [executives'] daughters wouldn't have been taken seriously at all in terms of getting counsel for an executive-level position" (p. 21). Apart from mentoring their daughters, the fathers are also now sensitizing them to possible discrimination at the workplace. Thus, there has been a shift in the role of the father from that of caretaker to that of counselor.

Researchers have found successful career wives to be intellectually bright, psychologically masculine, high in achievement motivation, and very goal directed; they also tend to marry late (Allen and Kalish, 1984; Chusmir, 1983; Rapoport and Rapoport, 1976; Stewart and Winter, 1974; Williams and McCullers, 1983). In her study of twenty two-career couples, Holmstrom (1972) found that the wives in her sample were not keen on getting married early, had long courtships, discussed their future careers with prospective husbands, and turned down men who were opposed to women pursuing careers. Sorensen and Winters (1975), who investigated parental influences on women's career development, found that successful career women identified with their mothers, who were themselves employed. These wives were also high on one or more of the following needs: need to establish self-worth through competition, need to accomplish concrete goals, need to know and understand intellectually, and need to avoid relations with the opposite sex.

Wives who pursue careers in engineering, science, and law possess masculine traits such as a willingness to take risks, assertiveness, and self-confidence and have profeminist attitudes (Chusmir, 1983). In other words, they eagerly maintain their feminine identity but are likely to perform much as men do in their jobs. The childhood experience of successful career women include play patterns that are traditionally masculine, and their adolescence was marked by greater unhappiness than was that of more conventional women. They also experienced less coercion from parents to fit traditional female roles (Williams and McCullers, 1983).

The husbands in dual-career families usually did not come from families in which the mothers worked, and as children they were close to their mothers. Many of the husbands continued to retain close ties with their mothers (Bebbington,

1973). The husbands' early experiences at home reflected caring and empathic responses among family members. They grew up in an atmosphere of harmony and social mobility. Such a background probably helped these husbands to be supportive and understanding about their wives' careers later in their lives. Such husbands were also not threatened by the career success of their spouses. On the contrary, they enabled their wives to make career progress by being emotionally supportive, and they derived vicarious pleasure from their progress (Bebbington, 1973; Rapoport and Rapoport, 1976). The husbands in Holmstrom's (1972) sample (in which the wives married only men who agreed that they should continue their careers after marriage) stated that they had given little thought to the issue of their wives pursuing careers before meeting them. After meeting their future wives, however, the men came to think it only natural that their wives would pursue careers after marriage. Data on more recent profiles of husbands in dual-career families are, unfortunately, not available. Even a recent book on men in dual-career families by Gilbert (1985) does not discuss the profiles of the husbands.

Husbands and wives in dual-career families, as compared to spouses in traditional families, have been found to be more inner directed—that is, they act on their own personal value systems in leading their lives rather than being externally oriented and directed by others' expectations and value systems (Huser and Grant, 1978). Compared to traditional couples, these spouses have lower needs for social exchanges or for being included, loved, or controlled by others in their external social and cultural environment (Burke and Weir, 1976b). These inner-directed couples acted out their own nontraditional parts and were very flexible in applying their personal values (Huser and Grant, 1978). Though no other major differences were found in the personality predispositions of husbands in traditional and nontraditional families, the wives in dual-career families said that they had more in common with wives in dual-earner families than with wives in traditional families. Rice (1979) summed it up by stating that spouses in dual-career families had strong needs for achievement, relied on external reward systems such as promotion in careers and the spouse's recognition of their ef-forts, hesitated to make long-term commitments, and protected their self-esteem from dependency needs and fear of failure.

Finally, although spouses often find dual-career life-styles to be highly rewarding, many such families also experience a nearly perpetual state of disequilibrium. Some of these families face discomforting situations as challenges, working out prob-lems and resolving issues on a trial-and-error basis, while others founder and end up in temporary or permanent marital separa-tion.

Understanding the stresses experienced by families and tracing them to the major dilemmas experienced by the couple will help dual-career members to examine their own value sys-tems and reorganize their lives if necessary. It will help organi-zations to assess the need to change their structures and evolve new policies so as to become more effective. Such awareness will also help counselors in their attempts to encourage spouses to work through their dilemmas and feelings of doubt, confu-sion, and guilt. Thus, the dual-career family members them-selves, their employing organizations, and those who guide and counsel them can benefit from an understanding of the dynam-ics that operate in the families and the problems and prospects that the members face.

TWO

Overlap Among Work, Family, and Personal Needs

The scene is Dick and Judy's residence on a Thursday morning at 7:30. Judy has just hung up the phone receiver.

Judy: Dick, the baby-sitter just called to say that she is not feeling well and won't be in today. As I told you last night, I have to make a presentation at the office this morning. You better take John and Lisa to school and call next door to see if Susan will baby-sit Melodie.

Dick: No! I can't do all that. I have a client coming in this morning. You ask Susan to take the kids to school and to take care of the baby. I've been asking you to check on what emergency services are available. Why didn't you?

Judy: Great! Why can't *you* find out what services are available, Dick? I'm busy from the time I get up till I go to bed at night. If you could give up a little bit of your tennis playing, we could get a lot more done in the family.

A two-career family, in contrast to the traditional family, has two principal actors, each of whom has a vested interest in his or her own career as well as in the other partner's career. Both spouses, of course, also desire to lead a family life and to be happy as marital partners. They endeavor to achieve these goals even as each spouse's life space encompasses at least three worlds—the work world, the family world, and the personal or private world. In addition, some members may want to get involved in church, community, or other nonwork activities. The demands, the activities performed, and the people encountered in each of these worlds are varied, complex, and interdependent in nature. As the two spouses involve themselves to a greater or lesser degree in all their different roles and sets of activities, they experience several types of gains and satisfactions, as well as some dissatisfactions and frustrations.

Figure 1 depicts the two main actors of the dual-career family—the husband and the wife—the multiple worlds encompassing the life space of the couple, the several demands placed on them as they enact their various roles, and the satisfactions and frustrations that the couple experiences both as individuals and as marital partners.

Overlaps in the Life Space of Couples

As noted earlier, every spouse in a dual-career family operates in at least three spheres on an ongoing basis—a personal world, an individual work world, and a shared family world. These three worlds are not segregated or compartmentalized units in their lives. On the contrary, they all overlap to a substantial degree.

The private or personal world of the individual is the physical and psychological space that the person retreats to from time to time. This personal world offers the spouse an opportunity to withdraw from the immediate family and work to do whatever he or she wants, such as resting alone for a few moments, exercising, engaging in hobbies, or visiting special friends. This personal world may overlap considerably with the other worlds of the individual, either spatially (if the personal time is taken at home or at work), physically (when there are interruptions from others), or psychologically (when the individual carries the concerns from the other spheres of life into his or her private corner). Thus, the personal or private world is rarely ever a segregated world. For some, the overlap is so great that a personal world scarcely seems to exist.

The work world consists of all aspects of a person's life that are related to his or her career, and the family world includes all aspects associated with his or her spouse and children.

Figure 1. The Multifaceted Dimension of Dual-Career Life.

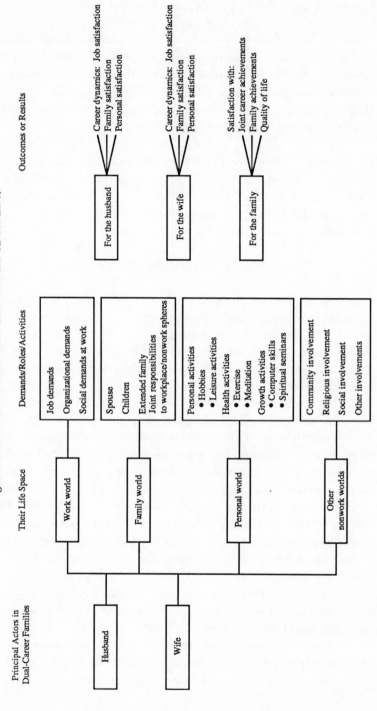

Usually, the workplace is spatially and temporally discrete from the family home, but emotionally, psychologically, and structurally the two overlap considerably. People do not simply shed the feelings, sentiments, and emotions that they have experienced at home once they step into the organizational world in the morning, nor do they cast off the anxieties, tensions, irritations, joys, and satisfactions experienced at the workplace when they return home from work in the evening. Their feelings travel with them and get superimposed on the environment in which they operate. Some of the patterns of family life are also set by the time and travel requirements of organizational systems (Davis, 1982) and by the shifts and schedules that people have to work (Pleck and Staines, 1982; Staines and Pleck, 1984). Thus there is an intrusion of the work organization into the family structure. The extent to which spouses allow spillover between the two worlds influences their behavior patterns—patterns that in turn influence the amount of satisfaction or dissatisfaction that they experience with regard to their careers and family.

It must be emphasized at the start, however, that the spillover between work roles and family roles has distinct gender differences. Although each of the spouses in dual-career families plays several roles, husbands for the major part still identify primarily with the breadwinner role and the wives with the homemaker role. Since the career role is deemed most significant by the husband, he will tend to let the family time and space be intruded upon by work activities. Thus, husbands more often than wives are likely to do office work at home or spend extra hours at the workplace after closing time. Wives who take on primary responsibility for the family role are more likely to allow family matters to intrude into the work sphere, as, for instance, taking care of an emergency at home by leaving the office early. These asymmetrical permeations of the home and work boundaries facilitate the husband's career progress but may cause the wife's career to stagnate. Not surprisingly, this creates tensions in the family (Greenhaus and Beutell, 1985; Holahan and Gilbert, 1979a).

Women with young children (less than twelve years of

age) are most likely to report high spillover from the family to the workplace, in contrast to mothers of older children and to all fathers regardless of the age of the children (Crouter, 1984). Many women professionals, including managers, also think more frequently about matters at home while they are at work than do their male counterparts (Richter, 1985). It appears that as long as society sees child-care and household work as the primary responsibility of women, mothers will allow spillovers from family to work. This will be reflected in such things as their prioritizing family over career and having lower energy levels at work. Both these factors are often construed as indicating women's low commitment to work, an opinion that may not reflect reality. It may often be the case that mothers of small children feel unable to give priority to their work because someone has to take responsibility for the children and husbands are generally not willing to share this responsibility. Thus, these wives may feel they are operating under severe constraints and think that their spouses enjoy the freedom to choose between family and work while they do not.

The asymmetrical permeation of boundaries and the gender differences involved in this process account for significant variations in the career progress of husbands and wives. By coming to understand these asymmetrical boundaries and examining culture's influence on how they get formed and sustained, we will be able to more fully comprehend current household divisions of labor, the parenting roles taken by partners, status inequalities, and competition in the dual-career family setting and the tensions this creates.

Meeting Two Sets of Demands

Consider the following recent headlines in the *Wall Street Journal* and the *Chicago Tribune*: "Working Fathers Feel New Pressure Arising From Child-Rearing Duties" (Wessel, 1984); "Executive Women Find It Difficult to Balance Demands of Job, Home" (Rogan, 1984c); "The Woes of Yuppie Love and Marriage" (Galloway, 1985). The last article describes the time and energy drain experienced by two-paycheck couples who are driven by career success and are too exhausted to enjoy the romantic side of their married life. The NBC television feature "Women, Work, and Babies: Can America Cope?" which was broadcast in March of 1985, highlighted the fact that American married partners might be becoming intimate strangers because of lack of time to be together, exhaustion, and a mismatch between role expectations and actual role behaviors. In the same vein, Rosen (1985) pointed out that even though women think that their careers are just as important as their husbands' and expect equal partnership in marriage, including the sharing of responsibility for child care and housework, reality does not match their lofty expectations and tensions mount in the family.

While different sets of issues produce stress for partners at different stages of their life cycle, the maximum tensions are experienced in families with young children when both partners are at important stages of their careers. If each is to achieve future career progress, both need to be dedicated to their work. However, this becomes difficult because of child-rearing responsibilities. At this stage, two major issues produce tensions for the couples. First, stresses build around the allocation of tasks or division of labor in the house and the sharing of home management responsibility. In nontraditional families, the traditional division of work in the home is not radically altered, and the working mother thus experiences considerable pressure (Edgell, 1980). In the dual-career family, this situation produces even greater tension because both spouses want to fulfill the demands of their careers. Second, competitive feelings may surface in the dual-career family if one partner gets an edge over the other in terms of career progress. We know quite a bit about the tensions experienced by wives in dual-career families. Not very much, however, is known about the nature of the actual stresses experienced by husbands, although their anxieties regarding career success have been surmised.

Division of Household Labor. With the increasing number of homes where both spouses work, it would seem that the roles of men and women should become more symmetrical—that is, men should become more involved in the family and women more involved in the workplace (Young and Willmott, 1973). However, time budget studies indicate that, as of 1976, husbands in two-earner families with children were spending an average of only 2.6 hours daily in family work and wives an average of 4.8 hours (Davis, 1982). Thus, although husbands may have increased the amount of their involvement in household activities, wives still bore the brunt of the responsibility for household work and management. There is also persistence of asymmetrical permeable boundaries between the home and the workplace for husbands and wives, and this also hinders the even distribution of home roles between the spouses (Pleck, 1977).

Why is a more equal sharing of work at home not occurring? The answer is that husbands still identify with the instrumental (breadwinner) role. They ascribe masculine properties to work that legitimizes their bringing work home and using family time for work-related activities. For wives, the permeation of the boundaries continues to be in the reverse direction because they still closely identify with the homemaker's role. For instance, it is the wife who will be late to work or take time off on the day that a child has to be unexpectedly driven to school or taken to the doctor. Since household responsibilities are considered to be feminine and expressive in nature, society expects the wife (who is nurturing and emotionally supportive) rather than the husband to cross over the boundary from the workplace to the family. In fact, there is an expectation that women will not perform well at the workplace because they cannot manage both the home (which is supposed to be their primary responsibility) and their work at the same time (Rosen, Jerdee, and Prestwich, 1975). Thus, cultural norms almost force wives to emphasize the home and husbands the workplace. And because it fosters such distinctive images of the two gender roles, society also perpetuates the gender-based self-identities of men, who at the conscious level might make an attempt to engage in ensuring an egalitarian distribution of the household tasks but then, perhaps at an unconscious level, find an escape through the legitimized route of spending more time at the workplace.

Parenting Roles and Their Effects. Most couples feel that their lives are incomplete without children, and the majority of prospective dual-career wives state that they want a career, a marriage, and a family in their future (Rosen, 1985; Rueschemeyer, 1981). Hence, professional couples do raise families, timing and spacing the birth of their children as best they can. Once the children arrive, however, schedules get disorganized, and even in the best-planned families, contingencies, emergencies, and frequent disruptions are unavoidable. Despite the fact that today's fathers are more involved with their children than their own fathers were with them when they were growing up, the extent of their involvement in child rearing is still minimal. It is the mother who still tends to the colic child in the middle of the night, rushes the baby to the hospital in a crisis situation, or attends PTA meetings. Time budget studies indicate few instances of shared responsibilities for child care in dual-career families (Carlson, 1980; Weingarten, 1978a).

Career women try to cope with the additional responsibilities of child rearing by modifying their work schedules and work commitments until the children grow up. This, no doubt, affects their career progress adversely. Not only does the cultural mandate require and expect such sex-typed behaviors in parenting, but the mother herself may feel guilty about "neglecting" her children during the day when she is at work (Johnson and Johnson, 1980).

Several women with young children in my survey expressed feelings of guilt about not giving enough time and attention to their children. One woman who held a middle-management position said:

> Personally, I find it hard being a mother, housewife, and career person. There are not enough hours in the day to adequately do all three. Being a housewife is not too difficult because I have a maid and my husband helps me too; I don't know how anybody can ever manage without these. But as far as being a mother, I never feel I have spent enough time with my child—never. But I have

talked to mothers who do not work, and they have
the same feelings a lot of times, and so I tell myself, "Now wait a minute, nobody feels they spend
enough time with their kids," and I comfort myself.

Another successful professional woman made the same
kinds of remarks when expressing her feelings of guilt about not
being with her child more as he was growing up.

I keep reminding myself from time to time
that even the traditional housewives do not always
spend all their time with their kids, since either the
kids are at school or the mother is off to a meeting or fund raising or something.

A mother of three children between the ages of seven and eleven
mentioned that by the time she unwinds after the day's work
and supper, the children have all gone off to sleep, and she expressed her unhappiness at not being able to spend much time
with them during the week. Not a single husband made such
comments during the interviews.

To overcome their guilt feelings, many mothers try to
overcompensate by planning a number of different activities
and spending time doing special things for and with the children. Mothers rationalize that the time that is not spent with
the children (quantity) is compensated largely in terms of quality time.

The mothers' overinvolvement and the fathers' under-
involvement with their children are, then, a function of the culturally embedded value systems of both spouses. A side effect
of these culturally normed behaviors is that the children, sens-
ing the lay of the land, generally look to their mothers for help
as they grow up and seldom reach out to their fathers. For instance, it is the mother's work that gets interrupted by phone
calls from the children, while they seldom approach the father
when he is at work. Even in families where the couples are professionally trained psychologists, the sex-role stereotypes with

regard to child rearing still persist (Bryson, Bryson, and John-son, 1978). Growing up in such environments scarcely provides children with models for a gender-free pattern of role behavior.

The overinvolvement of mothers in child rearing has at least two consequences. It drains their energy, and it reduces the amount of satisfaction and well-being that they experience in the family and at work. Working women enjoy less robust mental health than men not simply because they take on an additional number of tasks at home but more importantly be-cause they are overwhelmed by the incessant demands of their children which they constantly try to meet (Gove and Geer-ken, 1977). In the process, the mothers experience excessive fatigue, emotional depletion, and feelings of guilt whenever they cannot meet their children's demands. It is particularly wives with young children who get trapped in the time- and energy-consuming activities of the home and work roles. Both roles may be important to them, but they involve mutually exclusive sets of purposes and goals.

Poloma (1972) found that wives handle the dilemmas of role conflict and motherhood in one of four ways: (1) by ra-tionalizing that they are better mothers because they work and do not overmother their children; (2) by prioritizing the family over work so that the family demands are met without too much internal conflict; (3) by compartmentalizing their work and family lives; and (4) by compromising so that the neces-sary adjustments are made without totally sacrificing any one sphere. More often than not, wives compromise their own ca-reers, subordinating their professional ambitions to those of their husbands, since the latter enjoy greater status, power, and authority by virtue of their higher occupational status and earn-ing capacity (Hall, 1972; Hall and Gordon, 1973).

Role of Status and Power in the Allocation of Tasks. While cultural values play a significant part in how work gets ap-portioned in the family, the dynamics of status and power offer even more interesting insights into the behavior patterns of the spouses. The wife who earns less than her husband and who holds a less prestigious occupational position will often sub-ordinate her personal goals to his. However, the dynamics are different in families in which the wife's education equals or exceeds that of the husband and she earns as much or more than he does. The wives in these families seem to be able to negotiate a more equitable distribution of the household responsibilities and a fairer division of labor (Huber and Spitze, 1981; Maret and Finlay, 1984). As women increase their earnings either through occupational status or by virtue of their superior education, they establish a power base in the family, since success and achievement give them more confidence to exercise power. Husbands in such families even tend to bestow power on their spouses because, to them, a prestigious career wife may be a status symbol (Winter, Stewart, and McClelland, 1977). This acquired power then has a tendency to negate and override the prescribed cultural mandate of male superiority.

Consequently, in families in which wives are in high-status occupations with good pay, they expect and ask for more task-sharing behaviors from their spouses, and their husbands tend to meet these expectations (Bird, Bird, and Scruggs, 1984). When this happens, a more symmetrical distribution of roles becomes possible. However, when wives do not command such positions of power, true egalitarianism does not exist. The husbands might espouse values of equality but seldom match those espousals with appropriate kinds of behavior. For instance, it has been shown that some husbands encourage their wives to resume their careers after the birth of their children but do not in any way facilitate their doing so. As a consequence, the wives have to give up their professional careers (Hawkes, Nicola, and Fish, 1980).

Competition. A further source of stress comes from competitive feelings that may exist between the spouses. It is possible that spouses who are in similar career stages have a need to prove that each is at least as good as the other. However, the cultural imperative that prescribes male superiority in all activities, including cooking (Holmstrom, 1972), puts pressure on husbands to be a step ahead of their wives in their careers. The same cultural imperative forbids a woman to trample on the image of the subordinate wife by forging ahead of the husband (Epstein, 1970). Tension can develop in dual-career families, then, when the wife is successful in her career and advances to a higher position than the husband and earns more than he does.

In my survey, there were at least two wives who deliberately compromised their careers to avoid uncomfortable situations at home. In one of these cases, the wife would have received a significant raise in pay (an additional $30,000 per year) by joining another firm. Her husband, who was interviewed first, was the one who brought up the matter. He said that their family was very close-knit and that his wife, in fact, had turned down a recent offer that would have given her a very substantial increase in pay because it would have hurt the family had she accepted. He explained further that his wife felt she would be not able to spend as much time with the family if she took up the new job since it would be far more demanding than her present one. "It is your decision, I told her. And she chose to reject the new job offer." When his wife was interviewed later the same day, she did not bring up this matter on her own. However, at the very close of the interview, when asked, "What would you do if you were offered a job that would be very attractive to you? Would you be willing to make a move?" her reply was:

> As a matter of fact, I was recently offered a new job that meant a $30,000 annual raise for me. I discussed it with my husband, and I could read the tensions he experienced. He left the decision to me, but he raised so many issues that I knew he was uncomfortable about my new position. I have a good family life, and the $30,000 is not worth it to me to risk family problems.

Some women also feel competitive with their spouses, as in the cases of two wives in my survey who were at the same job level as their husbands. One wife said that she felt competitive since both she and her husband were working for the same organization, and she would not like to be passed over when the time for promotion came and her husband got promoted. "It is not the money that he would earn that would make the differ-

ence," she explained, "it is the feeling that my work is not recognized to be as good as a male's." During the interview with
her husband, when he was asked how he would feel if his wife
got promoted first, he said that it would definitely bother him
in the beginning but that he would soon get over it and be supportive of her career and future goals.

Another wife who held the same position as her husband,
but was paid $2,000 less per year, said that it did bother her that
she was getting paid less for the same job. "It is not the couple
of thousand dollars that really matters one way or another,"
she said, "it is the fact that for the same level of job the company somehow seems to be evaluating me as being less effective.
That makes me feel competitive in a way."

In her sample of dual-career families, Holmstrom (1972)
found that spouses did engage in a competitive race and that
this occurred regardless of profession. Competitive feelings
were aroused in men when they lacked self-assurance, felt inadequate or incompetent in a given area, or felt threatened, regardless of the objective opinions of their actual career progress.
Incidents that triggered competitive feelings included professional acclaim, publicity, and more control over work hours,
more publications, more grants, or a faster rate of success by
one partner than another. Those who harbored feelings of competition always found some basis for comparison even when
they did not work in the same areas as their spouses. Things do
not seem to have changed much since, judged by Doudna's
(1985) account of the competition among couples in various career fields—acting, television broadcasting, politics, and business.

Competition contained within bounds can be healthy,
especially when the spouses work in the same field. Healthy
competition energizes people and could very well increase their
productivity (Nadelson and Nadelson, 1980). However, excessive competition can be unhealthy and dysfunctional. When
both husband and wife consider their careers to be central to
their lives and both are highly productive, the covert and overt
forms of professional competitive instincts could very well
spill over into family areas and make it difficult to maintain
symmetrical relationships within the family (Johnson and John-

son, 1980). The most common mechanisms that wives have adopted to cope with competitive feelings in their husbands are to reject promotions, to try not to be too successful, and to keep a careful watch on how far they can outstrip their husbands without arousing strong competitive feelings.

Many wives, however, resent being put in a position where they are expected to make all the sacrifices. The statistics offered by Hiller and Philliber (1982) pertaining to wives who were pursuing traditionally male occupations—occupations such as engineering, law, medicine, construction, and skilled crafts—make sad and disturbing reading. Compared to families in which the wife's occupational status was lower than the husband's, where the divorce rate was 9 percent and another 9 percent of the wives chose to become downwardly mobile, Hiller and Philliber found that: (1) in families where the wife's occupational status was *higher* than that of the husband, the divorce rate was 15 percent, and 29 percent of the wives chose to become downwardly mobile; (2) in families where the wife's occupational status was *equal* to that of the husband, the divorce rate was 14 percent, and 23 percent of the wives chose to become downwardly mobile.

Stresses Experienced by Spouses

As we have seen, wives experience overload as a result of their household tasks and parenting responsibilities. Apart from the physical stress that these induce, they also produce psychological strain since the wives find themselves unable to devote sufficient time, effort, and attention to their jobs. If they are able to devote the requisite time and energy and become successful in their careers, the wives then become concerned about the competitive feelings that may be aroused in the family, which again are stressful to handle. These statements, though true, must be examined in perspective. The point at issue is not that husbands are to be derided and wives sympathized with. Husbands, more than wives, have to cope with internal and external pressures to prove themselves. For most of the current generation of professional women, pursuing a career is, in itself, a mark of success and achievement, and the pressure to reach the top is not as acutely felt by them as by men. This is clearly demonstrated in Rueschemeyer's (1981) study. Although none of the professional women in her small sample wanted to give up their careers, and many said that their satisfactions were derived from both their career and their family, not one said that her career was more important to her than her family. This, of course, will not continue to be true in the future. The percentage of women who believe that taking care of the home and children is more rewarding than having a career declined from 71 percent in 1971 to 51 percent in 1976 (Beck, 1976) and has probably dropped further since. But even today men, by and large, are more obsessed with career success than women, who have more diversified interests in life. Thus, from a self-identity perspective, the husbands might experience greater psychological stress if required to invest more of their time in family matters.

Men experience other stresses as well. Many wives expect perfectionism from men who participate in home roles, and this adds to men's frustrations and stress (Keith and Schafer, 1980; Parker, Peltier, and Wolleat, 1981). Added to all this, men have to contend with some of the anger that is natural to anyone who undergoes a role change—especially from a higher and privileged role to a less exciting one. The reevaluation of roles, which does not in any case come at their initiative, can be puzzling, confusing, irritating, and frightening to men (*Changing Roles of Women in Industrial Societies,* 1977). Thus, one cannot underestimate the conflicts and stresses that husbands experience in the redistribution of home tasks. The important point, however, is that until both husbands and wives can transcend the old cultural norms and effectively crossover roles without experiencing feelings of discomfort, the current stresses experienced by both partners will not be reduced.

In discussing stress, however, we should also consider the nature of the stress experienced—its magnitude, intensity, and frequency. Most housework results basically in physical stress. This type of stress can be alleviated by using labor-saving devices and hiring help. The home tasks can be shared between the spouses, albeit with some resistance on the part of the men.

However, it is the mental and emotional types of stress that are difficult to share equally, although even they can be minimized through supportive listening and problem solving by both spouses.

Today, when we talk about the strain on women that results from role overload, we miss the point if we consider only the expansion of their roles. What is even more traumatic for today's wife is the number, frequency, and intensity of the various stresses that she faces. She may often feel out of control, entrapped in a vicious cycle of events. Take, for instance, the case of the recently promoted wife who becomes pregnant with an unplanned child, or the wife who has just begun a new job but finds that she has to be with her child who has suddenly taken ill, or the professional who thought that everything was at last under control and is without warning informed that she is being transferred to another city. Consider the same wife being faced with different types of problematic situations intermittently. How can she deal with these stresses? The tables may be turned and, instead of the wife, the husband may face similar or different types of stressful situations. Can the spouses help each other to relieve at least some of these stresses?

Stress Management Models

Building support systems, going beyond egalitarian behaviors to practice equitable behaviors, and evolving different coping strategies are all mechanisms to reduce stress.

Support Systems

Each partner tries to muster his or her strength to handle stress. Support comes from three major sources—from within oneself, from one's spouse, and from significant others in the environment in which one operates. Inner strength and support are derived from a strong sense of the self (self-identity) and from knowing what one's goals are. This kind of support will be discussed more fully in the next chapter.

Enabling. The support that spouses give to each other is

termed *enabling* (Rapoport and Rapoport, 1965). Enabling can take the form of physical help, active listening, emotional support, encouragement, boosting the partner's self-esteem and self-confidence, information sharing, offering guidance, and engaging in collaborative efforts to solve problems and achieve goals. In the dual-career setting, the kind of support that the husband would expect most from the wife is emotional caring, affection, and tenderness. Wives also further their husbands' careers by playing supportive roles that are necessary for some professions, as for example, the dean's wife playing the role of hostess at parties. The wife often serves as the sounding board for ideas that the husband has regarding work issues. Not infrequently, when both are in the same professional field, husband and wife contribute significantly to each other's achievements.

The wife needs a good deal of support from the husband too. For example, she needs active listening, understanding, and emotional and physical support when experiencing stress. It is difficult for a wife to succeed in her professional life while still being happy in her family life unless her husband is understanding and supportive. To put it differently, the educated wife's career-family dilemma cannot be resolved without the husband's support (Bailyn, 1970; Kaley, 1971). As a matter of fact, the married woman with children is likely to experience very little role conflict when she has her husband's support through egalitarian role sharing and her job situation is also favorable (Holahan and Gilbert, 1979b).

Within the context of any marriage, the husband's attitudes must be positive, and his support should be given with enthusiasm if the wife has ambitious career plans and wants to achieve her goals. In fact, Holmstrom (1972), who studied a sample of dual-career couples, found that the husbands were supportive of their wives in every way because they perceived that their wives' aspirations were directed toward serious, life-long goals. These husbands encouraged their wives to work harder so as to keep up with competition at the workplace. They helped their wives with domestic duties and child rearing. They did not set up conflicting demands such as expecting their wives to make career progress while at the same time be attentive to all household details. Of course, the wives had also made sure that they married men who would support their careers.

The husbands who actively enable their wives to achieve their ambitions are those who have the capacity to understand and empathize with their wives' aspirations. Such husbands also usually exhibit a high need for affiliation (as opposed to a need for power and dominance) and have comfortably freed themselves from culturally prescribed masculine roles. Those who are more reflective and intellectually oriented (such as professors and scientists), in contrast to business executives of middle-class background, have been found to engage in more supportive behaviors (Birnbaum, 1975; Winter, Stewart, and McClelland, 1977). Education and occupation also exert influence on the extent to which spouses engage in mutually supportive behaviors (Lopata, Barnewolt, and Norr, 1980). When spouses enable each other to enhance their career prospects, they find great happiness in sharing each other's progress. Thus, each partner psychologically and emotionally invests the self in the other's career development as well as in his or her own development. There is a great deal of togetherness and sharing of work in such families (Rapoport and Rapoport, 1976).

Enabling can encompass other kinds of spousal support systems. A couple can support each other by fostering *interdependence*. Interdependent behaviors reflect a willingness on the part of the spouses to be dependent on each other at times and to be independent of each other at other times (Weingarten, 1978b). Allowing each person to enjoy his or her own private space as and when needed while also remaining supportive of one another calls for a spirit of give-and-take, and such reciprocity reflects supportive behavior. Thus, interdependence is a form of support. By the same token, *separation* can be a form of enabling or support as well (Douvan and Pleck, 1978). Couples at some stages in their careers—for instance, when they start their careers, when either or both are frustrated with their existing careers, or when one seeks a second career—may need to live separately while remaining supportive of each other. Thus, encouraging separation for the sake of careers can also be a form of enabling.

We can thus see that enabling or supportive behaviors come in various forms. Supportive behaviors are most often reported by families in which spouses take on egalitarian roles. In my interview survey, many couples stated that physical and emotional support were the main forms of enabling in their families. A male professional in a business organization, whose wife is a high-ranking public official, made these interesting comments:

> Managing a dual-career family is not easy. You first ought to know what you want to get out of life for both yourself personally and for the family as a whole. I have to manage my own career and be a big support for my wife's. The evenings are sometimes quite exhausting since I have to fetch the children from school, drive my daughter to the dance school, and many times also attend a reception as the spouse of a public official. Of course, my wife does the same for me also at other times. For us, it is always a case of deciding what is more important, which gets priority, and how best to fit all the things into our busy schedules.

His wife, who was interviewed separately the same day, said:

> My husband is very supportive. He is very helpful, flexible, and cooperative. There is no way I could handle my public office without his understanding and encouragement.

Support from the Environment. Spouses—wives in particular—need support from significant others in their environment. The attitudes and opinions of contiguous groups are important to a wife because they serve as guidelines about what she can and cannot do with impunity and validate her own identity and self-worth (Bailyn, 1970). For instance, the opinions of neighbors, of colleagues in her work setting, and of people in her husband's workplace are important to her because she is either directly or indirectly dependent on them for her emotional well-being and effective functioning. A neighbor who disapproves of her going to work and leaving her small baby in the care of a baby-sitter is obviously not one from whom she can seek help in a family emergency situation. If negative comments about her dual role are made by her colleagues, they are already biased against her. Likewise, the husband also needs understanding and support from the workplace when, from time to time, he has to prioritize the family over work demands. Current environmental norms are not conducive to the career success of family-oriented husbands.

Equity

Stresses that arise due to environmental constraints, such as a lack of jobs or the wife's or husband's being unable to pursue his or her career in the same location (for instance, a ski-trainer cannot pursue his or her career in the desert) can be handled through equitable approaches. Equity goes beyond egalitarianism. Egalitarian values exist when both husband and wife see themselves as equals. Sometimes, however, even equality is not enough if both spouses are to attain their career goals, and equity might be the answer. For instance, during the job search stage the family might decide that it will settle in the place where one of the spouses first gets a job. Though egalitarian in principle, the chances of the wife's finding a suitable job first despite having good training and skills may not be bright because of any number of reasons—she may be a professional in a field where the demand is less than the supply (for instance, liberal arts professors at the present time), organizations in certain areas may more readily recruit men than women for certain professional slots, and so forth. Thus, whoever happens to be the less privileged spouse may have to settle for whatever becomes available in the place where the other finds a job first.

It is in this context that the notion of equity—a concept that denotes the situation in which the couple face a fair and equitable set of opportunities and constraints—becomes important (Rapoport and Rapoport, 1976). For instance, the couple applying the notion of equity may decide that the husband will wait until the wife gets a job and then find a job in the place where she starts her career. Here the notion of equality is abandoned for the notion of equity. That is, the couple deliberately build into their decision model a truly viable proposition that favors the wife in the interests of fairness and justice against the inequalities that may exist in the situational context. (This illustration is used to make a point and should not be construed to mean that women are in general less qualified or lack opportunities to find jobs. Both men and women in fields where the number of available professionals outstrips demand may find their opportunities limited.) Equity is not related to gender but to the situation and could work in the interests of either of the spouses or even in the children's interests. For instance, a couple whose child had a disability said in an interview:

> I guess we could have better careers if we moved to the East Coast, but then Jerry [their son], who is still making adjustments here, would be put to great hardship. We have decided that staying here is the best thing to do, at least for now.

In all such instances, where a broader ideal is pursued with justice as the goal and without concern for self-interests, the notion of equity could be said to prevail. Sometimes, however, even when good intentions exist, environmental situations mitigate against the actual practice of equity. For instance, a couple might decide that the husband, who happens to be a professor of English, will first try to land his job and that the family will settle wherever he finds one. But the couple cannot afford to wait endlessly, and sooner or later it will be constrained to settle down where the wife finds an acceptable position, after which the husband may explore his options and career possibilities in that place. Thus, the very same adverse situational factors that equity is expected to resolve sometimes could make it difficult to practice equity.

Other Coping Strategies

The coping behaviors adopted by women who had to manage multiple roles were first systematically examined by Hall (1972), who described three coping strategies—structural role redefinition, personal role redefinition, and reactive role behavior. These concepts are equally applicable to dual-career couples. Briefly, the individual who uses structural role definition, which is a proactive strategy, solves problems by calling on outside assistance, by integrating roles effectively, and by eliminating or adding roles as appropriate. Personal role redefinition involves use of discrimination by the individual regarding how he or she manages roles and ensuring that personal interests are not sacrificed in the process. Reactive role behavior, the least effective of the three strategies, reflects a passive approach to handling role conflict. Couples can handle many of the stresses produced by role conflict through structural or personal role redefinition. (These are more fully discussed in Chapter Four.)

Our examination of the dual-career family as two actors playing various roles that overlap in an asymmetrical manner for husbands and wives provides us with insights into how and why there are disparities in the household division of labor and parenting responsibilities. It also offers us an understanding of how status and power issues play a part in the dynamics of the family and how competition can sometimes become a destructive force in dual-career homes. We further note that most of the tensions experienced in these homes spring from the overload dilemma, the identity dilemma, the role-cycling dilemma, and environmental sanctions. By examining the origin of the tensions, dual-career couples can themselves come to understand why they experience frustrations. They can then discuss the several different ways in which they can manage stress and develop appropriate support systems to manage their lives better.

By recognizing that occupational status, job positions, and earnings make a difference in the egalitarian values practiced in families, organizations can become sensitized to examine their pay and promotion policies to ensure that they are geared to notions of comparable worth. By remembering that: (1) maternal guilt is programmed in women through cultural conditioning, (2) identity dilemmas often prevent equal distribution of domestic responsibilities, (3) power equalization leads to more cooperative behaviors in families, and (4) women's occupational status sometimes becomes a competitive issue that might lead to divorce or frustration, counselors can develop appropriate techniques for helping couples cope with and resolve their problems.

❦❧❦❧

THREE

Quality of Life in Dual-Career Families

The level of overall satisfaction experienced by family members in the various facets of their lives—work, family, and personal spheres—keeps them in good physical and mental health and enables them to function effectively in their daily lives. Even in the best of families, however, it is not possible for the spouses to obtain maximum satisfaction in each and every one of the various roles that they take on, given the constraints of time, energy, and other resources.

The interrole conflicts experienced by family members as they try to juggle the many activities they perform, along with their frustrations while searching for ways in which to deal with these conflicts, also reduce the level of satisfaction that members experience. Because of these several constraints, the spouses try to optimize rather than maximize satisfactions from the various spheres of their lives. To put it differently, the partners try to derive the maximum amount of *total* satisfaction from all facets of their life space by compromising on what seems less important to them. By so doing, they try to achieve as much satisfaction from their lives as possible. This, in turn, enables them to experience good physical and mental health, as reflected in their being able to function effectively and to keep their personal, career, and family lives intact. We can say, then, that the quality of life in a family is ultimately reflected in the physical and mental well-being of its members. Figure 2 depicts the satisfactions experienced by the couple from each of the roles they play, the immediate results that follow, the interrole conflicts they experience, their level of effectiveness in coping

43

Figure 2. Quality of Life Experienced by Dual-Career Couples.

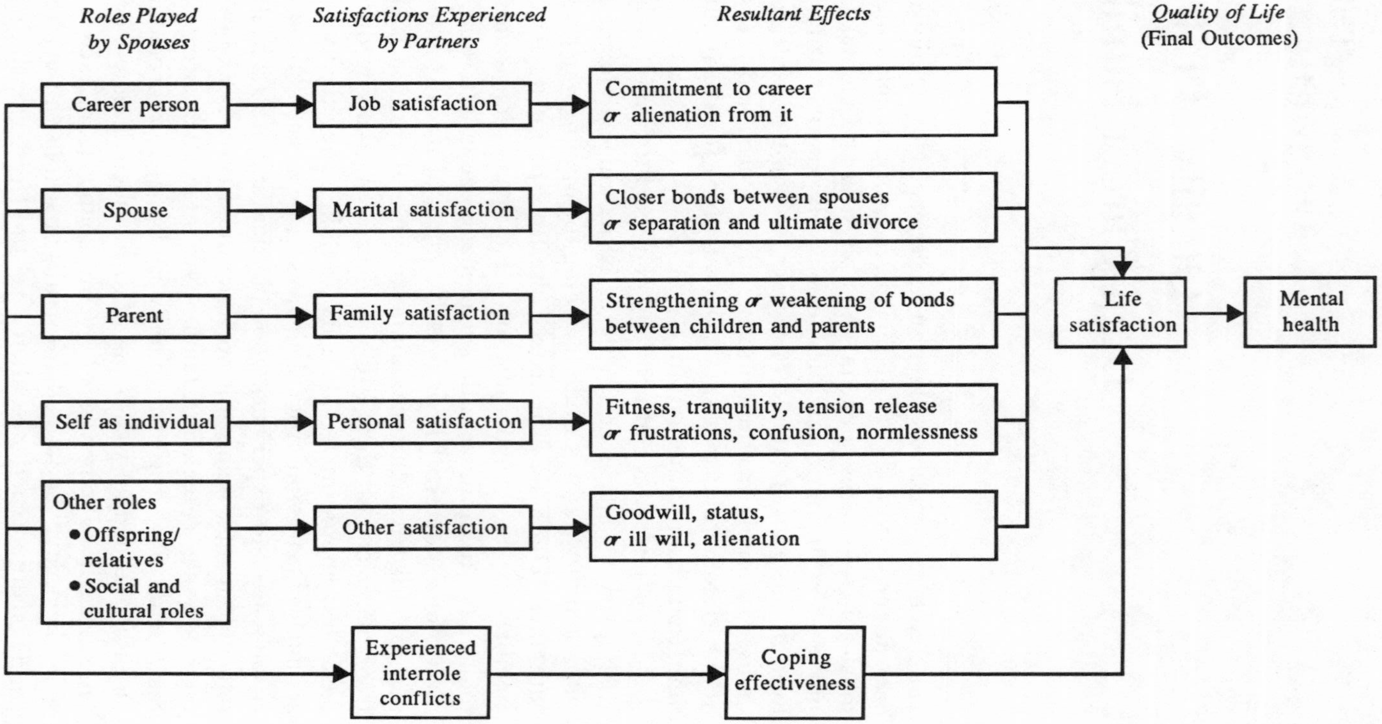

Roles Played by Spouses | Satisfactions Experienced by Partners | Resultant Effects | Quality of Life (Final Outcomes)

Career person → Job satisfaction → Commitment to career *or* alienation from it

Spouse → Marital satisfaction → Closer bonds between spouses *or* separation and ultimate divorce

Parent → Family satisfaction → Strengthening *or* weakening of bonds between children and parents

Self as individual → Personal satisfaction → Fitness, tranquility, tension release *or* frustrations, confusion, normlessness

Other roles
• Offspring/relatives
• Social and cultural roles
→ Other satisfaction → Goodwill, status, *or* ill will, alienation

Life satisfaction → Mental health

Experienced interrole conflicts → Coping effectiveness

with interrole stresses, and their experienced life satisfaction and mental health.

There is a difference in the quality of life experienced by husbands and wives in dual-career families. Professional wives, in general, experience lower levels of mental health (feelings of well-being) than their husbands. In essence, this is because they experience more frustration in simultaneously pursuing careers and maintaining homes with children (Gove and Geerken, 1977; Keith and Schafer, 1980; Sekaran, 1985a). It is not the greater number of roles the wives play that decreases their mental health but the frustration that comes from being unable to commit themselves to their careers as fully as they would like. The compromising coping strategies they have to adopt to handle their interrole conflicts vex them and impair their operating efficiency. The magnitude, intensity, and frequency of stress, as discussed in the previous chapter, also have adverse effects on the experienced well-being of wives. However, wives who experience feelings of success and self-esteem enjoy good mental health (Pines and Kafry, 1981).

In my research on dual-career families (details in Appendix A), I systematically investigated several issues to understand the nuances in the quality of life experienced by spouses (Sekaran, 1982a, 1982b, 1983a, 1983b, 1985a, 1985b). The first step was to find out if husbands and wives attached, at least psychologically, the same degree of importance to their careers (that is, considered careers to be integral parts of their lives) and to determine how they perceived their family and work worlds (that is, did they associate similar or different kinds of feelings and experiences with their family and work settings). The results indicated that both husbands and wives considered their careers to be equally central to their lives. They also mapped the various variables in their lives under four distinct categories: (1) those that were relevant to career enhancement, such as career salience or the importance they attached to work, self-esteem, and confidence in their own work competence; (2) those that helped them to operate effectively in their daily lives, such as supportive behaviors by their spouse, absence of excessive stress, satisfactions derived from the work and nonwork aspects of life, and mental health; (3) those factors that were seen as personal investments yielding some return, as for example, getting very involved in work and working long hours at the workplace and at home in return for more income through merit raises or promotions; and (4) their expectations from their organizations concerning certain facilities, such as day-care centers, and their satisfaction or dissatisfaction with the facilities offered. For a more detailed discussion on this refer to Sekaran (1983b).

Having found that there were few differences between the spouses in their career orientations, I next tried to determine the extent to which work and nonwork factors influenced their job and life satisfactions. The analyses of data yielded interesting results. The similarities between husbands and wives seemed to disappear when the job satisfaction question was examined, inasmuch as the husbands who stayed on the job beyond regular working hours experienced greater job satisfaction than did wives who spent discretionary time (beyond regular working hours) at work. This no doubt reflects the breadwinner identity of the husbands and the wives' concerns for family responsibilities.

The next step was to see whether the mental health of professional wives was indeed lower than that of their husbands and what factors influenced mental health. The results in both cases again indicated significant differences between husbands and wives. The mental health of wives was lower than that of husbands. And whereas husbands derived their sense of well-being from both work and nonwork satisfactions, wives derived their sense of well-being basically from the satisfactions derived from the nonwork spheres of their lives and by experiencing less interrole conflict. This again indicates that career wives value and identify with the nurturing (family) role to experience good mental health. The wives in this sample did not, or could not, place their careers above their families as men did, and hence their mental health was more influenced by how well they discharged their nonwork responsibilities. Thus the evidence again indicates that wives experience greater role conflict than men do and that, as a consequence, their mental health suffers.

Finally, I examined how family members derive their self-identity and self-concept from the work roles that they take on.

Examination of the anchoring of self-concept indicated that husbands derived their self-identity from their work roles irrespective of how capable they perceived themselves to be. The instrumental (breadwinner) role was very much in evidence here. In contrast, wives looked for self-validation through feedback from the workplace that was consistent with their self-image. In other words, if wives thought they were capable and the work environment reinforced their self-perceptions through promotions, merit raises, and other forms of recognition, their self-concept as career persons was heightened. Thus, their image of themselves as career persons seems to need reinforcement through external validation. This is understandable in that women entered the work world fairly recently.

Career wives also seem to be caught in a dilemma of how much time they should allocate to their careers and how much to their domestic activities. The data clearly indicate that when professional wives spend too much time on work-related activities, they are dissatisfied. When they are unable to give enough time to their careers, however, they become vexed and frustrated. These data reflect professional wives' career ambitions and their frustrations at not being able to allocate the necessary time and effort to make rapid career progress.

Thus, the series of analyses provided valuable insights into the quality of life of husbands and wives in dual-career families. All in all, indications are that even though husbands and wives might perceive their careers to be equally important and see their work and family worlds in more or less the same way, the wives encounter impediments in experiencing high levels of satisfaction at the workplace and enjoying a sense of well-being. The quality of life for wives, by and large, seems to get compromised. The results of my study and other recent studies in the area of dual-career families clearly indicate that the dual-career life-style is not trouble free. Why is this so, and what can be done about it?

Defining Success

The quality of life in a family is represented in the psychological success experiences or satisfactions derived by the individual members. Psychological success is derived by different people from different sources. Some derive success and satisfaction from career enhancement, others primarily from facets of the nonwork environment. Hence, if the quality of life experienced by both spouses in the family is to be enhanced, they should know what they want and in some way try to define what success means to them. In other words, they should know what kinds of satisfactions are important to them individually and jointly. The couple will necessarily have to make certain trade-offs, because of limitations of time and physical stamina, to achieve the satisfactions and success experiences that are most valued by them. That is, instead of trying to maximize all the outcomes from both the work and nonwork spheres—a nearly impossible goal for the two-career family—the spouses would aim at optimizing the overall gains and satisfactions derived from all spheres. But to do so, the couple must first decide what outcomes are desirable and what compromises will be made. If spouses are able to agree on the desired outcomes at the individual and family levels and choose the trade-offs carefully, this augurs well for the success of their dual-career life-style.

Satisfaction is a relative term, and *success* is a nebulous concept, both defying a uniform, standard operational definition. Each individual has to define what success means to him or her personally. In dual-career families, since there are two spouses, each of whom is functioning both in an individual capacity and as a partner of the other, successful outcomes take on a certain complexity. Both husband and wife have to individually define what success means to him and her in terms of career, family, personal, and other nonwork needs, and they also have to jointly define what the concept means to them as partners in the family. Unfortunately, there is little evidence to indicate that many families consciously arrive at decisions about how they want to enhance the quality of their lives.

Personality Predispositions

If psychological feelings of success are important for the well-being of dual-career family members, the next question that needs attention is how success gets defined at the individual and family levels in these families. In general, the definition of success is a function of six basic aspects of the person: need patterns, level of personal competence, self-esteem, priorities assigned to the various facets of life, self-concept, and self-identity.

Needs. Individuals have several needs, but there are at least four that manifest themselves in the workplace and in the dual-career home. These are the needs for achievement, affiliation, power or dominance, and autonomy. The part played by these needs in the work setting has been well documented (see, for instance, McClelland, 1965, 1971; Steers and Braunstein, 1976). The significance of these need patterns for dual-career family members has not been extensively explored, though studies are beginning to investigate issues such as power relationships and family dynamics (Winter, Stewart, and McClelland, 1977) and the career aspirations of spouses in families and their effects on job and marital satisfaction (Darley, 1976).

Substantial evidence indicates that these four needs are very important in defining success, both at the workplace and in the family. (To this list we could add another need that has not been explicitly addressed in the dual-career family literature—the need for parenting. The strength of manifestation of this need and the stage in the couple's life when it becomes dominant would definitely influence the family members' definitions of success, both at the individual and family levels.) Though all needs exist in all individuals, the potency or strength of the needs varies. One or more of the needs could be very dominant while others might be dormant. The pattern of needs also changes as the couple moves from one life stage to another.

When the need for achievement—the urge to achieve, accomplish, and be recognized—is very strong, the individual will define success primarily in terms of career accomplishments, recognition, and advancement. He or she will seek challenges and additional responsibilities on the job and will be very keen on performing well and getting positively evaluated. Where need for affiliation—the desire to be in the midst of people who are supportive and loving—is potent, the individual will seek satisfaction in life through gratifying interactions with others, whether they are colleagues at the workplace, members of the family, or friends in the community, church, or other social settings.

When the need for power is predominant, however, individuals will tend to take charge of the situations they find themselves in and exercise control over their environment. Such people may or may not be sensitive to the feelings of others around them. Their definition of success would encompass acquiring powerful leadership positions and taking on dominant roles in all the situations in which they find themselves. Those high in need for autonomy would not want to be, and tend to resist being, constantly instructed, watched, controlled, supervised, and restricted or curtailed in any way. Such individuals are likely to define success as being able to establish their freedom and operate effectively on their own without being subjected to behavior controls at the workplace or in the home.

Personal Competence. Personal competence, which denotes feelings of confidence in one's general abilities, interacts with the need patterns of individuals and influences their level of aspiration and goal achievement. Both the level of aspiration and the perceived level of competence influence how people define success. For instance, an individual who does not have a high degree of personal competence but is high in need for achievement might include in the personal definition of success the goal of reaching the position of vice-president in twenty years' time. Another person who experiences a high level of personal competence might define success as reaching the same position in seven years. Thus, definitions of success derive from both the need pattern and the perceived personal competence of individuals.

Self-Esteem. Self-esteem is a very important factor in how people define and achieve success. Self-esteem is present when the individual consistently regards himself or herself as a capable, successful, important, and worthy individual (Coopersmith, 1967). Self-esteem, a more comprehensive concept than personal competence, gets developed as individuals gain respect from others while successfully solving the problems that they encounter in their everyday lives. This concept is global in nature as contrasted to the term *sense of competence,* which refers to individuals' confidence in their own competence as they successfully interact with their work environment (Sekaran,

1985b). The vocational choices of individuals, their performance, and how successfully they accomplish their goals in the various spheres of their lives are all influenced by the degree of self-esteem they possess (Barnett, Baruch, and Rivers, 1985; Stake, 1979; Zuckerman, 1980). Individuals high in self-esteem will define success in terms of accomplishments and satisfactions in various facets of their lives, including their career, their marriage, the raising of their children, and their involvement in community and related activities.

Priorities in Life. Depending on how they prioritize the different aspects of their lives, individuals will assign different criteria for success. For example, to a particular individual, success might mean not only involving himself in career and family activities but also making a significant contribution to the community's advancement. For another individual, success might connote a peaceful, happy home that resonates with joy and laughter. Moreover, the same individual may prioritize different facets of her life at different times depending on her needs of the moment and the life stage she is in. For instance, most individuals assign top priority to their careers until they acquire a firm foothold in them. Raising a family will be paramount to individuals in their late twenties and thirties. Consolidating career gains will attain significance when people reach their forties and fifties. Later, they may give more of their time to preparing for retirement, and they may become more involved in church, community, or other activities. Thus, the definition of success will vary in the different stages of the life cycle of the couple. Success, then, is not only a multifaceted phenomenon but a very dynamic and nebulous one as well.

Self-Concept and Self-Identity. Self-concept provides one with a sense of identity as to who one is and how one presents oneself in daily life (Sekaran, 1985b). Self-identity thus reinforces one's self-concept. For instance, if a husband's self-concept is that he is an egalitarian, facilitating husband who puts family above all else, he would tend to be a supportive spouse who would physically, emotionally, and psychologically encourage his wife to attain her career and family aspirations. His self-identity, then, would be that of a family partner—not that of a male who is the sole or primary breadwinner of the family. Likewise, if a wife sees herself as not just a homemaker but as a capable, ambitious, and strong person who could go far in her career, her sense of identity will be tied in large part to her work role and not just to her homemaking role. Such a wife might decide not to have children or to have them only after she is firmly established in her career. Self-concept and self-identity, which mutually reinforce each other, also govern people's behaviors and how they present themselves in their everyday lives.

Since the definition of success is a function of so many factors, it is important for couples to periodically assess their needs, define what success means to them, and share their thoughts on this subject with each other. It is only then that spouses can attempt to reorder their priorities, renegotiate roles, and adapt their life-styles to meet individual and family goals. When this is not done—that is, when the changing needs and priorities of one or both partners are not made known—the spouses are likely to drift apart. Quite frequently marriages dissolve because the partners are not able to comprehend or tolerate changes in each other's behavior. For instance, the husband does not understand why his hitherto "good" wife has suddenly started to ask for an equal distribution of responsibilities at home, and the wife does not comprehend why the "caring and loving" husband of yesteryear has, of late, turned into a "work-oholic" who neglects his responsibilities on the home front.

Thus, family members should assess their own needs and orientations and define what they want to get out of their dual-career life-style. Unless they can in some way define what success means to them, the quality of life in the family cannot be enhanced for both members. One reason why the concept of success is not usually addressed by spouses in dual-career families is because the members—especially the wives—often get confused about what they want out of life. Being unable to divest themselves of what they learned in the early years of socialization, both wives and husbands experience the various dilemmas discussed in Chapter One and anchor their self-identity to their masculinity or femininity. Both then find it easier to revert to traditional roles and stereotypical behaviors.

As a consequence, career-centered husbands may well experience psychological rewards in their worklives as well as in their families (since their needs are also met there). As for the wives, while they have physically crossed the boundary of the home and stepped into the career world, most have not yet crossed the boundary psychologically and hence find themselves caught between the need to be a successful career person and the need to be a good homemaker. Thus, the husbands remain (or think they should be) aggressive, ambitious, analytical, competitive, individualistic, self-reliant, self-sufficient, unemotional, athletic, willing to take risks, and strongly career oriented (the stereotyped masculine properties). In contrast, the wives think that they should play the role of the affectionate, nurturing, gentle, soft-spoken, shy, sympathetic, tender, yielding, warm, understanding, compassionate, and sensitive spouse and mother who aspires to be a successful career person but generally ends up not being so. Herein lies the tension that prevents family members from experiencing a satisfying way of life.

Understanding and identifying their primary orientation (career/family/both) and sex-role identity (masculine/feminine/androgynous) will enable couples to come to grips with the incongruencies, if any, between their expectations and behaviors, both individually and as a pair. This, in turn, will help them to reduce their frustrations by closing the gap between their expectations and actual behaviors and enhance the quality of their family lives.

Accounting for Variations in Quality of Life

While the average dual-career family may experience tensions, a certain proportion of these families enjoys a fairly high quality of life as indicated by Rapoport and Rapoport (1976) and by my own interviews with dual-career families. It appears that some families experience high psychological success and hence have a high quality of life, some experience moderate levels of success and have a good quality of life, others experience more failures than success in various aspects of their lives and have a low quality of life, and still other couples simply end up in the divorce court. It is important to understand the family dynamics that account for these favorable and unfavorable outcomes.

One way to understand the dynamics that operate in families is to look at the typology of marriages. Two main factors are integral to dual-career dynamics—the couples' central life interest *and* their sex-role orientation. Both are personality predispositions, and the combination of these in the husband and the wife makes a big difference in how interpersonal interactions occur, how roles are played out, the extent to which egalitarian values operate in the family, and the kinds of satisfactions that are derived from enacting various roles. Previous categorizations of marriages have primarily been based on couples' orientations toward the career or the family and have not considered their sex-role orientations (Hall and Hall, 1979; Jones and Jones, 1980). Thus, they have not been able to fully explain why some couples experience a good quality of life and others do not. By taking into consideration both dimensions of the personality of the partners, we can examine the possible combinations of couples in dual-career families. This will enable us to see which types of couples are likely to experience a high quality of life and which are not.

Sex-Role Orientations and Central Life Interests

Sex-role orientations refer to the extent to which individuals have internalized traditional gender-based roles. Those who are traditionally oriented subscribe to the belief that men and women should take on the roles that are culturally mandated and socially accepted. Despite the fact that a large number of women now work outside the home, traditionally minded men and women still believe that men should assume the role of breadwinners and women the role of homemakers, even when the latter work outside the home. Having internalized these values, family members then conform to stereotypical role behaviors. The husband is not inclined to share the household duties and experiences identity dilemmas when he does. The wife takes the major responsibility for the household functions and feels guilty if she neglects them. At the same time, however, she is frustrated that she does not have enough time to give to her career.

Those who are nontraditional in their sex-role orientations do not agree that men and women should behave in particular ways and adhere to culturally normed patterns of behavior. The nontraditional husband will share the household work and parenting, while the wife will not feel psychologically bound to the home or feel that the family is entirely her responsibility. She will then be able to concentrate as much on her career as she would like to.

A third type of orientation is the androgynous one. Androgyny is typified in the individual who is capable of incorporating both male and female role behaviors in his or her personality. Such a person is equally comfortable either mowing the lawn or washing the clothes, repairing the car or cleaning the bathroom. Androgynous people experience no tensions in their daily tasks, whereas sex-typed individuals will have difficulty in engaging in reverse role behavior and avoid it since cross-sex behavior will be motivationally problematic for them (Bem and Lenney, 1976). (Incidentally, Bem, 1974, developed a scale to determine the sex-role orientations of individuals, which can be used to assess spouses' predispositions and the extent of rigidity or flexibility in their orientations.)

On the basis of these three sex-role orientations, we can have nine combinations of marital partners, as shown on the vertical part of the matrix in Figure 3. We can also have different types of marital partners on the basis of their central life interest. Central life interest denotes the priority that individuals assign to the work or nonwork spheres of their lives. To some, their careers are the primary interest in life while to others it may be the family that is of central interest. A few individuals will have difficulty discriminating between the two and will feel that both spheres are equally important to them. Thus, we can have three different orientations toward the main interests in life. Career could come first, family could come first, or both could be deemed equally central to the individual's life.

Again, on the basis of these three central life interest ori-

Figure 3. Eighty-One Possible Combinations of Sex-Role Orientations and Central Life Interests.

Central Life Interests

Sex-Role Orientations	1 HUS and WF Career	2 HUS Family WF Career	3 HUS Career and Family WF Career	4 HUS Career WF Family	5 HUS and WF Family	6 HUS Career and Family WF Family	7 HUS Career WF Career and Family	8 HUS Family WF Career and Family	9 HUS and WF Career and Family
1. HUS and WF both Trad'l									
2. HUS Nontrad'l WF Trad'l									
3. HUS Andro WF Trad'l									
4. HUS Trad'l WF Nontrad'l									
5. HUS and WF both Nontrad'l									
6. HUS Andro WF Nontrad'l									
7. HUS Trad'l WF Andro									
8. HUS Nontrad'l WF Andro									
9. HUS and WF both Andro									

HUS   = Husband   Andro   = Androgynous
WF   = Wife   Career   = Career
Trad'l   = Traditional   Family   = Family
Nontrad'l = Nontraditional

entations, we can have nine possible combinations of marital partners in a family—shown horizontally on Figure 3. It should be noted that sex-role orientations and central life interest, although allied, are independent. In other words, a nontraditional husband could be either career or family oriented, and a wife adhering to a traditional sex-role pattern could still place her career above her family. Such a person will probably try very hard to meet the role demands of the workplace as well as of the family. However, she is not likely to achieve both career and family goals to her satisfaction and is likely to become frustrated when one or both have to be compromised.

As the matrix in Figure 3 illustrates, we can conceivably have eighty-one different combinations of marital partners. Some of these combinations are highly conducive to marital happiness, and the quality of life in such families will be more than satisfactory. An ideal combination of such partners would be two androgynous spouses who are both equally career and family oriented. Such a combination would maximize the quality of life enjoyed by the couple since both partners would have the ability to fulfill their own desires as well as those of the other members of the family.

Some other combinations will also enable a couple to achieve an optimum level of overall satisfaction. For instance, a husband who is career centered and traditional and a wife who is family centered and also traditional will help each other to derive the maximum satisfaction from that part of their lives where they have the greatest involvement. The wife may or may not derive much satisfaction from the workplace, but overall there will be a good amount of satisfaction experienced by the couple, and the experienced quality of their life, though not as high as in the first combination, will still be good.

Some other combinations may induce stress in one or both partners as they find themselves forced to compromise some of their cherished desires. The quality of life in such families will be medium to low. For instance, a family in which the husband is career oriented and traditional and the wife is both career and family centered and very nontraditional will experience stress. The wife will expect the husband to share house-

hold work and child-rearing responsibilities since she is nontraditional in her sex-role orientation. But since the husband is
purely career oriented and is also traditional, he will not meet
her expectations. The wife will then feel forced to compromise
either her career activities or family activities or both. She will
give vent to her frustrations from time to time, and the husband
will consider that nagging. In such a case, the spouses will either
become reconciled to the state of affairs or place their hopes
on therapy or the simple passage of time. The quality of life in
such families will, at best, be medium and, at worst, low.

Finally, some combinations of partners will be so tension
provoking that they will force the members to cease operating
as dual-career families. Consider the case of a wife who is extremely career oriented and very nontraditional, married to a
partner who is very family oriented and extremely traditional.
In such a case, the wife will be inclined to neglect family matters because of her deep absorption with her career, and the
family-centered husband will become unhappy and angry because his spouse is neglecting her duties as a wife and mother.
He will be unable to reduce his level of frustration since, being
traditional, he will not want to take care of the things that need
to be done at home. In the face of daily arguments and quar-
rels, either the wife will give up her career or the partners will
get divorced. In either case the dual-career family has come to
an end.

Four Types of Couples

These four categories of couples can be referred to as
superordinate partners, synchronized partners, synthetic partners, and severed partners.

Superordinate Partners

Superordinate couples have the ultimate goal of realizing
life satisfaction for both partners jointly. They do not necessarily view their various roles as compartmentalized segments of
their lives but consider each role as an extension of the others
and as something worth engaging in. Their primary objective is

the physical and mental well-being of the family, and they center all their activities on this. Such couples do not necessarily achieve spectacular success in their careers since they have diverse activities that they engage in as families and are not keen on devoting their energies only to career success. The family is well integrated, and there is generally a feeling of considerable satisfaction and well-being in the family. These marriages consist of two partners who are both androgynous and value both career and other nonwork activities. They try to build interdependence among the family members—that is, their activities are sometimes independent and sometimes interactive. In an interview, a couple with an eight-year-old son had this to say:

> We like our jobs very much, but that alone is not enough for us. We like to be doing things together as a family. We opened a video shop two years ago, and all three of us go there in the evenings to see how business is doing and how the staff is managing the shop. It is exciting to meet new challenges and make our own business decisions, not another company's. Larry [the son] knows many of our customers and talks to them. He is already learning something about business! Our lives are busy but we have a lot of fun.

The superordinate couples, being androgynous, do not view activities or decisions from a gender-based perspective. Duties are performed on the basis of whoever is conveniently available and whatever needs to get done at the moment, instead of dividing activities and assigning specific roles. Such spouses are generally in high spirits and are always ready to further marital and family well-being while still remaining interested in their careers. Some couples that I interviewed on the West Coast deliberately carried out their activities in an interdependent mode, thus making maximum family interaction possible. These young couples were happy in their careers. At home, they spent time discussing work-related issues, but they also engaged in nonwork-related and leisure activities.

In sum, superordinate partners are androgynous spouses

to whom careers are important but not the only important interest in life. These couples usually create activities and interests in which both can get involved and interact jointly. In these families egalitarianism comes spontaneously, and equity-based values become a way of life.

Synchronized Partners

Synchronized partners help each other achieve their individual goals. These families may consist of either complementary partners or partners who are well matched in any number of different ways in their central life interest and sex-role orientations. In a complementary partnership one spouse's central life interest is his or her career, and he or she has a correspondingly low involvement in family matters. This is matched by the other spouse who has a relatively low involvement in career and high involvement in the family. Such a combination has also to fit the sex-role orientations of the spouses. For instance, if the husband has high family involvement and a nontraditional sex-role orientation and the wife has a high career involvement and nontraditional expectations of herself and her husband, the family will be happy. If, however, the husband is traditional and places greater emphasis on the family while the wife is nontraditional and has made her career her main interest in life, they will not be synchronized partners.

The following comments made by a wife depict the life of a synchronized partner:

> To me, my family comes first. I believe that the home is a place which offers the family members a good atmosphere to relax and enjoy each other after a day's work at the office. So I make sure that however busy I am, I take care of things at home and try to keep it always, or almost always, neat and clean. I enjoy doing things at home. My husband is very busy with his work and comes home late most of the time. He is happy to be able to relax in a comfortable couch and get to the din-

ner table for a hot supper. He plays with the kids
and puts them to bed, and, basically, we are a
happy family.

Here the wife who has the family as her primary interest and is
also traditional is ideally suited to the husband, whose primary
concern is his work and who is also basically traditional in his
approach to family tasks. If he helps his wife in *some* domestic
work and in *some* child care—but not too much—(otherwise the
wife's self-identity as the nurturing, efficient homemaker will
not be preserved), he will make her feel happy, appreciated, and
cared for. She nurtures him and is satisfied, and he is happy
with the division of labor. Helping each other to achieve their
individual goals accounts for the good quality of life experienced by such spouses.

A good quality of life can also be experienced in families
in which some compatible interests and orientations exist between the partners. For instance, if two partners who are androgynous have careers as their primary interest but also want
to have a fairly well-run home, the couple will be well matched
for each other and will optimize their satisfactions. A husband
had this to say:

Both my wife and I are very much involved
in our work and spend more time at the workplace
than most other couples do, but neither of us likes
to return to a dirty home in the evening. So we
take turns and tidy up the mess before we leave
for work in the morning. That way, even if we are
more hard pressed in the morning, we can at least
enjoy our evenings.

Synchronized partners, thus, could either complement
each other or be similar to each other. There could be several
combinations of central life interest and sex-role orientation
for synchronized couples. These families feel reasonably satisfied about the way they are meeting their career and family aspirations, and they experience a good quality of life.

Synthetic Partners

Synthetic partners are found in marriages in which one or both spouses feel that their aspirations are being compromised. This is due to some incompatibility in the mix of their central life interests and their sex-role orientations. The quality of life in these families is medium to low. In this kind of marriage, the wife (for whatever reason) may feel that she *has* to subordinate her career to that of her husband, or the husband may feel that he *has* to decrease his career involvement in the interests of the marriage. Quite a few dual-career families may well fall into this category. The following conversation between spouses typifies the frustrations experienced by synthetic partners:

Husband: I don't understand why the house is always such a mess! Can't you spend a couple of hours every week to put things in order? The children turn the place upside down searching for their clothes every single morning, and there is so much confusion here before we leave for work. I wish you would spend *some* time attending to your household responsibilities as well.

Wife: I don't know why *I* am always the one who is expected to do everything around here! I wish you would pitch in too and get things organized so we don't feel so rushed in the mornings.

Husband: Well, if that is the only way things will get done around here, I guess I will take the responsibility to keep the children's clothes organized and ready. They will be ready in the hangers before I go to bed at night. But I expect that you will take care of the weekly laundry and ironing.

Wife: Good Lord! What next?

A synthetic couple will inevitably experience frustrations and tensions from time to time. The couple may try to work out the problems on their own, seek outside help, or hope that things will simply work out as time passes. Makeshift agreements and periodic resolution of tensions, along with some degree of communication between the partners, help the couple to patch up their differences and keep their marriages going. But the quality of life experienced in such families is, at best, medium.

Severed Partners

Severed partners are so incompatible in their mix of aspirations and sex-role orientations that compromise and adjustment come to seem totally impossible, at least to one of the partners. Here we might have a nontraditional wife who is deeply committed to her career but not to her family married to a man who has high family involvement and low career commitment and is extremely traditional. A wife from such a family might tell her counselor:

> I don't think Mike [her husband] understands how important my career is to me. He resents my traveling so frequently and asks me to seek another job so that we can raise a family. I ask him who is going to look after the children, and he says we can somehow manage, and if it comes to that, I could get a part-time job. There is no way the two of us can see eye-to-eye on anything. He just doesn't know what I am talking about. I think the best thing for us is to split.

The frustrations for both partners in such cases are so high and the possibility of compromise so remote that the couple will often decide to end their marriage. Or if divorce is unpalatable to a wife, she may even be willing to give up her career. A wife might be willing to give up her career in the interests of keeping the family together when her husband is extremely career committed and very traditional but she herself is more committed to her family than to her career and has certain nontraditional expectations of her husband. For instance, she might expect her husband to help her in domestic work, get more involved in child rearing, come home in the evenings at a reasonable time, and forget about his work in the evening and have a pleasant conversation with the family in front of the fireplace. The reality may be, however, that the children do not even see their father during the week since he leaves very early in the morning and comes home very late at night. The wife may be concerned that the children are not getting enough love, and since getting a divorce is not going to solve that problem, she may decide to give up her career to provide more comfort for the children. In order not to destroy the marriage, she may thus sacrifice the dual-career life-style.

In sum, we have looked at four types of marital partners. Probably the majority of dual-career families today consist of synchronized and synthetic partners. Undoubtedly there are some severed partners and a few superordinate partners as well. This typology provides marital partners with a way to examine their own compatibilities and to determine to which of the four types their marriage belongs. They will then be able to confront the tensions, if any, in their own marriage and to see if one or both could change their behavior in mutually beneficial ways. This typology also suggests some plausible reasons why past research might indicate inconsistent findings in the satisfactions of dual-career couples. Future research should incorporate the variables of sex-role orientation and central life interest to see how different couple combinations account for variations in quality-of-life factors such as job satisfaction, marital satisfaction, life satisfaction, and mental health. Specific hypotheses—for example, superordinate partners will experience the greatest satisfactions in all spheres and thereby experience better mental health than the other three types of marital partners—will then become testable.

Mismatch of Couples in Past Research Findings

Past studies have reported the curvilinear effects of education on divorce; that is, when women were very poorly educated (did not even have high school diplomas) or were highly educated (had master's degrees and above), their divorce rate was high (Houseknecht, Vaughan, and Macke, 1984). But when they had two to four years of college education, their divorce rate was low. This phenomenon could well reflect a mismatch of spouses with reference to career and gender-role orientations as discussed earlier. For instance, it is possible that the highly educated wives (most of whom probably completed their education after marriage) were married to traditional husbands who were uncomfortable with the idea of their wives pursuing careers as a primary life interest. The wives may have been excited by the prospect of enhancing their career growth through their educational qualifications and may have paid greater attention to their careers than to their domestic roles. This, then, could very well be a case of mismatch between the traditional husband who expected his wife to accord secondary importance to her career and the nontraditional wife who wanted to give more emphasis to her career than to her family obligations. Husbands who married women who did not even graduate from high school probably became bored with them, especially if the husbands were nontraditional in their outlook and were inclined to encourage their wives to pursue careers.

Hornung and McCullough (1981) reported that men who placed little value on job advancement were more satisfied with their lives than those men who wanted to advance in their careers, irrespective of whether or not their wives were highly educated. These husbands were probably androgynous and considered the family their central interest. If their own career advancement was not important to them, they would not feel threatened by wives who surpassed them in status because of their high educational qualifications. These couples might fall into the category of synchronized partners. Not knowing the orientations and central life interests of the couples in these studies, we can only try to capture them in the light of the proposed framework so that future studies can test out the hypotheses suggested here.

There were contradictory findings with respect to the relationship between the wife's occupational status and the husband's marital adjustment and satisfaction. Burke and Weir (1976a) reported that husbands of working wives were in general less satisfied with their marriages and in poorer mental and physical health than husbands whose wives were not working. But Booth (1977) found this not to be the case when he investigated the same issue. In the first study, husbands may have been very traditional and expected their wives to be family oriented and to take full responsibility for homemaking. Thus, the husbands of working wives may have wanted their wives to pay only marginal attention to their careers. Those wives, however, may have expected their husbands to be helpful at home and to share the family burden equally so that they (the wives) could pay more attention to their own careers. These couples might then represent synthetic partners.

In contrast, Booth's sample of husbands of working wives may have been androgynous in their sex-role orientations and may have considered both family and career of equal interest for both themselves and their wives. They may thus have supported their wives and encouraged them to advance in their careers and derived satisfaction therefrom. Hornung and McCullough (1981) found that in the subsample of their study in which the wives' occupational prestige was higher than that of their husbands, the wives reported greater marital satisfaction but the husbands reported less satisfaction. In all probability this subsample consisted mainly of nontraditional, career-oriented wives and traditional, career- or family-oriented husbands. Staines, Pleck, Shepard, and O'Connor (1978) reported from their analysis of data collected by the Survey Research Center that wives' employment status did not affect husbands' reports of marital adjustment. This sample probably consisted of nontraditional husbands who were oriented toward both family and career.

Eiswirth-Neems and Handal (1978), who investigated the effects of husbands' and wives' attitudes toward maternal occupational status on family satisfaction, found that it was when the wife had a high attachment to her career that the husband perceived the family as less well organized and the family climate as not too satisfactory. The wives in that condition reported that there was less cohesiveness in the interpersonal dimensions of the family. This could very well represent a mismatched set of expectations and orientations both with regard to central life interest and sex-role orientation. Interestingly, Bryson, Bryson, Licht, and Licht (1976) in a study of psychologist couples found that even though the division of household labor was unequal, the wives accepted the situation without concern. Perhaps these were traditionally oriented wives who were both career and family centered and were married to traditional, career-oriented husbands. These synchronized partners could enjoy a good quality of life. It is highly probable that the differences in the findings among studies is a function of whether the couples were matched or mismatched in terms of central life interests and sex-role orientations. This is an empirical question to be tested in future studies.

In the previous chapter we reported studies indicating that women in higher occupational status were able to establish more egalitarian values in their families. It is quite likely that these high-status women were also married to nontraditional husbands. Hiller and Philliber (1982) were right in saying that the gender identity of both spouses is critical in determining their ability to sustain a marriage in which the *wives earn more.* They suggested that if both spouses have androgynous gender identities, both will be more comfortable with the situation. But if the wife is traditional, she will feel uncomfortable with her higher earnings even if she is career oriented; if her central interest is not her career, she will be confused by the situation. If the husband is traditional and is also career oriented, he will feel uncomfortable; if he is nontraditional and his wife is traditional, he may feel frustrated because he cannot influence his wife to retain her higher occupational position. Thus, in trying to account for the satisfactions experienced in marriage and the family, it is important to examine the congruent relationships that exist among the sex-role identity and the central life interest of both the partners.

The Future of Dual-Career Families

At one time at least, there was considerable skepticism about the durability of the dual-career life-style in this country (Parson, 1954). Even today, some feel that the dual-career life-

style is not a viable phenomenon because of the stresses it imposes on families, organizations, and society itself (Hunt and
Hunt, 1977, 1982). But some researchers have refuted these
misgivings, at least from the family perspective. Martin, Berry,
and Jacobsen (1975), for instance, stated that the intellectual
interactions between spouses who are both professionals promote the success of dual-career marriages. Through her research,
Bailyn (1973) found that the wives in dual-career families
posed no threat to this life-style and argued that the phenomenon is here to stay. Indeed, dual-career families will be successful and will contribute to the quality of life in society as a
whole if their members learn to give more thought to what they
want out of life and examine whether their personality predispositions are suited to achieve their goals. In other words, each
family has to define what success means to it, and husband and
wife must then design their life-style to achieve the kind of success they want. The probability that the partners will experience good physical and mental health and, hence, a good quality of life then becomes high.

If dual-career spouses have difficulty in clearly defining
success, they may seek the help of counselors. Counselors can
also help the partners identify their sex-role orientations and
central life interests and determine the type of marital partners
the couple happen to be. The couple can also be helped to see
the congruence or incongruence between their definition of
success and their orientations. Marriage counselors can also
help prospective spouses to articulate their expectations of their
future dual-career life-style.

Organizations will certainly benefit by recruiting individuals who have clearly defined their criteria of success and can
articulate them well in terms of work-related goals. Family-
centered members can be productive at work and contribute
greatly to the organization's success if they know what their
career-related goals are within the overall scheme of their definition of success. If individuals have defined that term satisfactorily to themselves, they will tend to be effective in both work
and nonwork spheres. It is only when organizations recruit individuals who have not thought through what they want out of

their work and nonwork lives that the organizations will suffer from members' ambivalent or sporadic efforts.

Given the increasing number of nontraditional families in the work force, organizations can no longer expect total dedication, twenty-four-hour commitment, and very high job involvement from all their employees. Organizations can, however, do much to increase dual-career family members' productivity and contribution to the system by recruiting those who have clearly defined their goals, tapping their needs at the workplace (their need for achievement, for example), utilizing their personal competence, and developing structures and processes that will help the members integrate their work and family worlds. By raising the self-esteem and sense of competence of members, organizations can effectively utilize their talents and abilities.

FOUR

Strategies for Improving Quality of Life

With steady increases in the number of dual-career families in our society, more and more people in organizations—managers as well as other professionals—come from dual-career families. The phenomenon accordingly needs to be addressed and understood from two perspectives: (1) how individuals manage their dual-career life-styles and (2) how managers in organizations who are themselves dual-career family members and manage others pursuing this life-style can influence their organizations to adapt to the changing composition of the work force. The first question will be addressed in this chapter and the second in the next three chapters.

Managing a dual-career life-style is far more complex and challenging than most other ventures that an average individual undertakes in life. It is paradoxical that dual-career partners will spend a number of years carefully preparing themselves for a professional career but plunge rather nonchalantly into marriage and decide on a dual-career life-style without giving much thought to it. It is not surprising, then, that these families often find themselves caught up in dilemmas. Many of the knotty issues discussed in the first three chapters can be dealt with by couples if they have thought through such issues as what their predispositions are, what they want from life, and how they should jointly work together to achieve their goals. Thinking through and defining what success means to them as individuals and as a family will give the couple a sense of direction. Defining their self-concepts and self-identities will help the couple to work through and sometimes even to transcend the dilemmas they encounter. Once couples have a clear sense of who they are and agree on where they are headed, they can sort out many of the anticipated and unanticipated problems that inevitably arise from time to time by means of open communication and joint problem solving.

Let us now look at some actual situations in which dilemmas arise and discuss what couples can do to minimize tensions. These situations can be chronologically divided into six stages: (1) making career decisions at the time of entering professional academic training; (2) deciding on a dual-career family life-style; (3) getting established as a dual-career family; (4) establishing certain norms for sharing household responsibilities and for settling status and power issues within the family; (5) expanding family roles from those of career person and spouse to that of parent as well; and (6) preparing for retirement.

Career Decision Phase

It is not too early to think about the possibility of becoming a member of a dual-career family when beginning professional training in preparation for a future career. This is especially important for those who are planning to enter professions that require a high degree of dedication and commitment. In many cases, the ability to pursue nonwork activities is severely restricted by the enormous amounts of time demanded by a job. Doctors, nurses, and certain kinds of research scientists belong to this category. Psychological preparation for pursuing such positions as male-nurse or woman-astronaut is also necessary since extremely nontraditional career roles can have implications for both workplace and family dynamics. At the workplace, there may be some uncomfortable and frustrating interactions, and one cannot be sure that even family members will fully understand and appreciate the nontraditional role holder.

This is not to say that there are professional careers that individuals should not pursue. Rather, as career decisions are made and professional training is acquired, individuals must also psychologically prepare themselves to become successful dual-career family members. It can normally be anticipated that one professional will marry another. This means that even at the time of training oneself for a future professional career, one should start thinking about the future integration of the work and nonwork lives of two professionals in a family. This involves taking a close look at one's own beliefs, values, feelings, needs, goals, and interests and seeing how they would mesh with a dual-career life-style. Actually, at some universities such as Brigham Young, Duke, and Southern Methodist, the implications of dual careers are now discussed in elective courses. The Harvard Business School even emphasizes such concerns as part of its curriculum in applied case analysis (Collins, 1985).

Deciding on a Dual-Career Life-Style

When two individuals with career goals decide that they want to get married, they should anticipate the many issues that they will encounter in the future and address them to the extent possible *before* they get married.

Some of the issues that partners should discuss are the needs, aspirations, interests, goals, and priorities of each as they relate to both careers and family. Both partners should explore their central life interests and sex-role orientations at this stage. Thoughts and feelings about whether both spouses will pursue lifelong careers, how many children each wants, and how the children will be spaced all need to be discussed seriously at this time. Exchanging information on such matters will give the couple some idea of how they fit into the marriage typology discussed in the previous chapter.

Couples at this stage should also exchange views on sharing household and parenting responsibilities and explore the extent of support that each will readily give to the other. Any serious incompatibilities that might surface at this time should be a red flag to the couple, warning them about the problems they will most likely face in the future as marital partners. Any discomfort and confusion should be confronted at this stage—if necessary, with the help of a counselor. This is also the time for the two to fully assess their commitment to career, marriage, and family. This will help many to avoid the "marry in haste and repent at leisure" syndrome. In particular, couples at this stage should discuss the following career-related issues.

Job-Seeking Strategies. If both partners are still in search of jobs, do they want to look for jobs in the same or different organizations? If both are unable to find jobs in the same locality, would they be willing to locate in different places and be commuter couples, or would they want to start the job search in a larger city where there might be jobs for both, or would one settle for a less than perfect job that would allow them both to be in the same place?

Career Commitment. To what extent will careers be important in the lives of the newly married couple? In other words, how much of their time will be spent in career-related matters and how much time will they spend together as a couple? Though this question might be difficult to answer at this point, it is an important one because careers are likely to be demanding and time consuming even during the initial career years. No matter how long and intense their academic training, the spouses will be expected to "prove" themselves before they are integrated into their organizations as capable members. This implies further training, apprenticeship, living with the discomfort of ambiguity, and not feeling a sense of competence until the work is comprehended and mastered and competencies have been demonstrated. Most careers demand a considerable initial investment of time, effort, and commitment to the organization that will take time away from the home. This could be frustrating to a newly married couple, especially if one spouse is more committed to his or her career than the other. It is important that the partners understand these issues and eventualities so that they do not start off their marriage on the wrong foot.

Handling Prospective Transfers. Some careers involve periodic job transfers. In such cases, what strategies would spouses pursue if one were to be transferred to another place in the next two or three years. Would they become commuter couples or would they operate on the basis of career precedence—

that is, would one person's career take precedence over the other's and would this pattern alternate? For example, if one person initiates a move to another location to further his or her prospects this year, will the next move be initiated by the other partner?

While these questions may not appear to be immediately relevant, it is important that prospective dual-career couples discuss as many of the issues relevant to their future life as possible. My research indicates that those who did so before getting married and came to an understanding on how various situations would be handled were able to commit themselves more fully to their careers and derive more satisfaction from their jobs than those who did not. This was particularly true for wives. It is not enough to vaguely talk about these issues; rather, the partners should thoroughly understand their orientations and know exactly how compatible their values and views are. The following remarks of a young divorced career woman highlight the importance of this:

> Before we were married, we kind of talked about our future, but we were so much taken up with each other that I did not think there would be any problem handling both the career and the family. During our courtship, Roger [her former husband] never gave me any indication whatsoever that he expected me to be a housewife first and last and be a career person only marginally. I took it for granted that he would fully support my career. He probably thought I would not be very career minded since I expressed a lot of sentiments about our happiness together and did not talk much about my career ambitions. To be frank, I did not myself have a good idea of how far I wanted to go in my career at that time. To cut a long story short, after we married, I realized that he expected me to be home when he got back from work, have the supper hot and ready for him every day; and to top it all, he insisted on starting a fam-

ily right away. My dreams of a happy life soon turned into days of arguments and constant badgering. We both ultimately decided to end the marriage.

Getting Established as a Dual-Career Family

If one or both partners are looking for jobs after marriage, they are likely to experience the stress of simultaneously adapting to their marriage and the demands of the job search. If one or both get turned down in interviews, it is possible that they might come to feel that interviewers discriminate against dual-career family members, especially against dual-career wives. They may be taken aback by such unexpected questions as, How would you manage a career and a family? and may be unable to respond to them in a satisfactory way on the spur of the moment. Between trying to establish a new home and hunting for jobs, the spouses might become tired and discouraged, and they might also begin to feel financial pressures. Depression may set in if the job search phase becomes too prolonged.

To minimize the hurdles in the job search stage, couples should think through several issues before they go for job interviews. The spouses need to have self-assurance, self-confidence, and a good idea of what they are looking for in their careers. Self-definition, self-understanding, and knowing what is important in life are important for determining one's goals (Stewart and Winter, 1974). These also help very much during interviews. The couple also needs to realize that most organizations have no knowledge of how dual-career couples manage their work lives and their families and might form their own stereotypes of the career commitment of the partners, especially of the wife. For instance, companies might assume that the wife will always follow the husband if he were to leave or be transferred to another city. This may or may not be true for individual families.

Since many interviewers find themselves in uncharted waters when hiring members of two-career families, they may want to get answers to several questions. The interviewers might

pose many of their questions in very subtle ways so that the
questions do not become too personal or infringe the legal
rights of the interviewees. Dual-career spouses, and especially
the wife, are very likely to be asked and should anticipate questions regarding whose career will assume priority, what their
family plans are, how any transfers would be handled, and what
would be the upshot if only one spouse succeeded in his or her
first job. The members should be prepared to respond to these
questions with confidence. This implies that the couple has
given serious thought to the issues and come to an understanding of their own predispositions. If necessary, they can seek the
help of professionals in these areas.

If couples interview for positions in the same organization, they should request separate interviews and negotiate for
terms as two independent people. They should not accept a
"package deal" unless it is a job-sharing assignment. Each
spouse should accentuate the professional side of himself or
herself in handling interview questions. For instance, an individual who is asked what would happen if his or her spouse were
to be relocated can reply, "Consideration of relocation would be
more a function of *my* career progress here than anything else."
Asked regarding how important a career is to her, an individual
could point to the considerable amount of serious preparatory
training that she has undergone.

The couple should try to support each other at this rather
trying phase in their early married life. If both have already
established themselves in their jobs before their marriage, this
phase will be happily nonexistent. Such couples can then concentrate on the next phase.

Norming Phase

This is the phase in which the couple establishes what may
be called its initial modes of behavior. Patterns of who does the
cooking, dusting, cleaning, vacuuming, laundry, mowing, car
washing, bill paying, and so on are implicitly or explicitly established in this phase. What the norms are and how they are set up
could very well reflect power and status relationships within the

family that might have far-reaching implications for the lives of the couple. For instance, a husband who does not voluntarily participate in household activities and is not asked to do so at this time cannot be automatically expected to pitch in or be easily persuaded to help the wife once the family expands and the roles of both increase. When one partner, but not the other, has to reduce his or her career commitment because of increased family demands, the incongruent status and power relationships in the family become very apparent. If both partners are happy with the situation, there is no problem. But quite frequently, the wife wants the husband to begin sharing the household and parenting responsibilities equally when the family expands. To have such expectations met, appropriate egalitarian norms should be set at the norming stage by expressing needs, discussing potential conflicts, and practicing egalitarian roles.

It is also possible that in these first few years one partner might advance more than the other in career, and feelings of envy might surface as a result. This needs to be handled in a way that is satisfying to both. At this phase some couples might also contemplate starting a family and therefore begin to experience role-cycling dilemmas. Handling these issues could produce tensions in the family during the first few years of the dual-career couple's life.

This is the time, therefore, for the couple to establish and to start practicing egalitarian values and behaviors. Androgynous couples will experience no problems in establishing egalitarian norms at home, and nontraditional couples will not experience difficulties arriving at a fair and equitable division of labor. Traditional couples, however, will have difficulty, initially, in making the allocation of home responsibilities between the partners both equal and nonsexist. But the time for establishing roles, redefining roles, and transcending sex roles is now —at the beginning of the couple's life together. A meeting of minds on how much time will be devoted to careers, how much to each other, and how much for personal activities is also essential from the very beginning of the couple's life together. If two-way communication, open expression of expectations, and supportive behaviors are established at this stage, the couple will probably live happily ever after.

If one partner advances faster than the other, the other may come to feel a sense of worthlessness at least temporarily. However, instead of entertaining feelings of resentment, anger, or guilt, the spouse should try to see the progress of his or her partner as a "family success." By the same token, "family solutions" can be generated for the other partner's advancement wherever possible—and it is possible in the vast majority of cases. Equity-based role redefinition, physical and emotional support, and active problem-solving efforts by both partners could well motivate the less successful partner to obtain extra training, to devote more time to career until success experiences occur, and to undertake more projects to demonstrate competence at the workplace. Such solutions generate healthy attitudes and raise the self-esteem of both partners, who will then enjoy each other's progress rather than harbor ill feelings toward one another.

When the couple is anxious to start a family but becomes concerned about possible conflicts between career advancement and family expansion, it needs to make conscious choices, knowing full well the pros and cons of each alternative. While a child may bring immense happiness to a family, its presence also raises numerous issues in the dual-career setting. Couples should be aware of and anticipate the changes that a child will bring to their lives and then make a decision about whether or not they are ready for parenthood. Once a baby is born, the neatly scheduled daily life of the spouses will become a thing of the past since the couple's entire existence will have to revolve around the biorhythms of the new arrival. Getting up several times during the night, arriving late at work when the baby-sitter arrives late, and having to miss work when the child is ill are all contingencies that will have to be built into the lives of the couple. Unless both spouses are fairly well established in their careers, career advancement may suffer, especially for the wife who will have to be away from the workplace when her children are born. Even if her job is waiting for her when she is ready to return to work, there could still be no guarantee that her absence will not jeopardize her chances or prospects for promotion.

Family Expansion Phase

The time when children arrive and the family expands is probably the most stressful period in the life of a dual-career couple, especially when there is more than one young child in the family. Children need a great deal of time and attention, and time becomes a scarce resource for the partners. Unless the couple happens to be androgynous, the wife is likely to experience extreme role overload at this phase. Emergency situations are also likely to arise from time to time, as when the child needs to be rushed to a doctor. Unless the couple makes alternative arrangements to meet such contingencies, it will find its normal work life constantly disorganized. If both the spouses frequently undertake work-related travel, life will become even more complex for the family. If, unfortunately, this is also the phase in which relocation choices have to be made because one of the spouses is being transferred, the family will come under extreme strain.

Parenting and Child Care. It is because this phase is so stressful that spouses should plan family size and timing with care. Reading books on parenting ahead of time can help the spouses prepare for the long and demanding days that they will have to spend with their children. Some books that offer useful ideas on co-parenting are *Parent Effectiveness Training* (Gordon, 1970), *The Father's Almanac* (Sullivan, 1980), and *Toddlers and Parents: A Declaration of Independence* (Brazelton, 1976).

Androgynous couples take turns minding the babies and the children and in general assume equal responsibility for them. My interviews with couples indicate that some spouses share child-rearing responsibilities by taking turns feeding, bathing, clothing, reading, playing, and alternately keeping night vigils when the children happen to fall sick. Such couples who fully shared child-care responsibilities told me that they had planned for such contingencies when they decided to have a

family. The children in such families were close to both parents
and did not depend only on the mother for help or love. The
more the couple engaged in co-parenting, the closer the family
became.

The couple should create structures to handle normal as
well as emergency situations. Hiring the right baby-sitter, identifying a friend or relative or neighbor who does not work and
will be willing to help out in emergency situations, having contacts with referral services, and finding care units for children
who are temporarily indisposed can all serve as support systems
for the working couple. In creating such support structures, the
couple should invest enough time and effort to establish suitable contacts and should work out alternative plans for handling
different situations. This investment will pay off in crisis situations. Both partners should get involved in these activities.

Hiring a baby-sitter who has training in child development is a wise decision. Trained kindergarten and primary school
teachers who like to baby-sit are usually available and can be
found through advertisements. Hiring the right individual even
if it costs more money will pay dividends far beyond the investment made. Some couples are willing to pay as much as
$20,000 per year for an all-day baby-sitter who cooks the chil-
dren's meals, does the grocery shopping, dish washing, and
laundry for the family when the children are napping, and takes
the children to school, museums, art galleries, libraries, and so
forth. Even though the parents may pay 25 percent or more of
their income for this kind of arrangement, they are relieved of
considerable anxiety and tension, and the children are the better off for it. These baby-sitters of course have to come with
good character references. *Working Mother* carried an article
titled "One-on-One Child Care: How to Find it, What it Costs"
(1985) that cites several alternatives, ranging from twenty-four-
hour live-in help to temporary baby-sitting assistance. There are
now agencies in big cities that screen employers and employees
and bring them together.

If parents want to place their children in a day-care center, they should check the sanitary conditions of the center and
the qualifications and credibility of the people who run it. They

should also make sure that the philosophy of the institution matches the child's temperament and makeup and the parents' own value system. Some of the parents I interviewed said that after they had put their children in a school, they found that it trained children to be aggressive and to retaliate when other kids teased them. This kind of behavior did not fit in with the parents' own views on how such situations should be handled. Thus, it is important that parents be comfortable with the value system and philosophy of the institution before entrusting their children to its care. This means that parents will have to spend time checking out various day-care centers and schools and talk to those who run the institutions and work there. But such efforts will help relieve the tension of the parents in the long run. Again, both partners should engage in these efforts, and all decisions should be jointly made.

Travel. When travel has to be undertaken by both partners, they should talk to their employers and seek their help in scheduling convenient travel patterns. Once employers know the difficulties experienced by dual-career spouses, they are usually willing to accommodate their needs. Relocation alternatives can also be explored with counselors and employee assistance and counseling professionals at the workplace.

Couple Time and Personal Time. Couples at this phase must make sure that despite their hectic schedules and responsibilities, they have set aside some time each day as "couple time" and "personal time"—even if each of these happens to be less than thirty minutes. Couple time allows spouses to talk to each other privately without distractions, and personal time offers an opportunity for each to spend some time alone doing whatever he or she desires. Periodic family trips on weekends or during vacation time can bring the family closer together and at the same time offer members a respite from the daily routine.

Work-Home Transition. The quality of time spent at home after work is a function of how effectively the couple makes the transition from work to home. If the partners are preoccupied with the difficult aspects of their workday at home, they will not be pleasant parents or congenial partners. It is, of course, difficult to come home in a relaxed mood after a tough day at work. But there are several ways in which parents can unwind and come home in the evening relaxed enough to listen to the children's narrations of their experiences at school, stories about their boyfriends and girlfriends, plans for the weekend, and so on (Mackoff, 1985). One way to begin the transition to home even before leaving the workplace is to devote the last hour at work to doing routine chores, and reviewing the day's activities, while tabling all unfinished business until the next day. Couples can also take some personal time to relax, exercise, jog, swim, or play tennis before they come home so that they feel relaxed and happy with the family for the rest of the evening.

Time Management. Time management becomes a critical issue at this phase. Effective time management contributes substantially to family and career effectiveness. Prioritizing goals and objectives, analyzing the current use of time, having a planned list of activities, and monitoring how effectively time is utilized are all a part of time management. Planning, organizing, delegating, and controlling activities both at home and at work are efficient time management techniques. Investing initial time in planning pays off ultimately, since it frees time for activities that an unplanned life forbids. The clothes will get laundered, the car washed, the house vacuumed, and the food cooked if everyone in the family contributes his or her share to the performance of these tasks. Rotating the activities will also help build androgynous behaviors in all members of the family.

Schwartz and MacKenzie (1977) offer several useful time management practices that can be used at work. They note that many tasks can and should be delegated to subordinates. Spending a few minutes with a secretary to go over what needs to be done during the day is a good time management strategy since the secretary can then screen all telephone calls and visitors, draft routine letters, and organize a good office system. All these help the professional to use his or her time more effectively. They also discuss eleven paradoxes that affect time management, including four critical ones: the paradox of the open door (although an individual may wish to be accessible for important matters, he or she may not wish to be continually interrupted with trivial questions or conversations of a social nature); the paradox of long hours (by working long hours, one may hope to accomplish more, but since productivity declines as fatigue mounts, this may not actually occur); the paradox of activities versus results (an individual may be extremely busy yet still fail to achieve the desired results); the paradox of efficiency versus effectiveness (if the wrong issues are being addressed, the effort is worthless, regardless of how efficiently the job may have been done).

Late Career and Retirement Phase

After their children grow up and leave home, parents experience the freedom to handle their work and nonwork lives in any way they choose. If relocation is necessary, the spouses will be able to follow a commuting couple's life with ease. As a matter of fact, professional women at this stage seem to actually enjoy commuter marriages (Gerstel, 1977; Gross, 1980). This is also the time in life when most people's thoughts turn to retirement. Couples could become perplexed and concerned at the prospect of shifting from a busy, programmed life to what they see as the boring monotony of retirement. They may thus picture retirement as an unpleasant journey into the future. Even for those who look forward to retirement, it may not turn out to be enjoyable unless the couple has invested some time in planning for this phase.

Developing new interests and involvements, perhaps in community affairs and voluntary services, will not only alleviate the loneliness of separation from children and/or a relocated spouse but will also ease the couple into a slow-paced retirement. Healthy activities, proper eating habits, good resting patterns, and periodic health checkups should help individuals to enjoy reasonably good health. Couples should plan at this time when each will retire, what activities will occupy them, what financial arrangements will be necessary for a relatively comfortable retired life, and so on. A new definition of success will emerge at this phase.

Having addressed the issues that may arise during specific phases in the dual-career couple's life, we can now list some characteristics in *both* partners, as well as some dynamics in families, that will help the couple to experience a good quality of life:

1. Mutual love, understanding, and respect for each other as two *individuals* who have their own needs, aspirations, and goals even as they both share a marital life with joint needs, aspirations, and dreams. In such a family, occupational status differences and other culturally imposed considerations do not influence the decisions that the couples make about their careers or the home. In other words, the spouses know what they want and pursue their goals unfettered by normative or environmentally set expectations.

2. A healthy team spirit that allows both to collaborate emotionally and professionally with a strong sense of togetherness. Team spirit pervades the family, and couples do not keep score. In such families competition gives way to joint problem solving.

3. Flexibility and a willingness to adjust to the needs of the situation rather than being unyielding and rigid about predetermined modes of behavior. Structural role definition and personal role redefinition help couples cope with situations either by seeking external help or by personally redefining roles to accommodate temporarily to the needs of the situation. Here the spouses resort to proactive role making (rather than predetermined role taking) to remain flexible.

4. A sense of fair play and equity to ensure that it is not only one partner who practices flexibility. Androgynous values help here.

5. A continuing redefinition of what success means to the couple. This requires that both partners be sensitive to each other and jointly define what success means to them individually and as a family.

6. The maturity to realize when to act independently, when to act in a dependent mode, and when to be interdependent.

7. Having or developing excellent communication *and* listen-

ing skills to ensure that small issues do not snowball into big problems.

8. Managing time effectively and building structures to make the transition between home and work a smooth one.

9. A strong commitment of the partners to the relationship and a high level of motivation to make a success of the complex life-style that they have chosen for themselves.

The more of these qualities that the partners cultivate, the fewer problems they will have in sorting out and handling the feelings of competition, jealousy, and so on that any two human beings are likely to experience from time to time, whether they be spouses, friends, colleagues, or siblings. The attributes listed above do not naturally exist in marital partners but have to be consciously developed by them. Couples can acquire these skills by attending workshops or through counseling. Indeed, when partners feel that family enjoyment and satisfaction are decreasing and that tensions between them are increasing, they should by all means seek counseling. In Chapters Eight and Nine, therefore, I will discuss the dilemmas of dual-career couples from the counselor's perspective. However, since the interface between career and family poses several problems for such couples, the next three chapters will examine what organizations can do to manage dual-career members effectively.

FIVE

Dual-Career Couples and the Organization: Challenge of the 1990s

The composition of the work force in America has changed radically during the past decade. According to the Conference Board (1985), today more than two-fifths of the work force—forty-seven million persons—is composed of spouses in working households; fewer than twelve million married men provide sole support for their families; and, compared to 1970, there are now five million more single-parent and other "noncouple" families. There are about three and one-third million dual-career couples who hold executive, professional, or technical positions, and the Census Bureau currently estimates that about one-sixth of all working wives earn higher salaries than their husbands. Though the primary focus of this chapter will be on the impact of dual-career families on organizations, I will also highlight how the changing composition and values of the work force have made it imperative for organizations to alter their structures, policies, and processes *now*. These changes are necessary not for philanthropic reasons but for the organizations' own survival and growth. As the Conference Board (1985) points out, variations in the family situation, combined with the new perspectives of a younger work force, have had a strong impact on organizations' effectiveness. We will examine the reasons why organizations should consider changing their traditional structures in this chapter and discuss what those changes should be in the next two chapters.

How Dual-Career Families Benefit Organizations

Members of dual-career families, whether working for the same or different organizations, can provide synergy and become valuable assets to institutions. For example, when organizations hire professionals from two-career families, they in a sense acquire the services of more than the individual or individuals they are hiring. As discussed in Chapter Two, coordinated couples who specialize either in the same field or in complementary fields can develop creative ways of handling their work and resolve technical and managerial problems in innovative ways. They can do this because of their common knowledge of work and organizational issues and because of their opportunities to gain insights into complex problems by sharing information. Even partners who do not work for the same organization or in the same field can discuss the challenging issues they face at work and gain better insights into the issues involved through these discussions.

Many couples I interviewed said that one of the joys they experienced in belonging to a dual-career family was the opportunity to jointly work through the problems they individually faced in the work setting. They said that they brainstormed, played the devil's advocate, and sometimes role played to resolve problems encountered in the work setting. They found this process to be exciting and challenging—something not experienced while discussing issues with colleagues, either because of lack of time or for fear of being perceived as "dependent on others to solve problems." One couple who were computer scientists in two different organizations narrated in detail how they discuss on a daily basis the technical problems that arise at work so that "each does not have to reinvent the wheel everytime." Another couple working in different fields related that they role played different kinds of interaction until they found a way for the wife to make her male boss more accepting of her.

Thus, career couples seem to have the knack of resolving the problematic issues they face at work, whether they be technical, administrative, or interpersonal issues. Creativity finds an outlet because the spouses have the unique opportunity to interact with each other away from the pressure-filled work atmosphere on a continuing basis and to share the excitement of contributing to each other's progress. These factors enhance the productivity of the organization, providing it with the necessary drive and synergy to meet its goals. Recently, Doudna (1985) described the synergy of the Doles (Elizabeth and Robert) this way: "They are a classic case of the whole being more than the sum of the parts: Dole plus Dole adds up to explosive political charisma" (p. 358).

The first three chapters of this book explored the critical issues for dual-career family members: (1) their need for flexible work patterns so as to balance the demands of the family and the career (Catalyst, 1981, 1984); (2) their need for revised employee benefit schemes that will allow the couples to start families when they feel the time is appropriate without jeopardizing their career prospects (Conference Board, 1985); (3) their need to be freed from anxieties about child care when they are at work (Immerwahr, 1984); (4) their need to expend energies in collaborative ways that further each other's career progress rather than to harbor feelings of resentment and competitiveness toward each other (Sekaran, 1985b); and (5) their need to maximize the overall quality of their chosen life-style— that is, to experience good physical and mental health (Sekaran, 1983b, 1985a).

By providing alternative work patterns (Meier, 1978), by creating innovative cafeteria-type employee benefit schemes (Gifford, 1984), by addressing the now hotly debated comparable worth issue (Smith, 1985b), and by developing organizational structures and processes that enhance the experienced quality of life for spouses—such as facilitating the relocation of professional spouses of transferred employees (Mathews, 1984)—organizations can ensure the sustained contributions of these productive and experienced members. In other words, by investing in these employees, organizations can reap rich dividends.

When employees face problems in simultaneously meeting the demands of the family and the workplace, the organization usually suffers in terms of (1) members' lost time at work, primarily because of child-care responsibilities; (2) turnover of personnel—sometimes due to members' inability to cope with unrelenting family and work demands and sometimes to the unwillingness or inability of the members to relocate as and when required by the organization; and (3) the more intangible adverse consequences of professionals' psychological alienation from work. Such alienation can result in unfriendly behaviors and discourteous treatment of clients, lowered quality and quantity of output, and higher wastage rates—all of which lower the profits of the organization. There are thus both hidden and manifest costs to the organization when dual-career members' stresses and strains spill over from the home to the workplace and from the workplace to the home. In any organization, there is bound to be some absenteeism, turnover, psychological alienation, and dissatisfaction. But with increasing numbers of dual-career family members on payrolls, these problems have a high probability of becoming exacerbated because of employees' dual commitment to work and family. Institutions thus face the challenge of working creatively to avoid these adverse effects and to turn dual-career members into organizational assets.

Let us first determine the cost of the dysfunctional effects of employee absenteeism, turnover, and alienation by means of a hypothetical situation and then see how, by providing certain types of benefits such as child care and parenting leave, organizations can actually increase their profits.

Hidden Costs

Let us examine the hypothetical case of a medium-sized company with an average annual sales volume of $25 million and with twenty-five dual-career professionals on its payroll. Let us assume that the average annual salary and perquisites of professionals in this organization come to $40,000. We can expect that some of the work hours of the professionals will be lost to emergency family situations, such as unexpected child-care responsibilities, as well as to vacation, jury duty, and personal leave. We can apply Cascio's (1982) formula (discussed below) to find the costs here. In addition, we can estimate the annual turnover rate of the dual-career family members due to various causes, including incompatibility of the spouses' work schedules, need for temporary part-time assignments, and forced relocation at 16 percent. This is based on Bureau of National Affairs statistics ("BNA's Job Absence . . . ," 1980) that give an average rate of 22 percent turnover of the work force for all companies. This works out to an average turnover of four dual-career members each year in our hypothetical medium-sized company. We can now determine the cost of these incidents, following Cascio's (1982) recommended methods.

Absenteeism. Cascio states that the hidden costs of absenteeism and sick leave can be estimated at 3 percent of the annual salary of members. In this case, for twenty-five professionals, the annual costs to the organization would be $30,000 (25 X $40,000 X .03).

Turnover. Turnover costs include: (1) separation costs (exit interviews, administrative functions relating to termination, separation pay, and unemployment tax contributions); (2) replacement costs (advertising for the position, preemployment administrative functions, interviewing candidates—at least three interviews for each position, and a number of different interviews for the person ultimately hired—medical examination, and postemployment dissemination of information); (3) training costs of the newly acquired personnel (informational literature, instructors' and trainees' salaries during instructional period, on-the-job training costs when both the newly recruited member and the trainer spend time learning and teaching); (4) dollar value increases due to inflation; and (5) lost time and forgone opportunities during the training of the newly hired persons until they catch up with the efficiency and the effectiveness of the more experienced workers.

These costs could total anywhere from two to ten times the annual payroll of employees in an organization (Report of the Committee on Human Resource Accounting, 1978). Let us estimate the costs of turnover and replacement of professionals in our hypothetical company to be five times their annual salary—the replacement costs of many professionals who are specialists difficult to recruit and replace would be much more. For each professional who has to be replaced, the organization will lose $200,000. For an average turnover of four members per year, the total replacement costs would be $800,000. These are extremely conservative estimates. In 1972, Flamholtz estimated that the replacement costs of *one* sales manager in an insurance company in 1982 would be $399,600! In 1977, the United States Navy estimated that it cost $86,000 to graduate a naval officer from the Naval Academy and $1,500,000 to train a competent fighter pilot (Wanous, 1980). Thus, the costs of turnover are high, and, as Cascio states, many organizations may be unaware of the actual costs they incur as a result of turnover of their personnel.

Negative Attitudes of Professionals. Even though Cascio recognized the problems with attempting to place a monetary value on employee attitudes and behaviors, he still demonstrated that providing conditions in the work setting that enhance the intrinsic motivation, satisfaction, and ego involvement of employees would lend itself to "dollarizing" attitudinal changes in employees. One method of doing this would be to arrive at an attitude index and then multiply it by the salary of the employees. It is not very meaningful to engage in such calculations in a vacuum, but since negative attitudes of employees are likely to affect sales (shoddy products and unhappy customers), we can conservatively estimate the sales lost due to the psychological alienation of professionals at 5 percent. With an annual sales volume of $25 million for our hypothetical company, the potential loss in sales due to dual-career members' negative attitudes would be $1,250,000.

Thus, the total hidden cost of dual-career professionals' absenteeism, turnover, and negative attitudes to the organization in our hypothetical case is $2,080,000 annually, or 8.32 percent of sales. However, organizations can avoid such adverse consequences by providing facilities to dual-career members that will considerably minimize, if not totally eliminate, the problems. Benefit schemes such as child care and parenting leave are inexpensive compared to the benefits they yield. According to a 1982 National Employer-Supported Child Care Project, 95 percent of the companies surveyed reported that the benefits of child-care assistance programs far outweighed the costs, resulting in a 65 percent decrease in turnover, a 53 percent reduction in absenteeism, an 85 percent increase in recruitment and retaining capabilities, and a 90 percent increase in employee morale (Lehrman, 1985).

We can now determine the cost of the benefits that would accrue to our hypothetical organization by providing child care, parenting leave, and even relocation facilities. Estimating an annual expenditure of $15,000 per year per member, the total cost of providing these facilities to the twenty-five professionals works out to $375,000. A tax write-off of 36 percent on this would lower the net additional cost to $240,000 ($375,000 less $135,000). By spending this amount, the company would not only avoid the loss of $2,080,000 in sales noted earlier but would actually increase its sales. By creating a climate conducive to the effective functioning of dual-career professionals, the organization would increase the productivity of its professionals, as a result of which we can estimate a gain of at least 5 percent in sales, raising the sales volume from $25 million to $26.25 million even during the first year. Investing $240,000 in dual-career members has resulted in losses being turned to gains. That is, on a net investment in employee benefits of $240,000, the net increase in sales (after the $240,000 has been deducted) is $1,010,000. These calculations for the twenty-five dual-career members in our hypothetical company are shown in Table 1.

This cost-benefit analysis concerns only the twenty-five dual-career members in our hypothetical organization. In the interests of equity, however, cafeteria-type benefit schemes will have to be introduced for all organizational members. This will, of course, increase the expenses for the organization. There might also be some heavy setup costs. At the same time, however, there will be corresponding decreases in employee turnover, absenteeism, and negative attitudes, as well as organization-wide increases in productivity. As the company's employee benefit expenses are reduced through economies of scale, moreover, the productivity gains for the organization are likely to be substantial if it follows the right managerial policies. Ferrara

Table 1. A Cost-Benefit Analysis of Facilitating Structures.

Costs of Ignoring Needs of Dual-Career Members	
Absenteeism (40,000 × 25 × .03)	$ 30,000
Turnover and replacement costs (40,000 × 4 × 5)	800,000
Poor attitudes of members (5% of sales)	1,250,000
Total Loss	$2,080,000
Loss as percentage of sales (2,080,000/25 m) × 100	8.32%
Expenses Incurred on Benefit Schemes	
$15,000 per member per year on child care/parenting leave/relocation (15,000 × 25)	$ 375,000
Less tax write-off @ 36% (375,000 × .36)	135,000
Net additional expenses incurred	$ 240,000
Benefits	
Gains in productivity due to improved benefits @ (5% of sales)	$1,250,000
Net increase in sales (1,250,000 − 240,000)	$1,010,000

(1983) recorded that improved performance resulted from quality of work life programs in organizations such as Fairchild Industries. Youngblood and Chambers-Cook (1984) found that the turnover of employees in a textile company in North Carolina declined from 8 percent to 3 percent after the establishment of an in-house day-care facility. Employees' job satisfaction and organizational commitment increased as well.

It is important to take into consideration the trends in labor statistics that indicate that single-parent professionals—both men and women—are increasing in numbers every year. Most of the structural policies and procedures aimed at dual-career couples will also benefit this group of professionals, which means that their productivity will increase too. Thus, organizations—especially medium- and large-sized ones—have everything to gain and nothing to lose by restructuring the workplace.

Since productivity is a key issue for organizations, considerable ingenuity is called for in making the appropriate changes to motivate the work force to give forth its best. The managing editor of *Consumers' Research* stated in the *Wall*

Street Journal (Lehrman, 1985) that even though firms cannot
afford to neglect employee child care, only 1,800 U.S. employers out of 6 million offer some type of child-care assistance.
Most employers, he explains, are just not aware of the problems faced by organizational members or the range of options
available to organizations for solving them. Lehrman urges that
companies use flexible benefit plans that cost them almost
nothing compared to the benefits they derive therefrom.

Why Changes Must Be Made

There are several other compelling reasons for organizations to contemplate structural and process changes: (1) the
changing composition of the work force; (2) the changing "organization man" ethic (Super, 1984; Yankelovich and Lefkowitz, 1982a); (3) changing definitions of career and success
(McDaniels, 1984); (4) emerging patterns of paths to excellence
(McKendrick, 1985a); (5) changing attitudes toward upward mobility (Kaye, 1982); (6) sex-role tensions between the genders
at the workplace (Sundal-Hansen, 1984); (7) obsolete organizational policies (Catalyst, 1981); and (8) the emerging dimension
of corporate social responsibility (Sekaran and Snodgrass, 1985).

Changing Composition of the Work Force. Consider the
labor statistics that indicate that (1) the male worker-to-popula-
tion ratio was 10 percentage points lower in 1984 than in 1950
and (2) there has been a truly impressive increase in the number
of female professionals during the period from 1972 to 1982—
a 59 percent increase among managers and administrators, 61
percent among engineers, 70 percent among computer specialists, 78 percent among accountants, 100 percent among techni-
cians, 100 percent among life and physical scientists, and 305
percent among lawyers and judges. These professional women,
however, still opt for a life-style that includes marriage and a
family (Rosen, 1985). The number of dual-career couples has
increased from 900,000 in 1960 to 3.3 million in 1983 and now
constitutes a fifth of all working couples.

Judging by the rate of increase among women who are
currently training themselves to be professionals, the number of

dual-career families is likely to grow at an exponential rate in the next decade. As highlighted by the Conference Board (1985), the relatively small number of two-career couples today belies the visibility they have in the business world and the influence they are bound to exert in the future on the personnel policies and practices of employers. In addition, the number of two-earner families, single-parent families, and unmarried working couples living together is steadily increasing. This population constitutes more than 90 percent of today's labor force. Organizations are already beginning to feel the impact of this new breed of employee.

Organizations have to acquire and use resources effectively and productively to make profits. By instituting policies, procedures, and practices that attract, motivate, train, reward, and help to retain qualified employees, organizations will increase their own productivity, profits, and growth. Since institutions cannot arrest the growth in two-earner and single-parent families, they really have no choice but to change their structures and processes to meet the new challenges posed by the changing composition of the work force.

Passing of the Organization Man. The "organization man" concept is fast eroding, and organizations can no longer expect employees to be totally committed to organizational work alone (Yankelovich and Lefkowitz, 1982a, 1982b). The reasons for this are many, and institutions need to be sensitive to the changes taking place. When organizations dealt only with traditional single-earner family members, they did not have to worry about the family aspects of their employees' lives. Men had their support systems at home, and wives were prepared to further their husbands' career aspirations. Companies could then order male professionals to undertake business travel, relocate, and accept overseas assignment—all at short notice. Such assignments were considered to be a recognition of and reward for good performance. The professionals were also expected to give 100 percent commitment to the organization as their talents unfolded. Companies could also train corporate wives to project the right image to people who counted.

Even when increasing numbers of married women began

to enter the labor market, most of them took jobs that they considered secondary in importance to their husbands' professional careers. Organizations thus did not have to make any significant changes in their policies to accommodate employees' families, since the wives remained flexible about their work and careers. Working women usually moved in and out of jobs as necessitated by family circumstances and the needs of their spouses. For instance, many wives withdrew from the labor market for childbearing and child rearing and reentered it only after the children had grown old enough to take care of themselves. If the husband was transferred, the wife moved along with him and found another job in the new place. When there were emergencies in the family, the wife took leave and attended to them. Thus, all problems and eventualities faced by the family were solved by the family, without the organizations ever becoming aware of or involved in them. But the situation has now changed.

As a result of the large increase in the number of educated professional married women who want to carve out careers for themselves, the dynamics of organizational and family commitments for men and women are starting to alter in irreversible ways. In two-career families, both spouses are forced to share family responsibilities. Total commitment to the job and the organization therefore becomes impossible for either of the spouses. Increasing numbers of dual-career members are now unwilling to relocate, and moving corporate spouses is becoming a new issue for organizations (Pave, 1985). Even in dual-earner families, wives who have acquired the necessary education and training to advance in their own organizations are now asking, "What about my progress in my job?" (Sekas, 1984). All this means that the husbands in such families are no longer free to concentrate solely on their careers and the needs of their employing organizations. Hence, organizations can no longer expect total dedication from their employees and must instead pay heed to the changing needs of employees in general and professionals in particular.

Changing Definitions of Career and Success. Organizations are also now facing the reality that employees place more and more emphasis on leisure activities. Consider, for instance, the many professionals—managers, department chairpersons, and scientists—who now take time away from their pressing job demands before the noon hour every day to jog or run. Leisure as a legitimate and essential pursuit closely aligned with one's career progress will gain increasing importance in the next decade. Even now, shorter workweeks, longer and more frequent vacations, and higher levels of interest in leisure pursuits are very much in evidence. These trends are likely to increase in the future. It is interesting to note that a recent report by Sears (1982) defines a career as the totality of work *and* leisure activities one does in a lifetime. This linking of work and leisure amounts to a "holistic" view of careers (McDaniels, 1984).

Given this perspective, as O'Toole (1981) remarked, it will become necessary for organizations to alter their expectations of employees in the coming decades. Organizations will increasingly have to adopt more flexible management styles to increase worker productivity and satisfaction. The working population is going to seek alternative patterns of work in the future and will look for self-fulfilment, self-actualization, and self-expression in both work and nonwork activities (Yankelovich and Lefkowitz, 1982b). Some progressive organizations have already started to provide organization-sponsored leisure programs and recreational facilities, including gymnasiums, outdoor tennis courts, and jogging areas. This does not mean that the professionals of tomorrow will not be work oriented and productive. But it does mean that they will be productive on their own terms—by balancing work and nonwork activities. In the case of nontraditional families, it would be a matter of balancing career, family, and leisure activities.

Different Paths to Achieving Excellence. Managers in the organizational world of today have to deal with a number of paradoxes. For instance, the literature on successful organizations extols the virtues of institutional excellence, hardworking, dedicated employees, and outstanding individuals who inculcate the virtues of the work ethic in other organizational members. However, most of the people who shaped successful organizations in the past were men from traditional families who dedicated themselves totally to their careers. These men created and developed their organizations and brought them to the state of excellence that recent books such as *Corporate Cultures* (Deal and Kennedy, 1982) and *In Search of Excellence* (Peters and Waterman, 1982) extol as models.

The future shapers of organizations, however, are likely to have a different definition of excellence and to have their own ideas of how excellence may be achieved. For them, excellence may imply an organizational system in which members, first and foremost, stay physically and mentally healthy and fit. We have already discussed many of the factors responsible for this changing definition. The slow erosion of the work ethic, the changing "success" ethic, the social milieu that is creating a work and leisure ethos, and the increasing number of dual-career family members in the work system are all factors contributing to the reconceptualization of excellence. Thus, the traditional belief that success and excellence are attained through total dedication, perseverance, and commitment to work will undergo a change (McKendrick, 1985a).

Current research also lends strong support to the theory that spending too many hours at the workplace is hazardous to health and family happiness (Bartolomé and Evans, 1980; Hall and Rabinowitz, 1977). Good mental health, it seems, requires the correct balance between career and nonwork (family, leisure) interests (Gysbers and Associates, 1984). It would no doubt be difficult for traditional managers whose lives revolve around their careers to live up to this philosophy themselves. However, becoming aware of the changing definitions of careers will help such traditional managers to avoid becoming frustrated by expecting total commitment from the new generation of employees, including dual-career professionals. Moreover, by balancing work and nonwork interests, employees may be able to produce higher quality work within normal working hours. Working beyond regular office hours (especially in the case of nontraditional family members who may have to share household work) will only fatigue employees, thus compromising the quality and effectiveness of their performance. As a matter of fact, one country—Sweden—is cutting down the normal workday from eight to six hours. While the economic growth rate and social values of Sweden may be different from those of the United States, American workers are among the most productive in the world and are capable of achieving excellence and high productivity within optimum working hours. Managers who work hard for long hours will feel less vexed with their subordinates when they reorient their thinking along these lines. This will also help them to conceptualize and attain success in new ways. As noted by McKendrick (1985a), a whole new corporate culture is developing in which competition is giving way to cooperation. Managers are coming to realize that the challenge for them lies in motivating employees through different approaches from those they found effective in the past.

An approach taken by Johnson & Johnson, Intermatic, and Hospital Corporation of America is to provide incentives to their employees to exercise and stay fit (Toufexis, 1985b). The companies look upon these programs as investments in their employees. Other companies encourage employees to take some time off from work during the day to exercise, relax, or meditate.

Shifting Attitudes Toward Upward Mobility. Concepts of job mobility have also changed among today's employees. Many professionals find satisfaction in doing what they are currently engaged in and do not care about moving up in their organizations. For instance, two male professionals whom I interviewed —one an engineer, the other a systems designer—said that they had just turned down offers for promotion from their technical jobs to administrative positions. The engineer told me:

> They offered me this promotion and my boss said it was *the* opportunity for me to climb up the ladder, but I did not care for it. In my line, I am an expert. When I get into the administrative side, I will just be pushing papers and that will bore me to death. I am just not cut out for that kind of job, so I politely declined. I guess my boss was somewhat disappointed.

Many effective, technically oriented employees become ineffective when promoted to managerial positions; they lose self-esteem and self-confidence and begin to consider themselves total failures. Organizational history is replete with such figures. Thus, vertical career ladders are not for everyone (Kaye, 1982; Raelin, 1984; Schein, 1978). Other alternative career paths have to be developed to keep professionals motivated. Sometimes managers welcome even downward career moves at particular stages of their lives—for example, when family demands become too much or when they want to ease into retirement. These needs for different career paths require structural changes in organizations.

Sex-Role Tensions at the Workplace. Sex-role stereotyping in the workplace produces tensions for both women and men (Good, Kirkland, and Grissom, 1979; Nelson and Quick, 1985; Unger, 1979). According to an article in the *Wall Street Journal* (Rogan, 1984b), a Gallup poll of senior executive women revealed that they felt that male chauvinism exists in organizations and that even at upper levels a woman is not taken seriously. These executives reported that men in senior management positions, who mostly come from traditional backgrounds and think that women should be subservient, feel psychologically uncomfortable in dealing with women. Seventy percent of the women executives polled said they were paid less than men of equal ability, 60 percent felt their views were not respected as much as men's, 41 percent felt that male subordinates resisted taking orders from women, and 29 percent felt that their personal lives were scrutinized more than those of their male colleagues.

With increasing numbers of women professionals entering the work force, such concerns and tensions detract from the effectiveness of all members. Issues of abilities, comparable worth, and equal treatment are dominant themes that organizations have already begun to contend with in the form of law suits (Smith, 1985b). As more and more dual-career members enter the work force, sex-role tensions will have to be managed in organizations. What is absolutely essential for managing these tensions is to create a culture that will "desex" the workplace. It stands to reason that if 50 percent or more of the work force is going to be comprised of women in the future, their talents need to be fully utilized. A vast human resource will be grossly underutilized if women professionals, most of whom will be from dual-career families, are prevented from giving their best.

Naisbitt identified an additional megatrend after the publication of his book *Megatrends* in 1982 that is of relevance here. This trend is the "shift from sex-roles to synergy"—that is, a "rethinking of masculine and feminine roles and making them into a new whole" (Zweig, 1983, p. 138). This shift implies that we go beyond the battle of the sexes to try to blend functional masculine and feminine qualities. This would be akin to the fusion of the right and left brain so essential for creativity, innovation, productivity, and capturing the best in human potential. In Chapters Two and Three we also noted that by treating women and men as equals at the workplace, we will bring egalitarianism to the family setting. Organizations will find themselves increasingly engaged in a search for creative ways to develop synergistic, androgynous structures in which sex-role stereotyping of occupations and roles will no longer have a place.

Change in organizational philosophy, culture, and processes will be brought about by sensitive and forward-looking managers. The main path to organizational growth and productivity in the future will be through the utilization of the *full* potential of all employees, including dual-career members. David Bloom, a Harvard labor economist, notes that "the growth of women in the work force is probably the single most important change that has ever taken place in the American labor market. Their arrival at high executive levels will be the major development for working women over the next twenty years" (Castro, 1985, p. 64). A partner in an executive-search firm adds, "More and more companies realize that a good manager is a good manager regardless of sex" (pp. 64–65).

Obsolete Organizational Policies. Some existing but obsolete organizational policies are not conducive to productivity in organizations (Catalyst, 1981). For example, a few organizations still enforce antinepotism policies. Antinepotism laws were rigidly enforced during the Great Depression. It was considered unfair for two people in the same family to hold jobs in the same company when numerous people were without work (Battaile, 1978). For quite some time now, antinepotism laws have been considered illegal and discriminatory. Yet many managers still entertain outmoded ideas in this area, even though couples working for the same organization are usually productive and the couples themselves derive satisfaction from working for the same organization.

Some firms also have conflict of interest policies that forbid the hiring of a dual-career member whose spouse works for a competing organization. Such policies may or may not be necessary. By retaining the conflict of interest policy, organizations may not be able to attract the best employees or may lose some existing valuable employees if their spouses go to work for another organization in the same industry.

New Dimensions of Corporate Social Responsibility. One indication of organizational effectiveness is the extent to which organizations help their members experience a high quality of work life (Davis and Cherns, 1975). With the increasing number of dual-earner families, organizations will have to start paying attention to both the quality of work life and the quality of life in general of both partners in dual-career families (Sekaran, 1985a). There are two reasons for this. First, by enhancing the general overall quality of life, the organization gains in terms of members' performance and productivity. Second, serious conflicts in the family frequently arise because of organizationally induced tensions such as fast career ladders for men but not for women (Kanter, 1977). When organizations pursue more equitable policies, they help the dual-career family to sustain itself as a unit. Although individuals are responsible for balancing the two facets of their lives, management must answer for practices and policies that make it difficult for professionals to manage the relationship between the personal and work spheres (Bartolomé and Evans, 1980). And it is highly likely that public sensitivity to such corporate responsibilities will become more pronounced in the future.

All the factors discussed thus far related to the entire work force, including dual-career members. The managerial challenge of the 1990s is depicted in Figure 4.

Figure 4. Need for Organizations to Change.

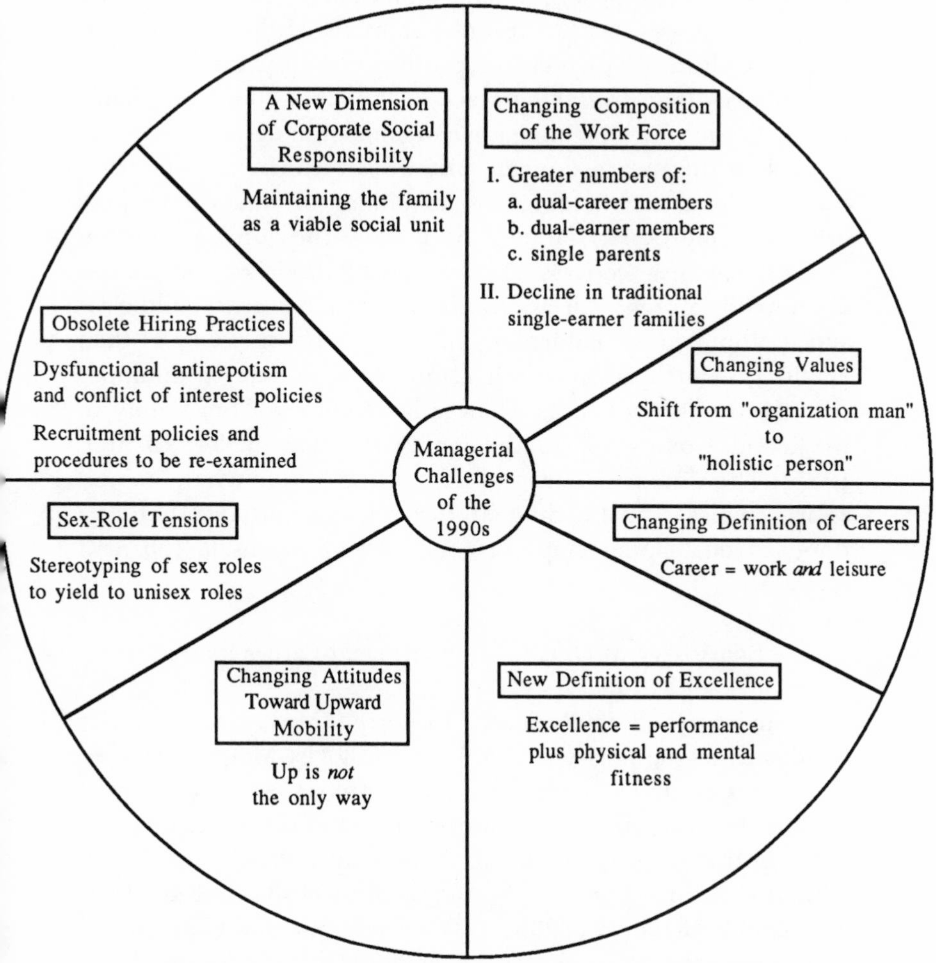

Managerial Challenges of the 1990s

A New Dimension of Corporate Social Responsibility

Maintaining the family as a viable social unit

Changing Composition of the Work Force

I. Greater numbers of:
   a. dual-career members
   b. dual-earner members
   c. single parents

II. Decline in traditional single-earner families

Obsolete Hiring Practices

Dysfunctional antinepotism and conflict of interest policies

Recruitment policies and procedures to be re-examined

Changing Values

Shift from "organization man" to "holistic person"

Sex-Role Tensions

Stereotyping of sex roles to yield to unisex roles

Changing Definition of Careers

Career = work *and* leisure

Changing Attitudes Toward Upward Mobility

Up is *not* the only way

New Definition of Excellence

Excellence = performance plus physical and mental fitness

With increasing numbers of nontraditional families in which the wives hold jobs that have the potential to lead to careers or in which the wives already are pursuing careers, employing organizations have a gold mine to tap. By changing the structures and processes hitherto geared solely to males, institutions can make significant progress. Currently, according to a survey of 275 corporations, American employees are working up to only half their capacity because they are ill prepared and ill managed (Thompson, Keele, and Couch, 1985). Organizations can, however, tap the full potentials of their employees, including those of dual-career professionals, by understanding the changes that are taking place in the labor force and facing the challenges through innovative organization designs.

In other words, organizations can enhance their effectiveness by understanding the dynamics of dual-career (and other nontraditional) families both from the nonwork and organizational perspectives. This will enable them to consciously develop structures such as alternative work patterns, child care, and multiple career ladders to enhance the productivity of their employees. Such design mechanisms will also help to minimize the adverse consequences of negative spillover from family to work and from work to the family (Crouter, 1984; Richter, 1985). The time to reflect and take action is *now* when the necessary changes can be thought through and initiated before a flood of dual-career employees hits organizations in the next few years.

Sensitivity of Organizations to Dual-Career Issues

In an article in *Business Insurance* ("Most Firms' Policies Outdated: Psychologist," 1982), psychologist Marjorie Hansen Shaevitz is quoted as saying that most companies see dual-career couples as a minority and do not understand the issues involved when both the spouses pursue careers. But the recent roundtable discussions sponsored by the Catalyst (1984) and the Conference Board report (1985) indicate that the consciousness of most organizations is slowly being raised in this regard. Thus, one senior vice-president remarked:

> It would be difficult today, I think, [for organizations] to be unaware of the growing number of dual-career families. I believe the business audience is hungry for direction and ready to experiment with new approaches. Many of the questions we are asking ourselves are with regard to: (1) pol-

icy-type issues (what organizational "rules" are appropriate for dealing with two married employees?); (2) what cultural values should the organization adopt to bring out "excellence" in the couples—organizations cannot presumably demand "workoholic" behaviors or view employees as "company couples"; (3) the entire area of employee benefits [that] is undergoing reexamination today largely because of dual-career families; some obvious issues are in the areas of redundant and overlapping benefits, vacation policies, parenting leave, and employee assistance programs; (4) recruitment policies and relocation facilities; and (5) reward systems that allow for other than vertical career paths to fit the family life cycle of employees.

The Catalyst survey of 1981 also indicated that companies were eager for information and knowledge about what other corporations were doing and how well new practices were working. These concerns are indicative of the felt need for restructuring institutions to take advantage of the dual-career family members in the work force rather than erecting barriers against them. However, the Conference Board study pointed out that relatively few companies make use of planning as a vehicle to proactively face the challenges of the changing demographics of the work force. Many corporations do not employ sophisticated information systems to monitor the characteristics of their own employees, much less do they use environmental scans to track current and projected trends in the demographics of the work force. Organizations are experiencing enough tension today, however, to make them ready and willing to explore the possibilities of introducing changes.

The Conference Board (1985) has constructed a profile of companies that are in fact becoming family-responsive in these changing times. Companies that are in high-tech or scientific fields, companies that have a relatively young work force, those with a high proportion of female employees, those located in "progressive" communities, nonunionized or largely nonunion companies, companies close to their founders' traditions, and those that make products for, or offer services to, the consumer market are found to be more sensitive to such phenomena as the emergence of dual-career families.

For all the reasons cited, it will be beneficial for organizations to start an audit of their own employees and determine what steps should be taken to enhance their members' and, thus, their own effectiveness.

SIX

Effective Hiring
Policies for Organizations

This chapter examines the ways in which organizations can effectively respond to the increasing numbers of dual-career families in the work force. The proposed changes in policies and procedures are designed to attract and utilize dual-career family members (as well as dual-career couples) so as to increase productivity for the organization, while at the same time increasing the quality of life for all members of the work force. An input-throughput-output model of human resource management will facilitate our discussion of current organizational practices and the changes necessary for the future.

A Human Resources Model

Organizations try to effectively deal with their employees from the time of recruitment to the time of retirement. We can discuss the various stages of human resources processing by means of an input-throughput-output model. The *inputs* into the system are the individuals who are recruited by the organization, while the *throughputs* are the ways in which these individuals are shaped or transformed so as to give the *outputs* or end results desired by the organization. The input and throughput efforts enhance organizational effectiveness as reflected in financial gains for the organization, a good quality of work life for members, and a good quality of life for society as a whole. Most organizational practices currently favor traditional employees, as depicted in Figure 5.

Inputs. In stage 1—the input stage—three functions become critical for the organization:

Figure 5. Traditional Input-Throughput-Output Model of Human Resources Processing.

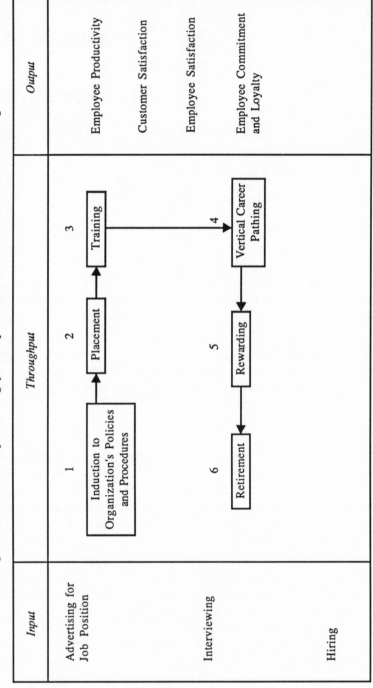

1. Advertising for positions that are to be filled in particular departments of the organization in ways that describe the position and indicate the types of individuals needed to fill the vacancies.
2. Interviewing the applicants.
3. Hiring the qualified applicants.

Throughputs. In stage 2—the throughput stage—organizations take various steps to ensure that the people recruited become productive employees. The transformation processes continue on an ongoing basis until the individuals retire. The critical steps at this stage are:

1. Induction into the company systems, policies, procedures, and norms through superiors and cohorts.
2. Placement of the individual on the job.
3. Periodic training on and off the job.
4. Designing vertical career paths for individuals.
5. Providing facilities, rewards, and benefits that motivate employees.
6. Monitoring the progress of the individual until retirement.

Outputs. After taking care of the functions in stages 1 and 2, in stage 3—the output stage—organizations look for, among other things, (1) increased sales, profits, and other measures of financial success through employee productivity; (2) increased employee involvement, satisfaction, commitment, and loyalty to the organization; and (3) an increased sense of social responsibility including a concern for such matters as safe products and protection of the environment (Sekaran and Snodgrass, 1985).

The current procedures and structures used by organizations in the input and throughput stages—for example, their processes for recruitment, training, and designing vertical career paths—are perhaps appropriate for a traditional work force. In the future, however, with increasing numbers of dual-career professionals in the job market, the functions performed by organizations in both the input and throughput stages will have to be greatly altered to meet the new challenges. Let us then examine existing practices, policies, and procedures, the changes that must be made, and what companies are doing in the various stages of the model.

Input Stage

Traditional organizational practices at the input stage are not tailored to the needs of the new wave of institutional members.

Currently, organizations advertise positions as and when vacancies arise, interview potentially promising applicants, and hire those who the interviewers feel are best suited for the job. Despite these efforts, it is possible that companies are still not attracting and making use of the best talent available in the labor market because of some existing dysfunctional policies on their books. For instance, if the organization has an *antinepotism* policy, dual-career couples who may be ideally suited for two different positions that the company has will not be recruited. Thus, existing policies and procedures followed by some companies may not only *not* be conducive to attracting the best among dual-career professional couples but may in fact be stumbling blocks to acquiring them. Additionally, antinepotism regulations enforced against spouses have been found to be illegal and discriminatory unless they are uniformly applied to all other types of relatives as well ("When Career Couples . . . ," 1976).

The second impediment could be an organization's *conflict of interest* policies that prohibit the hiring of persons with family members who are employed in competing organizations. Thus, organizations may fail to recruit a potentially valuable dual-career professional simply because his or her spouse happens to work for a competing organization. In the vast majority of such cases no real conflict of interest will ever arise. Also, as with antinepotism, there are some legal problems with trying to put conflict of interest policies into practice. Many civil rights lawyers believe that rejecting an employee because of the spouse's job violates the sex-bias provisions of the Civil Rights

Act of 1964 ("When Career Couples . . . ," 1976). More to the point, Shuman and Shuman (1983) described a suit that a woman marketing manager filed against IBM when the company required her either to stop dating a male marketing manager who had left IBM and joined a competing firm or quit her job. She won. Hence, organizations will have to carefully review their conflict of interest policies to ensure that they are not either losing out on potentially good professionals or making themselves vulnerable to law suits.

A third problem is that many of the *recruitment procedures* followed by organizations are not conducive to attracting either dual-career family members or couples. Usually, neither the advertising practices nor the interviewing procedures are geared toward dual-career professionals. If advertisements would specify that dual-career couples are acceptable to an organization or that the organization has facilitating structures for two-career family members (such as day care and flexible schedules), then more dual-career spouses would be encouraged to apply for positions in that organization. Further, the interviewing practices followed by most companies are outdated and counterproductive. For instance, several studies indicate that interviewers who do not favor the concept of two-career couples follow inappropriate interviewing procedures in talking either to the couple or to the individual spouses. They then make biased decisions that may be detrimental not only to the dual-career family members but also to the organization, since it misses the opportunity to hire qualified employees (Rosen, Jerdee, and Prestwich, 1975; Stringer-Moore, 1981).

Biases occur in several ways. Some interviewers simply do not think that a woman will be capable of managing both a family and a career. They may then automatically assume that the wife will be less than fully committed to her career and will sacrifice it to her husband's progress (Berger, Foster, Wallston, and Wright, 1977). Research also indicates that employers who offer jobs to a couple do not always treat both spouses as individuals in their own right. During job interviews, one of the members (usually the wife) may be ignored, and the combined salary offered to the couple may be lower than that offered to two competitive, independent employees. Even when offering a couple jobs, one of which might be below the qualifications of the individual, employers sometimes adopt an attitude of "we are doing you a favor" (Mathews and Mathews, 1980). When couples seek jobs individually, some employers insist on considering the husband's job status before making a job offer to the wife. Such an attitude forces the couple that might want to practice egalitarian values in career decision processes to resort to making nonegalitarian forced choices (Wallston, Foster, and Berger, 1978).

Whether a couple feels accepted or rejected during a job interview may often be a function of the attitudes of the recruiter toward dual-career couples (Pingree, Butler, Paisley, and Hawkins, 1978). It is possible that the style and process of interviewing have changed during the last five years, but institutions should nevertheless try to ensure the integrity of the interviewing process. Usually, people higher up in the organization and those who are themselves members of dual-career families are said to have better attitudes toward, and to be less biased against, two-career couples (Conference Board, 1985; London and Poplanski, 1976; Rose and Andiappan, 1978).

Apart from having unbiased attitudes, interviewers will also have to accurately assess the suitability of the interviewees with respect to their abilities, aptitudes, life interests, and career goals. Most interviews with dual-career members, however, seem to concentrate more on nonperformance issues than on the individuals' needs, skills, abilities, and career goals (Mathews and Mathews, 1980). Abundant research evidence indicates that some interviewers stereotypically assign lower abilities and skills to women than to men. Hence they are reluctant to hire women even though the women's academic and technical qualifications are the same as those of the male candidates (see, for instance, Rosen and Jerdee, 1974; Dubno, 1985). We can readily understand how such attitudes will thwart the goal of attracting dual-career members to the organization. It may be useful to highlight the following salient points from Reif, Newstrom, and Monczka (1975), who summarized the gender differences in work-related abilities and attitudes, so that institutions and their members can shed their fears about women's inabilities:

1. The Johnson O'Connor Research Foundation's Human Engineering Lab, which tested for differences between men and women in levels of measured abilities and knowledge required in regard to twenty-two business-related dimensions, found no gender differences with regard to fourteen categories. Women excelled in six—finger dexterity, graphoria, ideaphoria, observation, silograms, and abstract visualization. (Graphoria, ideaphoria, and silograms refer to the abilities to depict data graphically, generate ideas from available data, and organize them meaningfully.) Men excelled in grip and structural visualization. Because successful management depends on three important characteristics—objective personality, good English vocabulary, and abstract visualization—in the first two of which men and women are equal and in the third of which the women excel, it was felt that, at least theoretically, there should be more women than men in management.

2. Men and women are equally concerned about self-actualization at work and are equally disappointed with intellectually undemanding jobs. Both are equally interested in getting ahead on the job.

3. Female managers have more positive attitudes toward the formal organization and its ability to fill their needs than male managers do.

Thus, Reif, Newstrom, and Monczka (1975) strongly emphasized that the supposed substantive differences between men's and women's personalities, abilities, and attitudes about work do not really exist except in the minds of those who have traditional beliefs. The authors noted that they were not suggesting that women were superior to men; rather, they were arguing that women should be considered for positions purely on the basis of their qualifications, just as men are. Since several research studies indicate no gender differences between men and women, interviewers must be particularly sensitive to issues of personal bias and develop more objective evaluation skills. If not, opportunities to acquire two professionals who are likely to provide synergy to the organization will be lost. Thus, organizations may have to change existing policies and recruitment procedures if they want to tap the best available resources among dual-career professionals.

Policy Changes Needed at Input Stage

The changes needed in regard to antinepotism and conflict of interest policies, as well as the procedural changes required with respect to recruitment, will now be discussed.

Antinepotism. Unless some special reason exists for not doing so, organizations can safely discard all the antinepotism policies on their books (Gilmore and Fannin, 1982). However, companies do not have to allow couples to work in the same department or allow one spouse to supervise the other. If individuals who work together in the same unit get married, one of the members can be transferred to another department. Of course, this may not always be possible, especially if the individuals have technical qualifications in the same field or if they have already achieved high-level positions in the organization. In such cases companies should be able to fall back on an organizational culture and climate that calls for all employees (including couples) to follow professional norms of behavior.

In some cases, romantic relationships that created synergy and productivity for the organization when two professionals worked together in a boss-subordinate status has produced the opposite effect after marriage. The result was usually that one of the partners left the company (Josefowitz, 1982). In general, however, close relationships between employees will not be detrimental to the organization as long as the couples in question do not neglect the work side of their lives. In any case, the organization can establish norms of professional etiquette that will discourage romantic behaviors within the work premises (Jamison, 1983).

Conflict of Interest. Industrial espionage has always been of concern to some organizations (Hall and Hall, 1979), and rightly so, since market share, profits, and growth may all be tied to secret formulas. Manufacturing companies, scientific institutions, military systems, and governments are all concerned about guarding their secrets as are various kinds of service or-

ganizations. An article in *Business Week* ("When Career Couples
. . . ," 1976) reported the story of a senior vice-president and
creative director of a public relations firm who was dating a
woman working for another public relations firm. Both were
called by their respective bosses and asked for assurances that
their relationship was not compromising their job loyalty. Organizations cannot realistically do much more than this since,
in businesses such as telecasting and publishing, everyone might
have to quit if conflict of interest policies were strictly enforced. Formulating a written code of conduct is also not feasi-
ble since it is difficult to decide when conflict of interest is
endangered and when it is not. Moreover, as rightly pointed out
in the article cited earlier, it is extremely difficult, if not impossible, to police two individuals who are working for competing firms and have established some kind of relationship with
each other.

The *Business Week* article ("When Career Couples . . . ,"
1976) seems to indicate that couples have evolved their own
codes of professional conduct, which includes not sharing confidential work information with each other and thus protecting
their careers and their company's interests. In my own interviews with dual-career couples, a few spouses said that they
make it a point not to talk about work matters at home. Others
indicated that while they share their general work experiences
and anything that seems challenging or exciting at the workplace, they do not talk about confidential matters. Hence a simple oath of loyalty from all organizational members would be a
sufficient safeguard for most organizations.

In certain top security jobs and political systems, however, conflict of interest might become a key issue. Hall and
Hall (1979) mention the case of Robert and Elizabeth Dole; the
latter had to resign her government job to enable the former to
run for vice-president in 1976. But again, unless there are very
special and compelling reasons for not hiring or retaining an employee whose spouse works for a competitor, it may not be
necessary for organizations to have policies that forbid spouses
(or other kinds of relatives) from working for competing organizations.

Advertising Procedures. Policy and procedural changes are definitely called for in recruiting if dual-career couples are to be accommodated in organizations. Stringer-Moore (1981) has offered several suggestions to organizations on how dual-career members can be attracted to the work system and what procedures would help in the hiring of such members. For example, she notes that personnel departments can attract greater numbers of dual-career professionals into their systems by advertising the broadest range of job opportunities that exist in the organization at any given time. If an organization requires a diverse range of skills, it can more easily accommodate two spouses who might be proficient in different areas. Stringer-Moore also explains the pitfalls in hiring one spouse and then trying to discover or create a vacancy to accommodate the other. For example, a wife might not be willing to accept a job unless her husband is settled in the area too. But the company may become liable for legal action if it then creates a position and offers a job to the husband without going through normal hiring procedures (advertising for the job and so on). Hence, it is doubly advisable for organizations to advertise a full range of job vacancies at one time so that maximum opportunities exist to hire both spouses.

One way to do this is to coordinate the personnel requirements of the various subsystems by means of a central unit that could then periodically advertise the needs of the entire organizational system. The advertisements could state that the positions are open for all qualified people, including dual-career couples and members from two-career families. It could also describe the organization's employee-friendly policies, such as alternative work patterns (flexible schedules, job sharing, and part-time work) and child-care options. Carefully thought-out policies will enhance advertising effectiveness and will help the organization to acquire the best talent among dual-career professionals. Organizations can also build and project a favorable image by innovatively rethinking and implementing their hiring policies. The pioneers in this regard will, as with all other innovative marketing strategies, reap the highest dividends in the years to come.

Interviewing Techniques. Legally, interviewers may not ask interviewees personal questions such as the size of their families or the occupations of their spouses. Many interviewers, however, ignore the rules and do pose personal questions that are often resented by interviewees, even though they may reluctantly respond to the queries. According to Jablin (1982), the illegal questions most frequently asked of women are (1) do you plan to have children? (2) what are your marriage plans? (3) what does your husband do? (4) what would happen if you or your husband were to be transferred or relocated? and (5) who will take care of your children while you are at work? The most frequent question asked of men is, How would you feel working for a woman?

A trained interviewer, of course, can ask general questions that will elicit many of the responses that direct questions might fail to obtain. The interviews should directly focus on learning how applicants define success, how they propose to attain it, what their needs, abilities, aptitudes, and priorities are, and what strategies they would adopt to attain their personal and professional goals. Applicants who have thought through these issues seriously and have a clear idea of what their central life interests are, where their priorities lie, and how they will manage their work and nonwork lives can easily be differentiated from those who are vague about such matters. Thus, much information can be gained about interviewees without trespassing legal boundaries.

Eliciting such information, however, requires special skill development and training. If the interviewer is a dual-career family member, he or she can easily explore various career issues by introducing his or her own dual-career experiences. As long as the intent of questions is to explore career-related objectives, the interviewer is not likely to tread on the interviewee's toes. Dual-career members, more often than not, will volunteer information about circumstances that might cause problems later. For instance, one of the interviewees in the article cited earlier ("When Career Couples . . . ," 1976) stated that if her husband were working for a competing oil firm, she would rather volunteer this information than live in fear of what the company would do to her if it found out where he was employed.

If spouses apply for jobs in the same organization, they should be interviewed and considered for their jobs separately (Mathews and Mathews, 1980). They could, however, be taken out for lunch or dinner together, and this would allow interviewees and interviewers to explore any issues that might relate to the couple jointly. Such practices are familiar to faculty members in university systems.

Several research studies cited earlier in the chapter indicated that most interviewers showed biases against women (wives in dual-career families) in general and sometimes against dual-career couples. It is important that interviewers be trained to evaluate candidates as individuals who have or do not have the requisite qualifications, without stereotyping members as potentially more or less useful to the organization on the basis of their gender, marital status, or size of their families. The first step toward desexing the workplace would then have been taken. As noted earlier, people higher up in the organization and those who are themselves members of dual-career families are less likely to be biased. They are more likely to accurately assess the potential of applicants and make hiring decisions based on objective data. Some of these individuals can initially be included in the interview sessions until such time as regular interviewers are trained to discern the true ability of applicants and to ignore all the value-based noise that might otherwise enter into the hiring decision. Additionally, wherever possible, assessment centers could be used to add fairness and objectivity to hiring decisions (White, Crino, and DeSanctis, 1981).

The issue of salary differentials also may account for dissatisfactions experienced by dual-career couples who interview for jobs. If spouses are offered jobs in comparable positions but at different salaries, the employer should explain to each of them the basis on which his or her salary offer has been made, so that he or she does not feel cheated when comparing notes at home. Comparable worth is becoming a sensitive theme (Smith, 1985a, 1985b). If an organization has a sound reason for differences in salary offerings for similar types of jobs, it does not have to be apologetic or feel anxious about the situation. More experience, greater past achievements, and the like justify differential pay offerings (Duncan, 1974; Sandell and Shapiro, 1978). But if there is no valid reason for differential salaries, organizations will enhance their image as fair employers by offering the same salary to both spouses. Smith (1985b) defines four steps for organizations to follow: (1) define the pay strategy, (2) formalize it, (3) select a system that incorporates both internal and external analysis, and (4) be prepared to adhere to the program.

To summarize, the actions recommended at the input stage are to (1) do away with any antinepotism policies that may exist; (2) incorporate an oath of loyalty into employee contracts and do away with conflict of interest policies unless absolutely necessary; (3) revise advertising strategies and procedures; (4) develop a relevant interviewing strategy with a good set of questions that assess the definition of success, the career goals, and the growth potential of dual-career members; and (5) establish mechanisms to train interviewers and to include dual-career family members and higher-ranking people in the organization on the interview and selection board to ensure objectivity and fairness in evaluation. Apart from developing appropriate policies and procedures, organizations must also ensure that they are properly implemented.

These steps are necessary to attract the right kinds of professionals to organizations. Some of the changes, such as revision of conflict of interest and nepotism policies will usually not require much time or effort, while training interviewers will involve considerable time and commitment of resources. But by making these initial investments, organizations will more than recover the costs by attracting people who are productive and will give their best to the system.

Progress of Companies in Effecting Changes

Several studies shed light on how companies have so far dealt with the antinepotism and conflict of interest policies (Catalyst, 1981; Newgren, Kellogg, and Gardner, 1985; Kopelman, Rosensweig, and Lally, 1982). No documented evidence exists, however, on what changes, if any, companies have effected in their recruitment procedures to accommodate dual-career members.

Of the 374 companies in the Fortune 1300 who responded to the Catalyst (1981) survey, 82 percent allowed husbands and wives to work for them, although 74 percent said that both spouses could not work in the same department or assume the same function. Smaller companies had more such restrictions than larger ones. About 28 percent of all companies surveyed by Catalyst in 1981 felt that couples pursuing careers within the same company would be gainful to the company, about 29 percent thought that this situation would create more problems than it would solve, about 15 percent of the companies either thought the idea was bad or would not allow couples to work for them, and about 28 percent said they just did not care. Kopelman, Rosensweig, and Lally (1982) found that 76 percent of all the responding companies had no restrictions on husbands' and wives' working for the same company. This was particularly true in organizations employing a high proportion of women.

According to Newgren, Kellogg, and Gardner (1985), many companies have now greatly relaxed nepotism policies, although some still have certain restrictions on spouses working under the same chain of command. The authors report that about 90 percent of the 115 organizations they surveyed allow relatives to be employed in the same company. Their data indicate that 30 percent of the institutions specifically forbid the supervision of an employee by his or her spouse, while another 46 percent forbid supervision by a relative. With regard to conflict of interest, the authors found that about 4 percent of the firms prohibit spouses from working for a competitor and 7 percent forbid the employee's spouse to hold a key position with a major competitor. Of the remaining companies, about 12 percent obtain an oath of loyalty from employees, about 54 percent simply trust their employees, and another 23 percent follow other internal procedures to handle conflicts of interest. The authors found that industrial firms, as compared to service organizations, seem to be more concerned about the conflict of interest issue.

SEVEN

Developing Other Organizational Policies

Most organizations hire employees and give them some kind of induction into their systems, policies, and procedures, after which the individuals are placed on their jobs where they are given further training. In due course, employees also receive off-the-job training through professional seminars, conferences, or workshops. Companies identify and develop promising personnel and prepare them for vertical career paths. They then reward them through promotions in the expectation that these employees will remain with the company until reaching retirement age. But it is not unusual for companies to lose personnel to competitors long before retirement because of lack of flexibility in their policies (Conference Board, 1985), employees' unwillingness to relocate when they are transferred (Mathews, 1984), and so on. This is especially true with respect to dual-career family members. Many of the current practices followed by companies are simply not adequate to utilize the full potential of dual-career professionals, dual-earner jobholders, and single parents.

To maximize the contributions of all their members, organizations need to expand their roles and functions as shown in Figure 6. There is an urgent need to change socialization processes, develop alternative work patterns, redesign training and mentoring procedures and processes, revise compensation schemes, evolve different career paths for organizational members, and offer employee assistance and counseling for dual-career members.

Figure 6. How Organizations Must Change Their Roles and Functions.

Input Stage (Functional Elaboration)	Throughput Stage (Functional Expansion)	Output

Input Stage (Functional Elaboration)

Formulate nepotism policy

Formulate conflict of interest policy

Formulate new recruitment procedures

- Advertise for set of positions to attract dual-career couples
- Specialized interviewing techniques
- Egalitarian hiring procedures for couples entering male-dominated occupations especially

Throughput Stage (Functional Expansion)

1 Induction/Socialization

Couple counseling and orientation

Create organizational culture to treat dual-career couples as no different from other employees

2 Alternative Work Patterns

Job sharing
Flexitime
Flexiplace
Part-time jobs

3 Training and Mentoring

Matching with those who "made it" as dual-career families

a. Training for success and enhancement of self-esteem

b. Specialized training for women/wives?

4 Providing Facilities and Benefits

Revising benefit schemes
Revising leave policies
Introducing child-care policies

5 Career Pathing

Multiple career ladders:
- Horizontal
- Vertical
- Do not disturb
- Downward

6 Counseling

EAPs for:
- Career paths
- Travel
- Transfer
- Relocation of spouse
- Dual-career family workshops

7 Preparation for Retirement

Tapping Potential of Dual-Career Members

Output

Productivity

Customer satisfaction

Retention of valued employees

Quality of Worklife for Employees

Socially Responsive Behavior

Family Stability

EAPs = Employee Assistance Programs

Induction and Socialization

Two issues are important in the induction phase: (1) the socialization of dual-career couples into the work setting and (2) the integration of male and female members into the organization without unnecessary gender-based tensions.

Socialization of Dual-Career Couples. Currently, the number of dual-career couples is still relatively small, and hence the two-career couple phenomenon sometimes appears strange to other employees. The couples are often treated differently by organizational members, and the spouses themselves feel awkward and do not always fully understand what behaviors are expected of them (Mathews and Mathews, 1980). My interviews with couples indicate that when spouses work in the same department or in the same functional area, they feel that colleagues watch them whenever they confer with each other. Respondents reported that other employees sometimes think that couples use company time to engage in personal conversations and make family decisions. To remove this erroneous impression, some couples include a third person in the discussions, even though that person may be extraneous to the matter at hand.

In one instance, a couple holding the positions of president and vice-president in a bank took such extraordinary measures as traveling by two different cars and arriving at and quitting the workplace at different times. During an interview, the vice-president said:

> It is important that people here do not perceive us as a husband and wife who are also working for the same bank, but rather think of us as two individuals who are working for this bank. From the time we leave home in the mornings till the time we reach home in the evenings, we wear only our professional hats. The family hat stays in the coat stand, and we don't put it on until we reach home in the evening.

Wives, in particular, said that such precautions were necessary to preserve their professional identity. But these cumbersome modes of behavior seem demanding and unnecessary and might even impair the efficiency of dual-career couples. Thus, revised induction and socialization processes are necessary.

Dual-career couples working for the same organization must be offered counseling and orientation before they are placed on the job so that they are integrated into the system gracefully (Hall and Hall, 1979). This will help them to overcome some of the awkwardness they feel as career couples working for the same system. Such induction and counseling may be necessary until large numbers of career couples are absorbed into the system, thus taking the strangeness out of the dual-career family phenomenon.

Socialization for the Integration of Men and Women. While women careerists are still not commonly found in certain kinds of organizations, organizations as a whole are becoming increasingly staffed by women, and more than 50 percent of all bachelor's and master's degrees are now being earned by women (Castro, 1985) portending further increases of women professionals in the future. Since women employees form a significant proportion of the work force at all levels, except perhaps at the very top, their contributions to the system should be fully utilized. With growing numbers of dual-career families, the contributions of women professionals will significantly affect the productivity of organizations. Hence, their potential has to be fully tapped.

Unfortunately, however, current organizational patterns of interactions between men and women do not allow for this (Brass, 1985; Nelson and Quick, 1985). For example, since communication is more easy and comfortable between members of the same sex, men tend to interact with men and women with women. The more this happens within the organizational system, the more women get excluded from the kinds of informal interactions that provide much of the political information necessary for success on the job. Women, being smaller in numbers and "relative newcomers in organizations, are not as aware of informal networks or as adept at building them as men are"

(Brass, 1985, p. 328). For organizations to become productive, the socialization of *all* professionals to organizational nuances and norms is essential.

At present, there is considerable awkwardness in the interactions between men and women at the workplace because of confusion about appropriate norms of behavior. Because they adhere to stereotypes of male and female behavior, there is very little fruitful and mutually beneficial interaction among organizational members. There is also a tendency on the part of organizational members to downplay women's true worth and contributions to the organization (Albrecht, 1983). Once women are recruited into organizations, they are left to fend for themselves in a rather hostile environment, where it becomes difficult for them to succeed (Chusmir, 1983). Top management's support and a feeling of acceptance by one's colleagues are as vital for women to succeed as they are for men. Synergistic interactions among all organizational members, irrespective of gender or marital status, will increase the productivity of the organization. For this to happen, however, organizations will have to create a culture in which people are socialized to perceive both genders as contributing members of the work force and to shed their stereotypical perceptions of women as weak, vulnerable, and low in motivation (Brass, 1985).

Mary Cunningham (1981), former vice-president of strategic management at Bendix Corporation, has suggested that corporations should do three things to utilize women's talents: (1) channel more women into line responsibilities; (2) give them difficult assignments, and (3) share the critically important social activities with them by introducing them to senior managers, taking them to important lunches, and permitting them the visibility that is so essential for corporate mobility. She also suggested that top management not assume that women will not be interested in travel or relocation.

Top management in organizations should make concerted efforts to ensure successful experiences for women at work (Brass, 1985). They can serve as role models for other members in the work system in shedding traditional male-female patterns of behavior. In her discussions of sex and the workplace, Gutek

(1985) notes the importance of promoting professional behavior at work. She suggests that professionalism be stressed during the orientation of new members and that appropriate styles of address be discussed. Gutek states that managers at all levels should be role models of professional conduct. In addition, posters and other such materials can remind people to treat each other with respect, courtesy, and professionalism. By socializing all employees to act toward each other as organizational members rather than as people with different gender identities, the organization can be changed to a synergistic system (Sundal-Hansen, 1984).

But these are mere first steps. True integration will come only when women and men have access to the same kinds of information. Women, who are currently in small numbers in high-level positions, are seldom included in the power networks that dispense vital information and resources—a primary reason why men are more successful in organizations (Kanter, 1977). It is for the same reason that, although male and female MBAs start off with the same salaries, the women invariably fall behind by at least 20 percent within ten years. To succeed, an individual must be connected to the real sources of power and must have access to information. For instance, important deals are often concluded not in business meetings but during an informal gathering at a cocktail lounge to which only a select few individuals have been invited. Women are generally excluded from such encounters even if they hold significant positions in the organization (Lyles, 1983). It may be that men feel awkward about inviting a lone woman to meet with them informally (there are not very many women at the top), or it may be that the male executives simply do not think that a woman should be involved in top-level decision making.

Again, if organizations of tomorrow want to utilize the full potential of *all* people in the system, they should socialize women to acquire power and use it appropriately. This can happen only when their ideas are heard, discussed, and dealt with appropriately. They should enjoy such treatment from the very beginning of their careers in an organization. Sharing organizational information with women makes two-way interactions possible. Involving interested career women in the appropriate organizational and social network systems can only benefit organizations.

Programs of Organizations in Socializing Members. There is little published information to indicate that organizations are making special efforts to develop new patterns of organizational socialization that would produce synergistic effects, although Castro (1985) states that "as women have taken their place in management, both sexes have learned new ways of working together" (p. 65). Additionally, in their survey of 126 companies, Kopelman, Rosensweig, and Lally (1982) found that about 7 percent of them were providing training to their supervisors to deal with issues involving dual-career couples. Their study does not provide details as to what kinds of issues were handled or how the supervisors were trained, but it does give an indication that organizations are beginning to be sensitive to issues facing dual-career couples.

Nevertheless, much more has to be done to change corporate values. Effective human resource management requires that fundamental, difficult, and often threatening notions about personal and corporate values, beliefs, and assumptions be addressed (Beer and others, 1985). Managing corporate cultures involves implanting new knowledge and values, developing a shared vision, determining the desired change in beliefs, translating values into corporate behavior, reorienting power to support new values and behavior, and harnessing the management systems that have a high impact on change processes (Benningson, 1985). Top managers need to initiate these transformation processes and monitor progress until such time as the culture has changed and the organization has become synergistic. They can be the visible heroes who serve as role models to the rest of the organization, setting the climate for effective transformations in organizational culture. In addition, changes in policies, procedures, reward systems, symbols, and stories can be brought about with guidance and assistance from organizational consultants.

Alternative Work Patterns

Since time is a scarce resource, particularly for the two-career couple, organizations should design alternative work patterns for employees. As a matter of fact, some organizations already have incorporated job sharing, flexitime, flexiplace, and part-time schedules of work into their systems. When they are able to choose their own work styles, individuals bring greater concentration to their jobs and are likely to perform better. Alternative patterns of job arrangements might be an even more critical issue for dual-career and dual-earner families with small children than for childless couples.

Job Sharing. Meier (1978) has described job sharing as an arrangement whereby two individuals share a job and are jointly responsible for performance results. The two individuals are entitled to one salary and one set of benefits. This arrangement is particularly attractive to certain kinds of couples (for example, doctors, lawyers, editors, media specialists, and program directors). It enables the couple to share child care and professional and family responsibilities. For most families, however, job sharing for *both* partners may not be an attractive proposition because of the lower levels of income it would bring to the family. Meier describes the burdens that job sharing puts on the organization. The organization has to manage two people instead of one on the job and has to decide which kinds of jobs can be shared and what kinds of people are suitable to share jobs. Hence, companies will want to determine to what extent employees feel a need for job sharing before undertaking feasibility studies to identify jobs that would lend themselves to sharing.

Flexitime. Flexitime stipulates both a core time when all members in the organization are expected to be at the workplace and a flexible time chosen by the individuals when it is convenient for them to be at work. Flexitime seems to be the most popular work arrangement in many organizations. By 1990, 25 percent of the work force is likely to be on flexitime (McKendrick, 1982). Workers on flexitime enjoy the advantage of both full pay and flexibility in the use of their time.

One variant of flexible working hours is "seasonal hours"

(Conference Board, 1985). Some seasonal work schedules allow employees to take time off during the summer and work a greater number of hours during other times. Seasonal schedules tend to spread geographically rather than by industry. Some companies resisting the trend in Connecticut and Chicago have found themselves at a recruiting disadvantage (Conference Board, 1985). The compressed workweek is another variant of flexitime. Compressed workweek refers to the typical shortened workweek assigned to employees on a fixed or rotating basis. Employees work ten or more hours a day for three or four long working days and enjoy a three- or four-day weekend. Companies not presently on flexitime can assess the demand for it and then consider initiating a suitable form of this alternative work pattern, at least in some departments. But the Conference Board (1985) cautions that flexitime by itself does not provide sufficient relief to dual-career families with children.

Flexiplace. Flexible place arrangements allow employees to work any place they prefer as long as the work takes no more time to get completed than it would if performed at the office. Certain accounting, financial, billing, and editorial types of work can just as easily be done at home as at the workplace. This provides the flexibility of working when one wants to and attending to family matters when one needs to. It is a boon to employees with small children. Some professionals, such as artists and photographers, can more readily take advantage of flexiplace arrangements than can those who are closely bound to the workplace. In the future, however, as organizations make increasing use of computers and as information technology advances, many more professionals will be able to work at home and efficiently serve the needs of their organizations.

Part-Time Work. Some companies allow professionals to work part time, especially women after childbirth (Krett, 1985). Part-time work before retirement can also help ease employees into their new life-style. Law firms, hospital systems, banks, and educational settings offer more opportunities for part-time employment than most industrial and other service organizations. Part-time work has the same disadvantages as job sharing—lower remuneration and very few fringe benefits. However, professionals who do not want to invest all their time in work for one reason or another will be attracted to organizations that offer part-time work opportunities.

But to what extent have organizations actually initiated these alternative work arrangements?

"Job sharing is a concept that is still poorly understood by—or unknown to—many corporate executives" (Conference Board, 1985, p. 28). This statement succinctly describes the extent to which job sharing is used as a flexible work pattern. Campbell Soup is one of the few large companies that has job sharing, although Levi Strauss & Co. has also experimented with the concept. In their survey of 126 companies, Kopelman, Rosensweig, and Lally (1982) found that less than 2 percent of the companies had some sort of job-sharing arrangement. Meier (1978) states that job sharing occurs among physicians, media specialists, health educators, editors, program directors, and co-directors of personnel development. He also reports that Congress enacted legislation that increased part-time and job-sharing opportunities for federal workers. Newgren, Kellogg, and Gardner (1985) state that about 85 percent of American companies do not have job-sharing programs and that job sharing is more common in government, college, and service organizations than in manufacturing industries. Thomas (1982) found that 11 percent of the 378 companies that he surveyed in 1981 allowed job sharing but that ten or fewer jobs were shared in these companies since workers on job sharing missed the fringe benefits. Kopelman, Rosensweig, and Lally (1982) found in their survey of 126 large companies that only a very small proportion of the companies (3 percent) had job-sharing arrangements.

With regard to *flexitime,* Newgren and Gardner's (1980) survey of 115 firms showed that 37 percent of the industrial firms and about 31 percent of the service organizations used flexitime off and on but that very few used it consistently. Thomas (1982) found that 15 percent of the companies he surveyed used flexitime in 1978, which increased to 22 percent in 1981. Kopelman, Rosensweig, and Lally (1982) found that 53 percent of the 126 companies surveyed by them had adopted flexible working hours. McKendrick (1982) cited several organizations and types of organizations that used flexitime—insurance companies, the Port Authority in New York and in New Jersey, the American Bar Association, and some banks on the West Coast. He also reported that Transamerica Occidental Life had 3,000 employees participating in flexitime programs and SmithKline Beckman 2,000. Blitzer (1982) cited various organizations on the West Coast that have flexitime—for instance, Hewlett-Packard, Rolm Corporation (now part of IBM), and Levi Strauss & Co. Other organizations having flexible work schedules include Control Data, Honeywell, IBM, Transamerica Occidental Life, Seattle First National Bank, and Blue Cross and Blue Shield of Arkansas.

Turning to *flexiplace,* one Midwestern firm allows its employees to make use of "alternative work sites"; that is, they can spend some part of their day or week working in another company office in the area or at home (Conference Board, 1985). Informal arrangements in this regard seem to be more prevalent than formalized structures. Continental Illinois and certain high-tech organizations have flexiplace arrangements for some kinds of work. As far as *part-time* jobs are concerned, Blitzer (1982) reported that Bank of America had 10,000 part-time workers. New York's Citibank is said to accommodate mutually advantageous requests from full-time professionals to switch to part-time schedules. Atlantic Richfield, Transamerica Occidental Life, SmithKline Beckman, Hewlett-Packard, and Levi Strauss & Co. are among the organizations that offer part-time schedules for employees. Most firms are usually willing to accommodate employee-initiated requests for part-time assignments on a temporary basis (Conference Board, 1985).

According to the Conference Board (1985), the following companies have reported benefits as a result of alternative work patterns: Transamerica Occidental Life has experienced a 45 percent decrease in turnover and a 15 percent reduction in absenteeism since flexitime was introduced in the company. Managers in Kimberly-Clark felt that the productivity of employees increased after the introduction of flexitime. Hewlett-Packard, Control Data, and several other companies have reported that worker morale and satisfaction considerably increased after flexitime was introduced. Increases in output and employee sat- isfaction have been linked to alternative work patterns by Campbell Soup's president (Catalyst, 1984). It should be noted, however, that productivity increases resulting from these ar- rangements have not been conclusively demonstrated so far. But knowing the costs of turnover, absenteeism, and employee dis- satisfaction, we can safely conclude that structuring flexible work arrangements will benefit organizations.

There is considerable scope for organizations to explore and utilize the flexible work patterns discussed here. Companies should first take an employee survey to see what alternative ar- rangements employees want and then determine what types of jobs would lend themselves to those arrangements. Since investi- gating and installing new work arrangements will take time, or- ganizations could deal with employee requests on a case-by-case basis until such time as the new structures are in place.

Since organizations are likely to face a dearth of profes- sionals in the future once the baby-boom supply to the labor market gets exhausted, they need to seriously think of alterna- tive work patterns. Many experienced and talented men and women who are not now working because of a lack of part-time and flexible time and place arrangements may reenter profes- sional organizations as more liberal policies and flexible work patterns are adopted. Many service organizations and profes- sional systems will attract qualified dual-career couples more easily by adopting flexible work patterns. Other types of em- ployees are also likely to contribute more to the organization when they are not harried by family pressures and can choose their own work patterns (Conference Board, 1985).

Training and Mentoring

While alternative work patterns benefit employees direct- ly and the organization indirectly, training and mentoring bene- fit both equally. Training of employees is the responsibility of the organization, and almost all institutions offer various types of professional development programs. Unfortunately, most current training programs do little to enhance the sense of competence and self-esteem of trainees, even though this is one of the best ways to increase employee satisfaction and performance (Sekaran, 1985b). In other words, trainees mechanically go through training programs which usually impart technical, administrative, or managerial skills. Through creative role plays and experiential exercises that are oriented toward problem-solving issues at the workplace—for example, bringing about synergistic interactions among male and female professionals—trainees can experience a heightened sense of competence and self-esteem even as they go through the program. Among other things, training should also impart realistic performance appraisal skills so that managers and other professionals will be able to provide honest feedback—both positive and negative—to *all* members.

Whether or not special training and development programs are necessary for women is a moot point. Many, including Reif, Newstrom, and Monczka (1975) and Ritchie and Moses (1983), argue that since there are very few attitudinal, behavioral, and ability differences between men and women, there is no need for special programs for women only. If we are aiming to desex the workplace, such an argument seems not only sound but necessary as well. Berryman (1985) argues that organizations should offer training programs for both genders and suggests a model for androgyny training.

Mentoring is as essential for professionals as training, although it has not received much attention in organizations. Reich (1985) notes that mentors can develop abilities, foster creativity, arrange special projects, and provide visibility and advancement opportunities for the protégé. In my interviews, many professionals who had advanced in their organizations attributed their success to their mentors. One professional said:

> I joined this organization because I felt this would be an exciting place. The other professionals around here seemed to be friendly and willing to share information and help each other out. To me that is more important than money. I had another job offer from another company, but the place

seemed "cold." I accepted this job, and over the years my boss and other colleagues helped me a lot to learn the ropes and move up. They helped me to size up the clients, work in an assertive and confident manner, and be emphatic about putting forth my ideas. Peter [his boss], especially, would play the devil's advocate and help me to anticipate objections, problems, and protests that I would encounter whenever I had to present a new proposal to the department or to the client. Peter really mentored me and took great delight in my successes. But for him I would have perhaps not discovered my potential. He pushed me but always just enough for me to stretch and not break. Now I try to do the same for others in the company.

A developmental relationship evolves between mentor and protégé as goals are consciously set and plans are formulated for goal attainment (Clawson and Kram, 1984). Women professionals gain from the mentor relationship since it introduces them to the art of corporate politics and exposes them to key people in the organizational system (Berry, 1983). This helps them to gain visibility and power. Those on the fast track benefit immensely from the mentor relationship and can achieve their goals more quickly because of the guidance they receive (Berry, 1983). The only drawbacks of the mentor relationship are the feelings of dependency and, in some cases, the sexual tensions that might develop (Kram, 1985). Mentors of either gender who are themselves from dual-career families can bring to the mentor-protégé relationship the richness of their own experience in combining a career and family life. They will be invaluable to dual-career couples. A good mentor-protégé relationship will enhance productivity for the organization, while also providing satisfaction to the individuals in the relationship (Kram and Isabella, 1985).

Organizations have hitherto not played a key role in connecting members in mentor relationships. With more dual-career members entering organizations, structures can be established that will allow the organization to play an active role in connecting mentors and protégés. Organizations can, in fact, formalize the mentoring process to some degree by identifying key personnel who would be effective mentors for specific professionals.

Odiorne (1985) states that mentoring is a philosophy as well as a set of techniques. He further states that many men prefer to avoid the mentoring relationship with women and that this prevents many high-potential women professionals from reaching the top levels of organizations. Training, as just discussed, could help to overcome this kind of discomfort and hesitation. Several mentors may be necessary in the lives of successful individuals, whether male or female, as they continue to advance in the organization. Peer mentoring relationships develop in some organizations as professionals go through various career stages (Kram and Isabella, 1985). Such relationships are common in university settings.

Parenting Policies

Organizations need to rethink their benefit schemes and policies, especially as they relate to parenting. When to start a family and how to manage child care are vexing issues for dual-career couples. Unless a prospective mother is well established in her career, there is a tendency on the part of the couple to postpone starting a family. Postponing motherhood, however, could be hazardous to the health of the mother and child since late pregnancies carry more risk than those that occur during the normal childbearing years (Rosen, 1985).

After children are born, mothers have difficulty trying to arrange for child care. Since promotion and seniority may be at stake, wives try to get back to their work within weeks of childbearing (Clinton, 1983). The mother's level of anxiety and guilt in "abandoning" her child may produce high stress levels that are not conducive to her effective functioning on the job. As Meyers (1985) stated, it is self-defeating for company policies to require women to come back to work within eight weeks of childbirth. As the family expands, child care causes more and more concern and stress for the couple. Day-care facilities often do not work out well, and families may use as many as four different day-care facilities during the infancy and childhood of their offspring because no single arrangement is sufficiently reliable for continued use (Ornati and Buckham, 1983).

Traditional values dictate that the wife should stay at home and nurture her children. An NBC television white paper ("Women, Work, and Babies: Can America Cope") broadcast in March 1985 vividly depicted the way in which many husbands, who cannot themselves stay at home to care for the children, come to resent their wives for not performing their maternal duties and showed how a rift between the couple starts to develop. As the report also revealed, such situations become even more complex when the spouses have to travel frequently on business. Coordinating travel plans to make sure that at least one of the parents is with the children poses difficulties and causes stress for the couple since not all travel plans can be postponed. Thus, in the area of parenting leave, child care, and business travel, organizations will have to take a more creative role in relieving the tensions of employees.

Relieving Stresses of Parenting. Role-cycling dilemmas can be relieved for couples through parenting leave policies that guarantee a return to the job. The current paternal leave policies that a small number of companies have already adopted should be embraced by all organizations and applied both in letter and spirit. Providing child-care facilities will also enable parents to work without undue stress and tension when they return to their jobs.

Parenting Leave. Most organizations have not developed policies on parenting leave that address the concerns of dual-career members. Government subsidies for childbearing and child rearing would be very helpful, and federal tax exemptions would greatly motivate organizations to follow liberal and humane policies in this regard. Surely, it is somewhat ironic that organizations in a progressive country such as the United States lag behind organizations in some Third World countries. For instance, in India maternity leave is available to every working woman; it provides three months' full pay, with the option of also using vacation leave (on full pay) and accumulated sick leave (on half pay). A woman can thus go on leave for as long as a year, and she can return to her position without loss of seniority. It is no secret that Indian organizations do not have the assets or enjoy the level of profits that U.S. organizations do. If such systems can afford to be employee friendly, surely American organizations can!

Institutions can relieve the role-cycling dilemmas for couples by formulating policies that allow mothers to take maternity leave any time after one or two years' service without loss of seniority, and they can offer similar options to fathers. This course of action provides several benefits to the parents, the child, and the organization itself. First, it allows the couple to choose when to start their family. Thus, one of the major dilemmas they face is resolved. Second, the child experiences family closeness at a very critical time of his or her life instead of being left with outsiders. Third, it relieves the parents of guilt feelings in not personally caring for their child. Finally, what the organization spends in paying for maternity and paternity leave, it can recover from not subsidizing infant care for a whole year and through the increased productivity of the couple.

In suggesting that organizations liberalize their parenting leave policies, however, we should not ignore the legal problems that may arise for these organizations. Current laws classify maternity as "disability." Because of this, male employees have charged that they are discriminated against when a guaranteed return to the job is assured following maternity leave, since such guarantees are not given for other kinds of disability leaves. And the complaints of discrimination are even wider ranging. To take only one example, an audio engineer sued NBC when he was refused paternity leave (Haitch, 1982). One solution would be to establish similar types of maternity and paternity benefits, thus possibly nullifying any discrimination charges.

The need for day care for children is so keenly felt and so evident that it needs no elaboration. Rodriguez (1983) mentioned the following day-care options for companies: on-site day-care centers; day-care facilities operated by a consortium of different companies in the area; contractual arrangements with a community-based day-care center to take care of the employees' children; arrangements with families to provide day-care for children in their own homes; vouchers that reimburse parents, in part or full, for child care arranged by themselves (day-care expenses average as much as 10 percent of the gross income of working couples, according to LaMarre and Thompson, 1984); and referral services.

Ornati and Buckham (1983) state that from management's point of view, operating company-owned day-care centers is costly and risky because it requires about $100,000 a year to operate a day-care center, the facilities are sometimes underutilized, and the benefit is not equitable for employees who do not have children needing care. An equitable way to deal with the issue of day care is to offer employees a cafeteria plan of benefits (Cockrum, 1982). This arrangement lets employees choose whichever benefits they want within a prescribed ceiling from a package of different types of options, including child-care facilities. The cafeteria plan is rather expensive to set up initially, though it is said to be subsequently cost effective (Ornati and Buckham, 1983).

Stringer-Moore (1981) suggested a number of things that organizations can do to provide or facilitate child care, one of which is to set up interorganizational consortia of day-care centers. This would allow companies to share setup costs and operating expenses. Stringer-Moore also suggested that company vans or pooled vans be used to transport children to and from the workplaces of parents. She additionally suggested the formation of medical consortia where sick children could be tended on a temporary basis when they are laid up with relatively minor ailments.

Progress on Parenting Leave and Child Care. With regard to *parenting leave* facilities, the Catalyst survey of 1981 indicated that 96 percent of the companies gave some maternity benefits, about 9 percent offered paternity benefits, and 10 percent had some adoption benefits. The survey indicated that 65 percent of the companies offered maternity leave without pay but with the position assured on return. Among the organizations offering maternity leave were AT&T, Hewlett-Packard,

CBS, Security Pacific, and Continental Illinois. CBS granted six months' leave of absence to either parent following the birth of a child. Among the companies offering special adoption benefits were AT&T, Time Inc., Security Pacific, Control Data, American Can, General Mills, Xerox, and Procter & Gamble. More recently, Meyers' (1985) survey found that 120 companies, including Procter & Gamble, Merck and Co., CBS, and AT&T, offered maternity and paternity leave. Krett (1985), who surveyed 152 companies, found that a majority of the companies guaranteed the mothers' jobs on return. Sixty-four percent of the surveyed companies granted unpaid leave for a period ranging from sixteen to fifty-two weeks. Some companies paid partial salary from sixteen to twenty-six weeks, and others paid full salary for the same period. A few companies let people use vacation, sick, and personal leave.

Krett found that many companies expressed hostility to the whole idea of paternity leave. Norman and Tedeschi (1984) confirm that even though some companies do offer both maternity and paternity leave without pay, the companies consider fathers who take paternity leave to be eccentrics who are not serious about their careers. The authors state that even in Sweden, where men are paid 90 percent of their regular salaries during paternity leave, only 10 percent availed themselves of it in 1979, although that figure had increased to 33 percent by 1982. Meyers (1985) found that 37 percent of the companies surveyed, including AT&T, Procter & Gamble, and IBM offer paternity leave now as compared to 9 percent as recently as 1980. McKendrick (1982) states that the Ford Foundation in New York offers parenting leave for six months with two months' paid leave for both men and women.

As for *child-care* facilities, the 1981 Catalyst survey gives the following information pertaining to the 115 companies queried: 37 percent of the companies offered flexible working hours, 8 percent had flexiplace (so that the children could be cared for to some extent by the parents themselves), 29 percent gave sick leave when children were ill, 1 percent provided on-site day care for children, less than 1 percent provided subsidies for child care, 19 percent offered monetary support for community-based child care, and 8 percent took a cafeteria approach to employee benefits.

According to Meyers (1985), companies are beginning to realize that if they do not offer some kind of child-care assistance, they will lose out as a result of employee absenteeism and turnover. Her survey showed that companies such as Levi Strauss & Co., Hewlett-Packard, and Control Data offer part-time work arrangements, job sharing, and/or time off to care for sick children. On-site or near-site child-care centers for infants and toddlers were also offered by insurance and pharmaceutical companies. Meyers states that Stride Rite operates two child-care facilities to meet employee and community needs. Stride Rite spends $150,000 to $200,000 each year on these two centers, one of which at least has been in operation for the past thirteen years. PCA International has been successfully operating an on-site day-care center for employees for the past fifteen years (Blitzer, 1982). Several companies have developed consortium arrangements for local facilities for child care; these companies include Hewlett-Packard, Control Data, Honeywell, General Mills, Clorox, and Campbell Soup. Groups of employers in Chicago, the San Francisco Bay Area, and southern Connecticut are similarly resorting to consortium arrangements. Interestingly, San Francisco recently enacted an ordinance requiring developers of new downtown office projects to provide either space or money for day-care centers (Lehrman, 1985).

Some companies, including Measurex and Polaroid, have voucher systems that cover anywhere between 5 and 85 percent of the costs of child-care that is provided by authorized centers or personnel (Meyers, 1985; Ornati and Buckham, 1983). The employee presents the voucher to the facility of his or her choice, which in turn submits it to the company for payment. The voucher system gives greater leeway for the employees to select child care of their choice and at the same time relieves the company of the task of providing child-care facilities. This plan is suited for large companies with offices in a number of different areas. The amount of reimbursement depends, among other things, on the length of service of the employee.

As for other types of child care, Meyers (1985) reports

that Minnesota Mining and Manufacturing offers a sick-care program for children. In addition, 300 companies negotiate dis-
counts for employees at local day-care centers. Kinder-Care
Learning has a chain of 950 child-care facilities serving about
40 corporations. Three hundred large companies, including
IBM, offer referral services to their employees. Ornati and Buckham (1983) reported that insurance companies such as Connecticut General Life, Allendale, and Union Mutual Life have contractual arrangements with community centers with guaranteed
slots for their employees' children. Ornati and Buckham state
that some financial institutions have found that providing loans
to child-care organizations that are otherwise unable to qualify
for them is an effective way of expanding local day-care facilities. Companies that have established such loans include Citibank, Chase Manhattan Bank, and New York Life Insurance.
Ornati and Buckham also indicate that cafeteria benefits have
been introduced by TRW, Educational Testing Service, Energy
Group, American Can, and PepsiCo. IBM provides nationwide
computerized referral services for child care. Nontaxable salary
deductions for child care are provided by American Can,
Honeywell, and General Mills. Kantrowitz, Weathers, Doherty,
and Atkins (1986) indicate that sick-child care is now available
at some twenty companies. Some companies, for example, Minnesota Mining and Manufacturing, arrange to have a trained
child-care worker sent to the home of an employee whose child
is sick. The company also helps pay the bill.

Though some progress is being made with regard to child-
care policies, the Center for Public Advocacy Research says that
most corporations are waiting to see what other companies will
do in this area. This is not surprising, since there is no national
policy on child care. A statement made by Robert Beck, vice-
president in charge of corporate personnel of the Bank of America, during the 1984 Catalyst Round-Table Conference on the
Two-Gender Work Force and Corporate Policy, captures the essence of the problem. Beck said that since our society has excellent self-correcting mechanisms to solve imminent problems
when they occur (as evidenced by its handling of the energy crisis), it is a question of how long it is going to take to tackle and

solve the child-care problem. Lynn Povitch, senior editor of *Newsweek*, remarked that children are obviously being taken care of one way or another but that if we were to poll working parents today, we would hear many problems and complaints. She said that these issues are not discussed because "you are not supposed to bring these problems to work" (Catalyst, 1984, p. 25). An article entitled "Child Care: Where Companies Still Fear to Tread" (1984) echoed the same thought in saying that middle managers do not talk about child-care problems since they do not want to be seen as raising difficulties.

Benefits of Child-Care Facilities. It is estimated that as of early 1985, about 1,800 employing organizations (a fourth of which were hospitals) were providing some kind of child-care program. Many companies feel that less anxious parents are more productive employees. Nyloncraft, an Indiana plastics company, found that after the establishment of an on-site day-care center in 1978, turnover drastically declined, absenteeism fell to less than 3 percent, employee morale was up, and the company started making revenues of $25 million. Naturally, the management considered the establishment of the day-care center a sound decision (McKendrick, 1985b). Tiago Sportswear claimed a 50 percent decrease in turnover, and Intermedics experienced a 23 percent reduction in turnover and 15,000 fewer absenteeism hours in the first year after the installation of on-site child care (LaMarre and Thompson, 1984). In a quasi-field experiment with two textile companies in North and South Carolina, Youngblood and Chambers-Cook (1984) found that turnover rates went down from 8 to 3 percent when the companies converted rooms on their premises to day-care facilities. Rodriguez (1983) has reported a high negative correlation between child-care assistance and employee turnover and absenteeism and a positive correlation between child-care assistance and productivity. Despite the positive outcomes, very few companies operate their own day-care centers because they require large capital investments and involve high operating costs.

Recommendations. Companies should implement policies that allow an employee who has put in, say, two years of service to take a six-month leave for childbearing and child rearing, including at least three to four months of paid leave. This accommodation can be extended for the first two children of the mother. If the father is given similar privileges, the couple will be able to attend to their infant personally, full time, for the first twelve months of its life. All organizations should consider revising their parenting leave and child-care policies to obtain the greatest benefits from nontraditional professionals. Time off for taking care of sick children should also be made available to parents. If necessary, such time off can be paid back by working on weekends.

There are several options that companies can exercise with respect to child care. The least that very small companies can do is to set up information and referral services. Placing one person part time in charge of these services or subscribing to counseling services would be a good way to start. Small and medium-sized companies that cannot afford their own day-care centers can make contractual arrangements with community centers and thus guarantee a specific number of slots after assessing the demand for such child care. The voucher system is a good way to reimburse at least part of the costs of child care. Companies within a certain area can also provide loans to qualified entrepreneurs who may want to start day-care centers in the area. Cockrum (1982) suggests that all firms should consider cafeteria plans—whether the firms are small, medium, or large—and that the options should be voluntarily chosen by employees without pressure from personnel managers.

The dispensing of these benefits can become somewhat problematic when two spouses in a family work for different organizations. For instance, the two different organizations in which the two spouses work might both offer vouchers for child care. In such cases, organizations can require employees claiming the benefit to certify that similar facilities are not being utilized by the spouse.

There are numerous other measures that organizations can adapt. For instance, as a means of allowing parents to spend more time with their families and also as a way of handling unemployment problems, Sweden is currently reducing the number of hours that parents work in organizations (Kessler-Harris,

1985). Such policies could also be implemented in the United States. Whatever schemes are desired by a large majority of dual-career families and other professionals should be considered and tried. But records of cost-benefit analysis over the long run should also be judiciously maintained.

In summary, innovative child-care policies are good management strategies. They improve employee motivation, morale, retention, and productivity. But it is necessary for companies to first gather data on what kinds of child-care facilities are now being used by their employees, whether or not these facilities satisfactorily meet the needs of employees, and to what extent parents desire other child-care facilities. Information regarding current care of sick children should also be gathered so that policies regarding time off for the care of sick children and alternative arrangements for such care can be explored. After tabulating survey results, the company can examine the feasibility of incorporating the facilities most frequently mentioned by employees. And, after an initial feasibility study, dual-career members from all levels can meet as a committee to discuss, design, and implement further courses of action.

Career Planning and Career Paths

Whether it takes the form of upward or lateral moves, job redesign or relocation, career planning and development are highly valued by employees (Goddard, 1985). Goddard also notes that career dissatisfaction is reduced when career development is aimed not so much at questions of promotion as at personal development, work content, and job importance. These are particularly relevant to dual-career family members, who tend to look for challenge and excitement at work. Several experts assert that developing career paths that allow professionals to expand and exhibit their competence without feeling plateaued by vertical career paths is a good management policy (Bailyn, 1984; Gutzer and Maher, 1982). By offering career planning and designing appropriate career paths, companies can better retain their employees and improve productivity.

In the case of dual-career family members who perhaps

place equal importance on work and family, multiple-career ladders are a means to allow them to retain their self-esteem and contribute to the organization's goals. In other words, career planning is a vehicle to align individuals' career objectives with the organization's plans, needs, and goals. Career development of individuals and the development of the organization are synonymous in that sense (Schein, 1978). For many years, career development has been perceived exclusively in terms of vertical mobility. With the changing values, needs, and definition of success of present-day employees, however, multiple-career ladders need to be designed in organizations so that professionals remain motivated and productive on the job (Bailyn, 1984; Kram, 1983).

Like training and mentoring, developing career paths that suit the needs and inclinations of professionals with different life goals will help the organization as much as it does the individual. For a long time, the vertical move has been the only career path for promising employees. But career specialists now increasingly advocate several career paths, including horizontal or lateral moves and even downward moves. Employees may choose downward paths in times of failing health or family pressures and when they desire to spend more time with their families, community, or in recreation. Downward transfers help organizations in which promotional opportunities are on the decline.

Professionals in dual-career families cannot be solely work oriented, whereas those in single-career families can (Bailyn, 1979). What is needed, then, is a multiple model of career paths flexible enough to meet the needs of a variety of people who prefer to lead different life-styles. Bailyn states that the new pattern will not make professionals ineffective or unproductive. If the traditional model is the only path available to them, however, they will become so. She advocates that organizations adopt a long-range perspective on careers, come to a new understanding of what organizational commitment means to professionals, and redesign career ladders. When organizations pay attention to these issues, professionals' dissatisfaction and burnout also get reduced.

At present, career progress often requires relocation. For

some established nontraditional families, however, relocation is a stress-provoking situation. Many families with children wish to stay together, especially when they are reasonably satisfied with their current career progress. For such employees, if one spouse is transferred, only two options are available: one is to relocate, with the second spouse probably having to start his or her career afresh; the second is to refuse to relocate and take the consequences, which may include not ever being considered for promotion again, demotion, or even job severance (Challenger, 1985). The Catalyst (1981) survey indicated that while 40 percent of the husbands and 21 percent of the wives surveyed said that they had previously relocated for the sake of their own jobs, they felt that they would not *now* do so unless there was a net gain to them that was irresistible or unless both they and their spouses could maintain their careers at current levels. Fifty-eight percent of the wives and 60 percent of the husbands in the total sample considered the family their number one concern in life.

Layman (1982), who surveyed thirty-nine chemical and plastic companies, found that 56 percent of the companies experienced difficulties getting their employees to accept transfers to areas with high costs of living. Life-style and community environment were other aspects that influenced employees' acceptance or rejection of relocation. Thus, relocation will become more problematic in the future, since established couples will find moving unacceptable if it disrupts their family situations. For families with young children, relocation is especially difficult since it disrupts their schooling, requires them to make new friends, and so on. Organizations, however, need experienced and talented personnel to take charge of operations in new locations or to head branch offices when vacancies arise at senior levels. Hence, organizations will have to find ways of making relocation offers attractive.

What Companies Are Doing. With respect to career planning and career paths, Walker and Gutteridge (1979) noted that companies are not applying the career-planning and development activities that have been recommended in many articles. Their survey of 225 companies indicated that "career planning remains largely an informal, experimental, and fragmented activity" (p. 2). According to the *Career Development Bulletin* ("What's New in Career Development," 1979), a few organizations do consider career development too important to be left to personnel specialists alone. So some organizations have now formed top-level committees composed of the president, vice-president, departmental heads, and career specialists to deal with career development issues. These committees draw up plans for the career development of middle-level personnel in the organization and closely monitor progress. Southern New England Telephone established a personnel planning committee network to facilitate multiple careers over the individual's work life. Many organizations periodically conduct career development programs and workshops; the major elements of these programs include orientation of the employee to career development, career planning and guidance counseling, assessment techniques, and self-guided career planning. Thus, organizations are now beginning to understand that career planning helps them to engineer their human resources with respect to placement, promotion, transfer, training, and development.

Some companies are developing strategies to make relocation more attractive and less problematic for couples. For instance, Kopelman, Rosensweig, and Lally (1982) found that 27 percent of the 126 companies surveyed by them assisted couples to develop strategies for coping with their transfers in advance and also helped spouses to relocate. Layman (1982) reported that many of the 39 companies in his survey had programs to help the spouse of the transferred employee find a job. They acknowledged, however, that it was much easier to relocate a spouse who simply needed a job than one who was pursuing a career. Levi Strauss & Co. tries to accommodate two-career families by lining up interviews for the spouse of the transferred employee. IBM pays up to $500 for counseling and job-hunting expenses incurred by the couple for the spouse's new placement. Thus, companies now go beyond paying moving expenses and helping to sell the current residence of the employee to offering help to the spouse of the transferred employee to continue his or her career in the family's new location. These efforts include engaging a relocation assistance firm to help spouses find new placements, counseling spouses on opportunities available, and forming consortiums of companies to create job banks (Mathews, 1984).

Minor (1984) lists about 100 companies that render different types of relocation services—from estimating the costs of relocation to helping the spouse of the relocated employee search for a job. Union Carbide, AT&T, and Diamond Shamrock, among others, provide job search facilities for spouses. Many insurance companies on the East Coast have created job banks to accommodate the spouse of the transferred employee ("America's New Immobile Society," 1981). Citibank and Hewlett-Packard, among other organizations, have developed networks for job placement of trailing spouses. These will be the strategies of the future. Computer-assisted search facilities will match individuals and jobs all over the country.

Action Plans for Organizations. Bartolomé and Evans (1980) suggest that organizations broaden their values and create multiple rewards and multiple-career ladders through use of Schein's Career Anchor Model—the managerial anchor, the technical anchor, the functional anchor, the creative anchor, the security anchor, and the autonomy anchor. Using these different career anchors, organizations can create multiple-career paths for individuals and discard the one-dimensional vertical ascendency model. Indeed the pressure to move vertically is intolerable to many technical-level staff who would much prefer to stay where they are.

Thus, institutions should let people continue to do the work they enjoy doing rather than pressure them to move in an unwanted direction. If members are promoted and thereafter find themselves not liking the role or fitting the slot, they should have the option to move downward without losing their status as useful and valuable members of the organization. If such a flexible climate can be built and fostered in organizations, multiple-career ladders—vertical, horizontal, static, and downward—can be created that will neither demean the individual nor hurt the organization. After all, the organization wants only a small number of motivated and ambitious individuals to climb the organizational ladder; the system will come under severe stress if too many such individuals start competing for the few positions at the top.

Hall and Richter (1984) suggest several career strategies for organizations to deal with the baby-boom generation of workers. For instance, the authors recommend that career paths be restructured by adding intermediate job levels, by offering more opportunities for advancement, by enabling lateral mobility, by structuring task forces in which employees are exposed to a variety of skills and challenges, and by formalizing entrepreneurial activities through encouraging and rewarding innovations.

Travel and relocation are two factors that are, in many cases, closely linked to mobility—whether upward, horizontal, or even downward. Two-career families experience problems when they have to travel extensively and frequently on company work and when they have to relocate. Organizations can do a few things to help ease their discomfort. Travel is absolutely essential for some purposes; at other times it may not really be critical. Company personnel sometimes travel to gain information about how another plant conducts its operations. Many times information of this nature can be obtained over the telephone. It would be useful for companies to examine their travel allocation plans and see if all the travel undertaken is entirely necessary (Stringer-Moore, 1981). With the rising costs of travel and the increasing sophistication of information technology, companies may want to substantially reduce the amount of travel that their members undertake. Some kinds of training programs now available on cassettes reduce the necessity for employees to undertake travel to attend workshops. Stringer-Moore (1981) calls for better "travel time management" by companies, suggesting that they critically examine the travel schedules and examine whether travel is necessary at all or could at least be decreased in duration and frequency.

Dual-career couples will be more amenable to relocation if their organizations help the spouses of the transferred employees to relocate without having to sacrifice the career progress thus far made by the individuals or to compromise their current life-styles. Companies can also schedule relocations at times that will cause the least disruption to the children's education. The companies should have special arrangements with local schools to accommodate the children of transferred employees. Many organizations are already doing a number of things to make relocation attractive for families. Despite the difficulty of finding people who are willing to relocate, organizations feel that there will be a significant number of relocations in the future (Catalyst, 1981). The number of work-related family moves was estimated to be between 260,000 and 300,000 during 1984, and the estimated costs of moving a family of four members a distance of 1,000 miles in 1984 was $40,000 (Minor, 1984). Minor indicates that organizations are increasingly using the help of relocation services since this reduces relocation costs by 4 to 15 percent. By all accounts, it seems important for organizations to increase their counseling services, improve their job listing and placement technology, and make the entire relocation package more attractive. Extensive use of reputable relocation services, job banks, and computer-assisted job searches; arrangements for placing the children of the transferred employee in schools at short notice; and consortia of organizations within an area sharing job information and relocation costs as suggested by Mathews (1984) might be the way for the future.

While substantial evidence exists that more and more established dual-career members are reluctant to be transferred and relocated, it should not be taken for granted that all dual-career members will be unwilling to relocate. There are families in which the spouses are highly career oriented and do not mind pursuing their careers at two different places. Maynard and Zawacki (1979) state that some couples feel no need to choose between their jobs and their marriages. They accept the job and adjust the relationship through different life-styles, such as pursuing commuter marriages. The authors emphasize the fact that some women are even willing to relocate overseas. Hence, we must abandon traditional views of who should be considered for relocation.

However, since some employers have the erroneous impression that dual-career members will not relocate, career spouses are sometimes not considered for promotions when relocation is involved. Le Louarn and DeCotiis (1983) found that American managers tend to view dual-career family members as less suitable for relocation. However, this was not true for managers who were themselves members of dual-career families or who understood the life-style of dual-career family members better. The same researchers also found that employers were unwilling to select, promote, and transfer dual-career employees because they were considered "high-risk" individuals as a result of the complexity of their life-styles. Some employers therefore overlook dual-career family members for promotion, should relocation be a part of the requirement. This leaves some dual-career employees with the feeling that they are being discriminated against.

When making relocation decisions, therefore, organizations must first determine the individual's reactions to relocation. If they are favorable, it would be a good idea to have his or her spouse involved in later discussions, since open communication between the company officials and the spouses is the best way to explore the benefits for both sides. Sometimes an employee might turn down an offer for relocation because of its adverse consequences for his or her spouse's career but not indicate that this is the reason (Challenger, 1985). As Walker (1976) suggests, companies can enhance the careers of both spouses, as well as further their own interests, by opening up lines of communication between all parties rather than simply expecting employees to adjust to the companies' requirements.

It is possible for organizations to develop attractive relocation packages. They can make arrangements to help a spouse reestablish his or her career in the new place. They can also offer attractive incentives for the children of the transferred employee. Young children may become depressed at the thought of having to leave friends and schools and move to an unknown place. Baxter Travenol Laboratories gives travel kits for the children of relocated employees that offer a positive perspective of the move. Materials in the kits have individual items suited to the age of the children. The items focus on the new community, friendships, surroundings, and so on. Children seem to find the travel kits appealing (Conference Board, 1985).

Hall and Hall (1979) suggest that organizations develop

flexible career tracks, involve members and their spouses in career planning, decision making, and problem solving, create support services for career couples, and help them to develop skills in dealing with conflict and life-career management. Thus, organizations should take a multipronged approach in dealing with relocation. In addition to developing job banks, circulating the resumé of the transferred spouse among prospective employers in the new area, and helping the children to find new schools, organizations can also consider restricting the area of relocation so that commuting by family members becomes a viable alternative to moving the whole family. However, if more and more professionals, whether from dual-career families or not, become unwilling to relocate, companies may have to reconsider both their recruitment and their promotion policies. They may have to recruit and train more employees locally, and promote executives *in situ* rather than constantly shift them from place to place.

Counseling Services for Dual-Career Couples

While trainers, mentors, and colleagues at the workplace can offer advice and support with regard to work-related issues, they do not have the necessary training and expertise to offer counsel to perplexed dual-career members as they try to make decisions regarding various trade-offs between career opportunities and family happiness. In-house organizational counselors can be of particular help to members since they are familiar with organizational policies and practices. An additional reason for having counseling available to members is that the counselor-counselee relationship is of a confidential nature. A high level of trust can therefore be established between the parties for the delicate issues to be addressed. Such an environment of trust and faith is not likely to exist in other kinds of relationships. Thus, organizational counselors perform a unique role, and their services can avert, or at least minimize, employee alienation and dissatisfaction and save the company from constant turnover of personnel.

Whether full-time organizational counselors paid for by

the organization are necessary would depend on the size of the institution and the number and magnitude of the problems that require employee counseling. Some institutions, however, are already beginning to establish employee assistance and counseling programs (EAPs). These may be managed as in-house programs or contracted to an outside agency. About a fifth of the companies who have EAPs run their own programs (Conference Board, 1985). Currently, assistance and counseling are rendered in traditional ways—helping employees to deal with alcohol and drug abuse, manage their personal finances better, handle stress, and cope with health problems. The Bechtel Group, Anheuser-Busch, Tampa, and others have EAP for counseling on the personal and work-related problems of employees. Counseling centers for relocations are also made available by some companies (Groh, 1984).

Organizations such as Control Data, Wells Fargo, and Equitable Life Assurance have person-to-person counseling over a twenty-four-hour hot line under employee advisory resource programs. EAP programs facilitate employees seeking out their services whenever needed and also make provision for referrals from supervisors or medical staff. In the context of dual-career members in organizations, the services of EAPs can be vastly expanded to assist dual-career spouses from the time they enter organizations to the time they retire.

EAPs can counsel dual-career members either on an individual basis or as groups. For instance, dual-career couples can be counseled, as discussed earlier, to shed their concerns about the possible misperceptions of others as they interact with each other at the workplace. This can be done immediately after they are hired and before they are actually placed on their jobs. As dual-career family members settle down in their jobs, they may need special counseling on how to manage their careers. Apart from individual help and referrals, EAPs can (1) conduct workshops and seminars on managing conflicts as members try to juggle their careers and family lives, (2) form support groups of members of dual-career and dual-earner families, and (3) offer training programs that develop and build dual-career management skills. EAP can also provide employees with information and guidance that will help them make decisions with regard to career paths, relocation, and other issues that bear on family and career priorities. In my survey, organizational members expressed a particular need for counseling that would allow them to assess themselves realistically in making career decisions.

EAPs can also help dual-career family members by highlighting the several different alternatives for solving such problematic situations as relocation and frequent travel. For example, simply suggesting that a family member ask her superior to alter travel schedules or to give her travel assignments less frequently seems to ease tensions for employees. Some managers just do not realize that dual-career family members face unique problems. EAP counselors can offer the extra push to get employees to talk out their problems with their superiors. Relocation is another issue that is difficult for employees to deal with by themselves. On the one hand, relocation may be accompanied by advancement; on the other hand, it disrupts family life. Relocation counseling can alleviate spouses' fears about the new life that awaits them if they accept relocation (Challenger, 1985). EAPs can also give relocated employees information about networks available to those who want to initiate job searches in the new place.

EAPs are also very useful in helping members to plan for retirement. Retirement means different things to different individuals and affects the self-concept of individuals in different ways. Retirement could be a good experience for those who have planned for it. If no planning has preceded retirement, however, individuals may see it as a dark, empty, vague, tense, and restrictive experience (Rosen and Palmer, 1982). The timing of retirement of couples in nontraditional families is important. Retirement affects household division of labor, life-style, and decision making in the family, all of which have consequences for the life satisfaction experienced by couples. Joint retirement is good for some families. In other cases, it is better for the wife or the husband to work beyond the other's retirement (Scanzoni and Szinovacz, 1980; Streib and Beck, 1980). EAPs can help couples come to the right decisions regarding retirement.

EAPs can also operate in the supplementary form of hotline telephone services. Family members who feel uneasy about face-to-face encounters, at least initially, with an employee counselor can avail themselves of these services and get a feel for what the process is like before approaching the counselor in person.

Executives whose firms offer EAP—AT&T, United Airlines, and General Motors, among others—feel that its costs are inexpensive when compared to the costs of such alternatives as long-term disability or replacement of employees. Even a few lives saved or problems solved, they feel, is justification enough for having EAPs (Conference Board, 1985). If they offer the extended services for dual-career and other nontraditional family members recommended here, EAPs will become even more valuable.

Responding to Future Demands

Professionals usually take pride in their work and are productive when they are relieved of undue stress and the organizational environment is conducive to effective functioning. By designing structures and processes that contribute to employee success, organizations ensure their own profitability, employee satisfaction, family stability for employees in nontraditional families, and a high societal quality of life. As Miller (1985) points out, employee retention and productivity, both of which influence company profits, are a function of organizational members' ability to view their work and family life as complementary rather than as conflicting. Organizations can do much to enhance members' overall integration of the various aspects of their lives. By reconceptualizing what kinds of organizational systems would best suit the current professionals in the work force and by effecting the necessary structural and process changes in organizational design, institutions will benefit themselves and the nontraditional work force and, ultimately, will enhance the quality of life of our society itself. The proposed courses of action for organizations are depicted in Figure 7.

A prerequisite for change is the commitment of top man-

Figure 7. An Action Plan for Organizations.

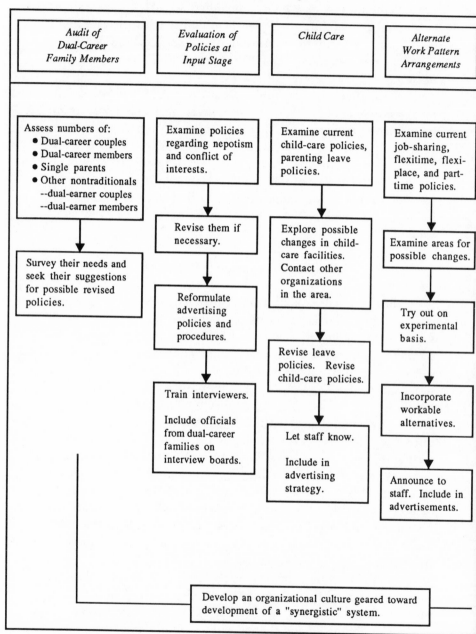

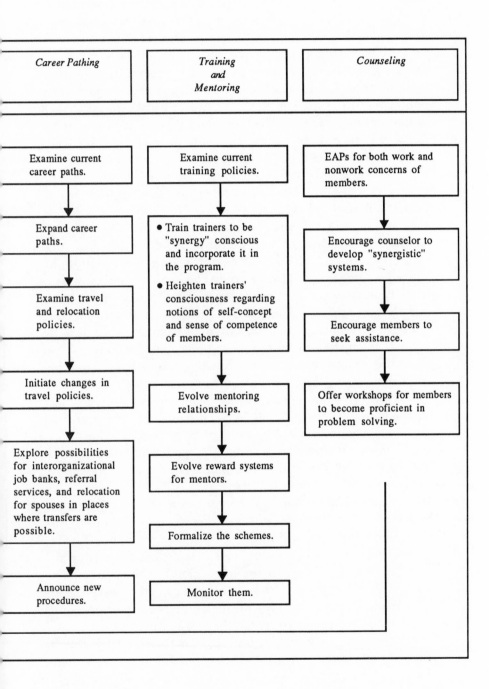

agement to initiate, implement, monitor, and evaluate change. Thus, by taking a proactive stance now, before dual-career family problems become even more acute, institutions will be able to capitalize on the productivity of the new wave of professionals now entering the work force in large numbers. As already noted, the first action in the proactive process is to take stock of the existing values, philosophy, and culture in the organizational system and see what changes are necessary to create the right climate to tap the potential of organizational members.

Previous chapters highlighted two specific areas that require a changed organizational philosophy and culture. One involves defining careers in a holistic way. In this view, employees achieve excellence through balancing work and nonwork activities rather than through meeting the demands of the work ethic alone. This trend calls for a change in management philosophy and style. Managers will have to be flexible and use employee-friendly approaches to achieve organizational excellence. A second shift in organizational culture is the move toward creating synergistic systems. If the full potential of all members is to be tapped, organizations must eliminate sex-role stereotypes and masculine images of organizations. Supervisors, first-line managers, personnel directors, human resources counselors, and all others who have an impact on the organization's progress must be made to realize that old ideas, prejudices, structures, and processes have to creatively yield place to a new ethos if organizational effectiveness is to be achieved. This culture, needless to say, will be egalitarian, humanistic, and employee responsive.

Changes in technological innovation should be matched by changes that create organizational systems devoid of sex-role identities. Only then will organizations become more effective. The new values should pervade the entire organization, from the president's office down to the lowest level in the system. The changes should be a function of conscious and painstaking efforts made by top management, including the use of appropriate symbols and rituals to spread the new culture.

One way to effect such changes is to recruit large numbers of competent and qualified women for responsible high-level positions. Properly socialized and trained, these women would successfully establish themselves and change the excessively masculine images of many organizations. When equalization of power in organizations finally occurs, the potential of their human resources will be much more fully tapped than it is now. Starting with a new vision, organizations can initiate action plans at the input and throughput stages to energize the system and make the workplace an exciting milieu to be in.

Conclusion

Today, more than ever, the progress of society is closely linked to the productivity of organizational systems. With the growing number of dual-career and dual-earner families in the work force, organizations play a vital role in preserving the stability of the family unit. Society's progress, in a sense, rests with organizations. For perhaps the first time in the history of our country, society will look to organizations to maintain its core values, chief among which is the preservation of the family system as an integral unit, and will at the same time expect organizations to provide opportunities for individual growth and development. Thus, organizational effectiveness will, in the future, encompass financial success or failure (measured by sales, profits, and other dollar figures); quality of work life (assessed by the degree of employee satisfaction, motivation, morale, and commitment to the organization); and the added dimension of social responsibility, which includes the preservation of the family as a viable social unit. In other words, since our society values the family subsystem as integral to its well-being, organizations will, in the context of dual-career families, be obliged to take some responsibility for not putting such families at risk (because of unbending rules and an unwillingness to be flexible).

As we have seen, organizations must be proactive in making changes in their structures and processes to capitalize on the strengths of the increasing number of nontraditional family members that will be joining the work force in the future.

The multifaceted dimensions of dual-career families and the spillover from one sphere of their life space to the other were discussed in Chapter Two. Despite the fact that organizations can do much to reduce the tensions of dual-career family members and offer them various types of assistance, there are certain other factors that induce stress in the couple for which they need comprehensive help and counseling—as, for instance, dealing with feelings of competition, nonegalitarian values, and the like. I will discuss such factors in the next two chapters.

EIGHT

Counseling Needs of Dual-Career Families

In the last chapter, employee assistance and counseling programs (EAPs) were discussed as ways to help dual-career members to deal with personal problems or issues that arise at the workplace. Dual-career couples, however, also experience certain dilemmas and problems outside of work and need help in sorting out some of the more intricate and complex issues that arise in the nonwork spheres of their lives *as a couple*. Some of the tensions and stresses experienced by couples and the complexity of the dual-career life-style are captured in articles such as "Juggling Job and Junior" (Lublin, 1980), "Love on the Run: When Two Careers Means Two Homes, Couples Pay the Price" (Kantrowitz and others, 1985), "Career and Family: The Juggling Act of the '80s" (Watkin, 1983), "Competition Between Couples: The Dark Side of Success" (Doudna, 1985), and "The New Improved 1983 Model Husband: Is He for Real?" (Broderick, 1983). Considering the couples' lack of training and psychological preparedness for managing a complex and intricate life-style, it is actually laudable that dual-career families are doing as well as they are. This chapter and the next offer some psychoeducational perspectives on dual-career couples so that those in helping relationships can obtain a broader view of their problems. The objective is not to offer insights into the counseling processes itself but to provide a framework for understanding the interconnections among the various factors that become stressful for dual-career couples.

General Dilemmas

Chapter One discussed the five dilemmas of role overload, identity, role cycling, social network, and normative or social sanctions. Issues of power and status that emerge within the family due to cultural conditioning and adherence to traditional norms preclude egalitarian values from being practiced in most families (Hiller and Philliber, 1982; Jones and Jones, 1980). Nonegalitarian patterns of behavior get reinforced and accentuated by the sex-role differences thrust on employees and the gender-based differential patterns of task allocations and treatment at the workplace (Hiller and Philliber, 1982). Neither the family nor the organizational system has yet faced up to the reality that the incongruency between what is useful to be practiced (equality) and what is being practiced (inequality) is a stumbling block to achieving individual, family, and organizational effectiveness (see, for instance, Bird, Bird, and Scruggs, 1984). The incongruities generate problems within the family as to who should be responsible for what family tasks, how children should be cared for, how finances should be handled, or how time should be utilized.

Dissatisfactions experienced at the workplace, difficulties coping with frequent travel, relocation dilemmas, and several other work-related frustrations experienced by both spouses exacerbate the tensions at home (Bryson, Bryson, Licht, and Licht, 1976; Cooke and Rousseau, 1984). Boredom, inertia, guilt, anger, withdrawal, depression, rigidity, blaming, fighting, demeaning each other, neglecting the family, and turning to work as a sanctuary from family tensions are all dysfunctional coping mechanisms that couples adopt to deal with the various problems faced by them (Parker, Peltier, and Wolleat, 1981).

Interviews that I conducted with dual-career families indicate that couples who genuinely desire to practice egalitarianism often become confused by certain intrapersonal and interpersonal ambiguities. They perceive irreconcilable discrepancies between their felt needs and how *they* have decided to reformulate their roles. Some examples of such conflicts are:

1. A felt need for affection, closeness, and emotional depen-
   dence, along with a need to be independent and assertive.
   For instance, one manager said:

   > Sometimes everything goes wrong at the
   > same time—the business deals I was sure of slip
   > through my hands, all of a sudden we'll have my
   > parents or in-laws visiting us, and the child will fall
   > sick! Those are the times I feel like throwing up
   > my hands and crying on my husband's shoulders,
   > but then I have to catch myself and say, "Janet,
   > you are stronger than that!"

2. A need for privacy, combined with resentment when one is
   left alone for a long period of time. A lawyer working for
   a business firm said:

   > When I come home from work, all I want is
   > peace and quiet and some privacy. But when my
   > wife is gone for the whole evening for some party
   > or some such thing, I feel terrible and have this
   > feeling of being "deserted."

3. A need to be empathic but a fear of coming across as con-
   descending, especially when one's career is on the upswing
   and that of the spouse's is in reverse. A hospital administrator who had received a promotion said:

   > Carl [her husband] was trying very hard to
   > get the new position that was created in his office,
   > but his boss felt that he should wait a couple of
   > years before he would be ready for promotion.
   > Carl took it badly. My heart went out to him, but I
   > did not say anything lest he get offended.

4. A continued need to be treated as "special" or as "superior" carried over from the workplace to the home, where

adjustments have to be made to become egalitarian. A wife
who was pursuing her career as a technician said:

> Sometimes I think Bob forgets to hang his
> "boss" hat at the office when he comes home. He
> expects that everything will be done for him on
> schedule and gets upset with the children or me be-
> cause we were not on time, or did not have some-
> thing ready for him, or whatever. Every once in a
> while I have to remind him that we are his family
> and not his employees at work.

Added to these conflicts, the unrealistic expectations that
some couples entertain about themselves can cause immense
vexations and frustrations. Some couples want a perfect home,
a perfect marriage, a perfect family, and a great career (Rosen,
1985). But as noted in Chapter Three, there is always a trade-
off between career progress and family satisfaction. If both
spouses are equally concerned about career ambitions and marital happiness, success can be "managed" by couples who are
androgynous and understanding. But if couples want everything
—career, marital happiness, children, and family happiness—
something has to give or be compromised. Among couples subscribing to traditional values, the wife often tries to be a super-
woman who can manage everything perfectly. In the short run,
she may succeed. Over the long haul, however, she will suffer
from fatigue, tedium, and frustration.

Couples who think of success only in terms of career advancement sometimes find themselves feeling unhappy, despite
the fact that they are doing well in their careers. To handle
these feelings of unhappiness, they may concentrate even more
on their work, which will drive them even farther apart. Or, not
knowing what has gone wrong, they may resort to counseling.
Such situations offer counselors an opportunity to ask the couple to discuss their expectations and to redefine success in a
way that will lead to greater overall satisfaction. Many couples
also grossly underestimate the demands that a child can make
on their time and life-style. Couples in my interviews repeatedly

stated that they had not realized the extent to which the arrival of a child would transform their lives. All their thoughts and activities, they said, had come to revolve around the new addition to their family without leaving much time for anything else. Counselors can sensitize spouses to the fact that raising a child needs special effort, considerable energy, and a great deal of patience and stamina, so that couples can make more informed decisions regarding family expansion.

Unrealistic expectations begin to surface even before partners actually start a dual-career life. For instance, graduating students at first imagine a rosy future, seriously underestimating the difficulty of obtaining two satisfactory career positions in the same city, and then panic when they are unable to find jobs. Oddly enough, their next step may be to get married, presumably in the spirit of "let's see what happens next." In my many conversations and talks with MBA students, I found the same pattern of initial nonchalance, sudden panic, and "marriage first and career decisions next" operating. Because such young people are not fully aware of the problems they will face, they often compromise their careers and put their marriages in jeopardy. Many of the problems of a dual-career life-style can be anticipated and combatted, however, if couples can be counseled concerning what they will be faced with at the various stages of their lives.

Issues During Different Life Stages

Chapter Four discussed problematic issues at different periods in couples' lives and suggested some ways in which couples themselves could minimize tensions. Here, delineating their life stages somewhat along the same lines, we will detail the underlying causes for the tensions experienced so as to provide a framework for holistic counseling.

We can conveniently examine the problems that dual-career couples are likely to face in the context of five stages in the life-cycle: (1) the "prelaunching" stage, a period when prospective dual-career couples have an opportunity to discuss their future before actually settling down to a dual-career life-style (say between the ages of twenty and twenty-four); (2) the young married couple stage when there are as yet no children (say between the ages of twenty-five and thirty-four); (3) young parenthood, when there are children under six years of age in the family (say between the ages of thirty-five and forty-four); (4) mature parenthood, when there are teen-agers in the family (say between forty-five and fifty-four); and (5) the preretirement stage, when children are on their own and parenting responsibilities are over (say fifty-five until retirement). These life stages follow the pattern suggested by Holmstrom (1972) and Jones and Jones (1980).

These demarcations in the life stages are appropriate for dual-career couples since they segregate the periods when different types of concerns tax the minds of the couple. For instance, during courtship, the couple may be happy in love but may have nagging worries about how they will fit both careers and a marriage into their lives. The first few years of married life before the children are born is usually a period when couples work toward career success; in fact, success may be the major preoccupation of either or both partners at this stage. The third stage, that of raising a family with small children under six years of age, is a significant point in the lives of the couple since several trade-offs between family and career now have to be made in terms of time, effort, and priorities. Stage four with teen-age children is a relatively less stressful period in terms of child-rearing responsibilities, although it may prove difficult to deal with teen-age emotions and one's own career progress and career moves at the same time. The preretirement stage creates a vacuum in the family since the children are gone and couples have to face an altered life-style. Thus, these five stages denote significant break points in the life of the dual-career couple from the time they contemplate getting married to the time they retire.

Stage 1: Couples Launching Dual-Career Life-Styles. This is the stage when both partners seriously consider getting married and launching a dual-career life-style. As early as 1972, Holmstrom came up with evidence that couples who agreed beforehand that careers were important for both tended to have successful dual-career lives. My own research indicates that couples who had fully discussed their priorities and had agreed on their future life-style experienced higher levels of job satisfaction than those who had not (Sekaran, 1982a). Couples may get confused as they talk about and try to understand their aspirations, interests, goals, career and family orientations, and sex-role identities. They may also be unable to differentiate between minor discrepancies and incompatibilities, on the one hand, and major substantive issues, on the other. This could easily cause depression in the couple, and they may require the help of counselors at this stage.

Research indicates that most young women professionals graduating from universities prefer egalitarian roles and consider their careers to be at least as important to them as are their families but that most young men prefer the traditional life-style in which the man's career is given precedence over the woman's (Rosen, 1985; Yogev, 1981). While such men may profess egalitarian values, they may not actually practice them (Kassner, 1981). When women find this to be the case after marriage, they get vexed with the mismatch of perceptions between the partners. Counselors can help prospective couples to be honest with each other and to seriously explore their sex-role and career orientations. Counselors can even administer paper and pencil tests and help the couple enact role plays to understand their own orientations. Such counseling as is necessary can be then offered to the couple. This will minimize unmet expectations for the partners in the future.

Counselors can also ensure that the couple are psychologically prepared for a dual-career life-style and look upon marriage as a firm commitment to each other rather than as something they can escape from through divorce if things do not work out. Most importantly, counselors can help family members define their self-identities and immediate and future goals. This will offer the couple a sense of direction in life. As emphasized by Thomas and others (1982), young people about to get married need more realistic preparation for life than they generally receive, and counselors can play a very important role in this phase of their lives.

Stage 2: Young Married Childless Couples. This is the
time when spouses work hard to build their careers, and they
may even help one another solve problems that arise at the
workplace. The partners also try to understand each other more
fully as they live together under the same roof as married partners. Many life patterns are set implicitly or explicitly at this
stage, including patterns of emotional support. According to
psychiatrist Edward Parsons, couples cheat themselves of much
needed nurturance because women seem to be irritatingly independent and men are afraid to cuddle them, and women,
though wanting to be cuddled, are afraid to ask for it for fear of
regressing to the old dependent female role (Rosen, 1985). It
would be good for couples at this stage to understand that the
comfort zones of men and women are different. Men may be
more inclined to desire privacy and to want less intimacy because they fear close human connections, whereas women may
have more of a tendency to fear separation and hence to want a
greater sense of "connectedness" (Galloway, 1985). Understanding this psychology will help both partners to meet each other
halfway and thus experience greater satisfaction both individually and jointly.

If both spouses are very career oriented, this could very
well be a time when competitive feelings develop, especially if
one progresses faster than the other (Hiller and Philliber, 1982).
This could put some strain on the relationship unless the partners are sensitive to each other's emotions and help one another
to deal with their feelings. It is not uncommon for the person
who lags behind to entertain feelings of worthlessness, hostility,
and jealousy, on the one hand and to experience a sense of guilt
about entertaining such hostile feelings, on the other (Doudna,
1985). But the spouse that rises faster in his or her career may
also feel uneasy. Among university couples, the husband frequently gets promoted faster than the wife, and in the movie
world wives often progress and attain fame faster than husbands
(Doudna describes the competitive feelings among professional
couples in various walks of life).

Mixed emotions are bound to arise when there are seem-
ing disparities in the growth and development of people who

started their careers at the same time. The successful spouse may feel helpless to comfort the other and may simultaneously resent that his or her success cannot be fully enjoyed because the other is depressed. Partners sometimes deal with these situations by rationalizing the events. My interviews indicate that husbands sometimes tell themselves that their wives are progressing because they are women and organizations are emphasizing female advancement, while wives might conclude that they cannot progress as rapidly as their husbands precisely because they are women! Though these feelings might provide some temporary consolation and comfort, they will not put an end to the resentment and frustrations of the partners.

Counselors can help couples to transform competition into cooperation by encouraging the couples to vent their true feelings and to resolve their anger and frustration. The air then gets cleared, and the couple can interact with each other in a collaborative, problem-solving mode. When the spouses are able to recognize their tensions, bring them out into the open, and work toward resolving them, they will be on the road to resolving their conflicts and to removing any feelings of isolation and depression that they may be experiencing.

This could also be the period when the couple becomes anxious to start a family. Many couples, however, may not fully understand the trade-offs between career and family satisfaction and make hasty decisions, only to regret them later. A couple needs to know that the arrival of a child can be a very stressful time for the couple, especially for the wife if the husband is traditional in his sex-role orientation. The partners also need to realize that if the husband happens to be traditional, he is likely to feel neglected and somewhat resentful of the attention bestowed by the wife on their baby. This, then, could be a period in which the couple start to drift apart if they do not share the child-rearing process (see for instance, Gappa, O'Barr, and St. John-Parsons, 1980; Johnson and Johnson, 1977). Even if husbands share these responsibilities, taking on a work-family role may depress those who still abide by traditional value systems. The careers of such husbands, as well as their mental health, may suffer when both spouses seek to juggle their family and work obligations (Keith and Schafer, 1980). Keith and Schafer suggest that counselors help traditionally oriented husbands to adopt healthy attitudes toward role transition since there are costs attached to sticking to old beliefs while still wanting to be part of a dual-career family. Families in which one partner, but not the other, desires a child can also be helped to sort out their conflicting ideas and to arrive at a mutually acceptable decision.

Stage 3: Young Parenthood. This can be a stressful period. The hectic schedules of the workplace and the home (where the children become the center of constant attention) would seem to put the personal and marital lives of the partners "on hold." Spouses aspiring for high-level positions in their organizations will experience considerable stress if they are not able to devote as much time to their careers as necessary. Again, ambition and success may seduce one or both of the partners, and marital and family life may come to be neglected. If the spouses have to travel frequently or if one is suddenly transferred to another place, the complexities of the situation can become extremely tension producing. Unfortunately, these are, as corporate psychologist John McNulty points out, the most "crucial years" in the career lives of many couples, and young executives often feel that they have the least control over the demands of their jobs precisely when they are climbing up the career ladder (Watkin, 1983). Thus both the career and family place heavy demands on the couple, and unless both partners are androgynous, there could be crisis episodes in the family.

The NBC program on "Women, Work, and Babies: Can America Cope?" which was aired in March of 1985, depicted very poignantly the unequal responsibilities of parents. It showed women trying to adjust to multiple-role stresses and explored the feelings of competition and the sense of dissatisfaction that women experience at this stage. Some families break down under these pressures. Many traditional husbands complain that their wives do not spend enough time with the children, and most nontraditional wives complain that the children have "absentee" fathers. Psychiatrist David Rice (conversation with the author, January 1986) states that at this stage couples do not talk to each other very much, sex ceases to be enjoyable, and there is no longer any time for friends. Moreover, even though many couples openly discuss the "inequity" in role sharing, they treat it as a "temporary disadvantage." As women try to adjust to their "temporary disadvantages," however, feelings of dissatisfaction can begin to fester.

At this time, the temptation could be great for men to turn more and more to work and stay longer and longer hours in the organization (Bartolomé and Evans, 1980). But such behavior would only add to the marital problems because then the wife would become even more overstressed and resentful. Martin Goldberg, director of the Marriage Council of Philadelphia, says he is amazed at the small amount of time that couples spend together. He says that even weekends are heavily scheduled with errands and that couples spend this time battling with each other because neither knows how to spend their time most fruitfully (Rosen, 1985).

This is a period when mothers experience intense guilt and anxiety if they are not with their children during the day. For this reason some might be tempted to overindulge their children (Nadelson and Nadelson, 1980) and allow them to take control of the home and act like "little bosses" once the parents get back from work. This could be detrimental to the children. Counselors can help mothers to get over their feelings of guilt and also help them to transcend their culturally conditioned need for taking on major responsibility for the children to the near exclusion of the father in the parenting role. Moreover, the insecurity and guilt feelings of the mother seem quite unwarranted since research indicates that children of working parents evince more self-reliance, creativity, and responsibility than do children of traditional parents (Johnson and Johnson, 1977).

The dual-career household with young children has a hectic atmosphere. Husbands, especially, feel rushed and out of control. A kind of inertia sets in as they come to feel overwhelmed with activities (Winter, Stewart, and McClelland, 1977). Both men and women feel emotionally drained after dealing with the professional, family, and financial aspects of their lives (Jones and Jones, 1980). Humphrey (1983) labels the fatigue and exhaustion at this stage of life the "young parent syndrome." He states that wives who play several different roles are fatigued and lose interest in their sex life, while their husbands who are less negatively affected by fatigue might become dismayed, angry, and hurt at their wives' apparent lack of interest or coldness.

Humphrey suggests that therapeutic resolutions to the problem are possible. Counselors can provide help in this regard by pointing out to couples that concealing anger and stress (Rosen, 1985), attaching low priority to being together, and not knowing how to unwind from the day's stresses (Mackoff, 1985) can all result in lower levels of intimacy. A relaxed atmosphere, peace and quiet, using the transition from office to home as a period of decompression, and making intimacy a priority and planning for it (as one does for a party) are all essential if couples are to experience connectedness and intimacy (Galloway, 1985). The time crunch that dual-career couples, in particular, experience is an impediment to the spouses' experiencing marital satisfactions, and this could well lead to inhibited sexual desire. Sex therapist Helen Singer Kaplan estimates that about 50 percent of the patients in sex therapy clinics and about 20 percent of the population in general suffer from inhibited sexual desires (Rosen, 1985). Counselors can highlight how important it is for spouses to deliberately plan to spend some "couple time" each day and to be by themselves in a relaxed manner.

Stage 4: Mature Parenthood. This stage will not be as hectic as the earlier one. However, parents may become concerned about their teen-age children with regard to drugs, alcohol, and sexuality. These and other issues are particularly on the minds of dual-career parents since both partners are away from the house for a major part of the day. Feelings of anxiety and guilt that one might not be acting the part of a good parent, along with fears that their children are in the wrong company, could nag the couple. Teen-age children can also be trying, since they can easily stir up discomfort in the family if they feel neglected or cheated in some way or if they do experience other tensions (David Rice, conversation with the author, January 1986). With teen-agers in the family, spouses may also find it easy to avoid confronting the differences and problems between themselves and instead come to the counselor with their children's problems. Thus, counselors may have to deal with individual spouses, the couple, the children (individually or as a group), and the family as a whole to resolve many of the problematic issues at this stage.

This could also be a stage when one spouse is transferred. This is a particularly vexing issue since the children will be in school and may not want to move. The spouses may also be at the age where it is difficult for the trailing spouse to establish a career in a new place. In addition, if things are not going well at work (promotions not forthcoming as anticipated), individuals could begin feeling normless and ambivalent about themselves. This would affect the home sphere as well, and one or both of the spouses may resort to dysfunctional coping behaviors, such as drinking and excessive smoking, or begin to ignore their career or family obligations. For other couples, however, this could be a period in which the partners have consolidated their career gains and are now taking on the mentoring role. Relieved of career tensions, such couples may become more family oriented and shift their interests to community and social matters and derive a sense of satisfaction from participating in them.

Counselors can help worried parents of teen-age children with good counseling. They can encourage the couple to develop trust and openness in the family. They can also encourage children to share their problems, as well as their success experiences, with their parents. This could be the time when, with the help of the counselor, parents and children come closer together by engaging in such activities as taking family vacations together. Family members can also learn to be interdependent. Interdependence among family members is necessary for members to unwind, celebrate, commiserate, clarify, sympathize, and enjoy (Weingarten, 1978b). Counselors can help the family come closer together and enjoy each other at this stage.

If a decision about relocation becomes necessary, counselors can help couples take a "balance sheet" approach to the decision, negotiate simultaneously for two positions, arrange for commuting, go separate ways to pursue short-term opportunities, or simply reject the relocation offer (Maynard and Zawacki, 1979).

Stage 5: The Empty Nest. This is the stage in the life-cycle when the children have left home and husband and wife are once again alone. Contrary to stereotypes, there are indications that men, more than women, suffer from the empty nest syndrome (Mall, 1979). Most women, it seems, feel happy and relieved at this stage, but men suffer from regret at not having been closer to their children as they were growing up and thus feel a sense of lost opportunity (Mall, 1979). For some couples this could also be a time of crisis in their marriage because they cannot use the children as a buffer for their emotional disagreements but have to confront one another face-to-face. If direct confrontation becomes a problem, they may seek geographical buffers by accepting any relocations that come their way (David Rice, conversation with the author, January 1986).

Many couples, however, begin to engage in leisure and community activities at this stage. Career women may now feel free to pay more attention to their work lives, may accept relocations easily, and may even be willing to consider commuter marriages. Hence, they may see this as a period of autonomy, freedom, and achievement (Gerstel, 1977).

Since many dual-career couples marry late, they may now be approaching the final stages of their careers. The most preoccupying thought for many at this stage would be retirement, which they might consider as either a pleasant or an unpleasant venture into the future. Since most professionals' identity is linked to their work, retirement, which is the end of their professional lives, is a time of identity crisis for many (Hall and Hall, 1979). Even for those who had looked forward to retirement, it may not be as enjoyable as they might have dreamed unless they have put in the necessary time to carefully plan for it in terms of activities, life-style, financial arrangements, and so on. Planned retirement is important for the peace, life satisfaction, and mental health of both partners. Developing alternative interests and activities for retirement is important if couples are to lead a long, healthy life. Counselors can help couples to explore their alternatives and to make financial plans for retirement. Counselors can also show them ways to ease into retirement by developing new interests and hobbies and perhaps by traveling.

Specific Counseling Concerns

Defining success and being effective in interpersonal communications are critical to the well-being of two-career families. Since both involve the heart as well as the head, counselors can often help couples by providing advice and guidance.

Defining Success. As discussed in Chapter Three, it is important for families to periodically share with each other what they want and expect out of life. This requires spouses to assess their changing needs from time to time and examine the congruence of their personality predispositions and career orientations in the context of new definitions of success. The shifting emphasis between careers and the family as the couple go through the various life-cycle stages needs to be articulated, understood, and shared by the couples. It is very easy for the partners to forget that there are always some trade-offs to be made and that there is no such thing as a "super" dual-career family. It is simply not possible to be dedicated careerists, perfect spouses and flawless parents, all at one and the same period of time. By gently reminding the couple that making it to the top in a career is not the only way to define success, the counselor can help the couple to weave a different pattern of success in their life—a pattern that they might eventually find to be highly satisfying. While opportunities for reaching middle-level positions in one's profession may be numerous, there are fewer opportunities at the top. In hindsight, many professionals may feel that their painful and lonely journey to the top was not worth the struggle and the sacrifice of family life. Since career-oriented couples who are also fond of their family life are particularly likely to experience anxiety, restlessness, and exhaustion during transitional periods in their lives, counselors can offer good advice as the individuals talk matters over with them. The counselor's help to couples in jointly generating their definition of success could make a big difference to the quality of life experienced in families.

Effective Interpersonal Communication. One of the most important first steps to effective communication between spouses is to build into their relationship trust, openness, and a willingness to communicate with each other about their emotions and experiences on a daily basis. If feelings of trust, cooperation, and collegiality are built into the relationship from the very beginning, the couple will be able to interact without fear of hurting each other or being rebuffed. Lack of communication and listening skills seem to be the main barriers to the interpersonal effectiveness of many dual-career spouses today. Listening is hampered when either spouse fails to consider the other as an individual having his or her own independent needs and aspirations but instead insists on establishing a superior-subordinate relationship. This builds a wall between the partners and hampers both listening and effective communication (Bartolomé and Evans, 1980).

Couples can be effective dual-career partners or they can be "duel" career partners. Although not in the context of dual-career couples, Bartolomé (1983) very forcefully pointed out that tragedy and waste shadow the personal lives of executives who lack communication skills. He says that executives frequently admit to difficult and painful problems at home, loss of vitality in their marriages, and difficulty with children, all of which turns them into slaves to their work. The author argues that executives wrongly assume that managing a family is easy and that getting along with children does not require any effort. Many male and female executives feel very competent in their work but not at home. Many do not confront problem situations because they are afraid of being unable to handle the conflicts that may arise.

Bartolomé further says that as long as people consider family life a duty rather than a pleasure and an opportunity, they are likely to stay longer at work than they need to. When family life is enjoyable, however, they start organizing their work so as to leave time to interact with family members. Bartolomé suggests that spouses abandon the thought that having a good family life is easy and that it does not call for any particular effort or skills. He advocates that executives develop interpersonal sensitivity in their personal lives. He theorizes that often the apparent insensitivity of male executives is just a mask to hide a hypersensitivity that could be transformed and put to work. He feels that building a good family life is like creating a company or building a bridge, neither of which is easy but both of which can be done. People have to work at building a family. In the dual-career family setting, working at it means keeping the lines of communication open and communicating with each other freely and honestly.

In my interviews with dual-career couples, the members time and again pointed to effective communication as one of the most important factors accounting for their happiness. One member said:

> We need to listen to each other. Communication is not just talking, but also listening. Unless we listen to each other, we will be just stating our own points and get frustrated with the other. Sometimes when I talk, my husband will not reply; he will be busy reading a newspaper. I just take the paper away from his hands and tell him that I am talking to him and expect him to listen to me. He will cup his ears and turn to my side! We always talk about things that bother us. We have made it a rule not to snap at each other even if we get angry, but discuss matters in a mature way. It is not always easy, but we have practiced it by agreeing on a penalty of more home work sharing for whoever fails.

Walker (1976) pointed out another problem that hinders good communication. He noted that while a husband and wife might be able to relate their feelings individually to a counselor, they do nothing but indulge in recriminations when together. Walker says that high-achieving male executives feel that they have to be supermasculine, supertough, and superstrong. They then act at home in an obtuse, arrogant, problem-solving mode that angers the wife and diminishes her self-esteem. Although these executives have needs and feelings of dependency, they never express them for fear of being seen as "weak." Walker suggested that frank and open communication between the family partners as individuals and not merely as husband and wife or father and mother would help marriages. He compared marriages to space travel, where a slight midcourse correction is often necessary for successful goal accomplishment.

There is another incompatibility between the spouses that needs to be overcome. Hawkins, Weisberg, and Ray (1980) found in their study that wives wanted open and full communication with their spouses but that their husbands were less eager for the same. Wives also wanted less controlling behavior from their husbands than the husbands actually engaged in. The authors also found that wives seek open and full sharing of views but that husbands often avoid such sharing. Operating in such an environment, many wives hold back from effective interactions. They do not express their expectations of help, support, and understanding for fear of disapproval or rejection. Another problem that hinders effective communication is that many wives (and some husbands) expect perfectionism from self and spouse (which annoys the spouse) thus thwarting or limiting effective interactions between the two.

Good interpersonal communication can help resolve the many conflicts and tensions that arise in families. Conflicts between the couple can be time based, strain based, value based or behavior based. While value-based conflicts are more difficult to resolve and might require third-party intervention, the other kinds can be dealt with through open communication, honest discussion, and joint problem solving. These are the kinds of skills that counselors can develop in the couple.

As Jones and Jones (1980) stated, two-career marriages are cooperative ventures that require frequent consultative decision making and adjustment. Couples can be helped to see and learn the most useful ways of dealing with situations. For instance, if there are conflicts with regard to financial matters, counselors can suggest that each spouse contribute a monthly sum for household expenses but that each partner also maintain his or her own account to which the balance of his or her salary is credited. Gifts and other personal expenses usually come out of these individual accounts.

Various decisions can be made by the couple as they relate to careers (for example, whether to take a new assignment or reject it, relocate or not relocate) and to the family (such as having children or not, using hired help or not). But once the choices are made and the priorities assigned, it is better that the frustrations and regrets that these choices may entail be addressed in a problem-solving mode than that the couple begin to blame each other for the decisions. Parker, Peltier, and Wolleat (1981) pointed out that couples who keep score experience power struggles and sex-role tensions, as a consequence of which there are denial, blaming, repression, psychosomatic reaction, withdrawal, and "going crazy" behaviors exhibited in some families. The authors suggest that couples would benefit by accepting each other as individuals; sharing work-related concerns and happiness; scheduling personal and family time; asking for and offering mutual support; sharing expectations, goals, and needs; using support systems from outside; and seeking help from employers regarding adjustment of work schedules if necessary.

Skinner (1980) suggested that couples establish their priorities among and within roles, compartmentalize family and work, and compromise career aspirations if that is required to meet other important role demands. Taking enough personal time to relax, learning to achieve smooth transitions between work and home, and having backup plans to meet emergencies (such as developing a relationship with a neighbor who will be willing to open the door for the plumber during the day or drive the children to school) all contribute to enhancing the quality of life.

While dual-career couples do experience stress because of the complexity of their life-style, it is this very complexity that offers them the challenge and excitement that many thrive on. The motivation to succeed is so powerful that people accomplish the difficult balancing act merely by believing that they can (Rosen, 1985). Multiple roles can be self-enhancing when they are well managed. Health risks are also usually less for active people. Thus, there are numerous mechanisms built into the life-style that can raise the self-esteem and well-being of the couple, enabling them to experience a series of successes. Professional counselors can make these success experiences happen by helping dual-career couples to realize and articulate what they want, emphasizing positive attitudes, teaching them to operate androgynously in a problem-solving mode, and enhancing their awareness of self and others.

Thus, counselors and others in helping relationships can do much to help dual-career couples achieve their goals. The specialized training and experience of these professionals can help the couple to maintain two careers and a family successfully. In the next chapter I will offer a systemic view of both the tensions and the counseling needs of dual-career members and also give an overview of some of the strategies to bring about needed changes in couples' attitudes and behaviors.

NINE

An Integrative Framework for Counseling Dual-Career Couples

Treating the individual problems that are brought to the attention of counselors in isolation may not get to the root of the more complex dilemmas that couples experience. Rice (1979) expressed concern over the lack of clinical literature to document the themes and common problems faced by dual-career couples. His book discussed such issues as structural problems and conflict syndromes in dual-career marriages and also described some special therapeutic techniques for dual-career couples. With the increasing number of dual-career families, there is a growing need to understand more fully the problems, issues, and dilemmas that such couples face. A holistic approach to dual-career couples' problems can help counselors be more effective with their clients. When counselors are aware of the whole range of issues and dilemmas faced by a couple, they can help members explore in a more fundamental and thorough manner the nexus of issues that might be presented to them as "a problem" by the client or clients.

Counselors can obtain a good idea of the multiple origins of the problems faced by a couple by looking at the whole panorama of issues that result from the five major dilemmas faced by dual-career families. This enables those in helping relationships to take a systemic approach to counseling. Some issues will be more critical at particular stages of the couples' lives than at others, as discussed in the previous chapter, and some counseling may have to be addressed more specifically to the

husband or to the wife (the wife may have to be taught to compartmentalize work and family responsibilities, while the husband's sensitivity to the family environment may have to be enhanced). In all cases, however, relating issues to the five major
dilemmas is likely to make it easier for counselors to offer help
in a holistic way.

Issues, Problems, Feelings, and Tensions

The five dilemmas that couples face will now be discussed
from the perspective of the range and intensity of feelings they
generate in the couple. Examining the root causes of these feelings, attitudes, and behaviors will help counselors to formulate
appropriate strategies for counseling.

Dilemmas of Role Overload. As discussed in previous
chapters, strains due to overload are likely to be felt by both
spouses since the work of a full-time homemaker has now to be
redistributed between two people, both of whom are also pursuing careers. Tensions between the spouses arise with respect
to (1) sharing of household tasks (disproportionate allocation
of tasks, with the wife bearing the heavier burden), (2) parenting responsibilities (higher levels of physical and emotional
stresses experienced by wives in child rearing), and (3) attempts
to balance the several roles and responsibilities of the spouses in
a satisfactory manner (not sacrificing the career for the family
or neglecting the family for the career). Since the majority of
spouses still cling to the traditional gender-based norms of role
taking and role behavior, they are perplexed as to how to make
couple-based roles effective and functional for the family as a
whole. This ambivalence creates excessive role overloads for the
wife. Some families try to reduce the imbalance by hiring outside help to take care of such household functions as cleaning,
washing, and dusting. In other words, there is some structural
role redefinition on the part of the wife. However, this still
leaves other tasks to be handled by the family, such as daily
cooking, paying bills, and attending to the social side of business and family life—most of which are handled by the wife. In
addition, families with children have to shoulder the parenting

functions from the time they get home from work until they leave for the office the next morning. The wives take on the bulk of the parenting responsibilities, and this imposes additional strains on them.

Caught in the bind of wanting to discharge her family duties and responsibilities without unduly imposing on her spouse who is traditionally not expected to be responsible for the home, and being physically and emotionally drained from overwork and exhaustion, the wife tries to manage her life as best she can. She goes about her duties at home and at the workplace to the best of her ability, perpetually carrying with her feelings of resentment, frustration, guilt, restlessness, vexation, and anger—feelings that she can neither understand nor sort out. On the one hand, she feels fortunate in being able to pursue a career, but, on the other, she is frustrated that she is unable to put more time and effort into her career because of her family obligations. She also feels tension because she wishes she could get more help from her husband, but at the same time she feels guilty about wanting to impose *her* responsibilities on him. Dilemmas of overload and identity are experienced simultaneously, and the wife does not know what to do.

As a result, she may begin to snap at family members, become overly critical, or become intolerant or unresponsive. Thus, what might sometimes be seen as the wife's acceptance of inequitable division of labor in the house (Bryson, Bryson, Licht, and Licht, 1976) or wives' lower threshold levels for desired support (Sekaran, 1983b) may have seriously undesirable side effects on behavior. Sometimes the wife may try to resolve the tensions by giving up her career in favor of her household and parenting responsibilities. But this is likely to turn out to be ineffective since it does not address the real problem. The problem is not work, family, or the children per se, but the couple's inappropriate way of handling the overload (Nadelson and Nadelson, 1980). If the wife gives up her career, the chances are that she will come to resent this sacrifice and that her resentment will be reflected in dysfunctional coping mechanisms. Thus, giving up her career would still not help either the wife or the family.

Husbands also feel stressed when they have to take on additional household work. Husbands feel that by taking on household responsibilities they may compromise their careers. This vexes, annoys, and irritates them and makes them resentful of their wives' demands. One consequence of all these physical and mental tensions is that conflicts frequently arise between the two partners. Conflict might manifest itself in immediate outbursts, or tension may build up gradually, only to explode later. Unless the tensions are analyzed and relieved as they occur, they become more dysfunctional and unresolvable with the passage of time. Role-related conflicts arise between couples because the sharing of roles and responsibilities does not allow the spouses enough time for their careers (time-based conflict) and because their role expectations do not match their actual role behaviors (strain-based conflict). However, couples can resolve both time-based and strain-based conflicts through proper role behaviors and time management. Counselors can help couples to differentiate between time- and strain-based conflicts and to evolve appropriate strategies to avoid them in the future.

Identity Dilemmas. Problems of identity arise when dual-career couples still identify, at least some of the time, with their traditional gender-based roles. This causes confusion, internal tensions, and disharmony because the spouses, although realizing the need for androgynous behaviors, are not able to shake off the traditional belief that wives are primarily homemakers and husbands primarily breadwinners. Couples often have difficulty rejecting their old values because no new models are available to them (Gross, 1980). Because of the role confusion stemming from identity dilemmas, their self-concept, self-identity, and self-esteem get blurred. When self-identity is not clear, spouses are unable to define what success means to them individually and jointly, and they find themselves unable to plan for the achievement of goals.

Because identity gets blurred from time to time, mixed signals are intermittently passed between the spouses who may be trying desperately to establish egalitarian values but who periodically revert back to stereotypical sex-role values and behaviors. Issues of status, power, and dominance emerge as one spouse reverts back to traditional role values that are overtly or covertly resented by the other (value-based conflict). Conflicts also arise because of the incongruence among expected, preferred, and enacted behaviors (behavior-based conflicts). The unpredictability of these episodes may cause partners to mistrust and fear each other. The following remarks by a hospital administrator typify this situation:

> Pat [her spouse] and I would like to think we are an egalitarian family. Most of the time, we do treat each other as equals—this is easy for us since we are in comparable job positions and earn about the same. But when I least expect it, Pat will say something that sounds very sexist. For instance, just the other day, when it was his turn to baby-sit when I had to go to an office party, he said that if God did not mean to place the responsibility for children on the mother, He would not have decided to let her carry the babe in her womb. Now this is off the wall, and I would never have expected Pat to say something like this, but he did! I do get annoyed with him at times, but most of the time he is okay. I just have to watch it and put him wise whenever he gets into one of "his moods."

Other kinds of confusion also emerge when self-concept and self-identity are not clear. Spouses come to feel awkward in seeking emotional support, intimacy, and solace from each other. The wife thinks she is supposed to be on her own when she pursues a career, and the husband may find himself unable to express his feelings, even though he may need the same emotional support from his partner as she does from him.

By helping the spouses to define their self-concept and establish their identities, counselors can resolve or greatly minimize many of these problematic issues for the couple. Counselors can especially help couples to establish egalitarian and nurturing roles and behaviors. Values clarification, self-awareness enhancement, increasing interpersonal sensitivity, acculturation to androgynous behaviors, training in communication skills, and enabling spouses to act as counselors to each other when inappropriate behaviors occur are the many ways in which counselors can help couples.

Dilemmas of Role Cycling. Couples experience stresses when they go through role-cycling dilemmas. When wives are career oriented but also want to have a family, they may find themselves confused about when to start a family and up to what time starting a family can be safely postponed. Fresh dilemmas arise when children are born. For example, the couple at this stage has to make child-care arrangements and ensure that their children are getting appropriate physical and emotional sustenance. Not having sufficient time, energy, or knowledge to deal with these concerns, couples experience tension and internal conflicts. Many have qualms about spending as much as 25 percent to 50 percent of their combined earnings on child care and feel that there must be less expensive ways of bringing up children. Many wives try to cope with these tensions by giving priority to their domestic parenting role and lowering their career ambitions. For highly career-oriented wives, however, such a decision may produce emotional turmoil. They may feel resentment toward their husbands, who have not lowered their career ambitions for parenting.

Such conflicts would disappear if wives could compartmentalize the family and work spheres of their lives. Unfortunately, however, most career wives are unable to emotionally separate their work and nonwork environments as their husbands so (Johnson and Johnson, 1977). This adversely affects their career progress. Also, in trying to meet the incessant demands of their children, they experience a high degree of role strain that impairs their physical and mental health (Gove and Geerken, 1977). Wives experience additional strains as they constantly shift gears between two incompatible roles—that of the nurturing wife and mother and that of the aggressive, rational professional career person (Gray, 1980). Through proper counseling and guidance, much of the stress, guilt, and confusion experienced by couples can be alleviated. Wives especially can be helped to see their role as that of both mother and career person. Counselors can help couples realize that once out of the womb, the child is the responsibility of *both* parents.

Network Dilemmas. Scarcity of time sometimes compels couples to exclude even close relatives and friends from their social circle. Apart from creating feelings of guilt and fear, this also forces couples to seek emotional support, comfort, and closeness within the confines of the marital relationship. Should the couple be separated because of travel, training, or other contingencies, they may start to feel abandoned. Most husbands feel lonely and lost during such periods since they are not emotionally close to anyone other than their wives. Husbands are likely to build resentment toward wives whose careers take them away from home. As Gross (1980) suggests, what husbands may miss is not only their wives but also their "inherent" right to importance and first place in the family. They may also resent the shift in parenting responsibilities and household maintenance when the wife is gone, despite the fact that they think that her career also "counts" (Gross, 1980).

A whole range of issues and concerns may develop simply because the husband cannot freely relate to persons outside his immediate family. Having paid little attention to relatives or colleagues in the past, he may find it awkward to turn to them when his wife is gone. Tensions of this nature may result in marital conflicts that are difficult for the initiator to spell out or the other spouse to understand. Becoming more expressive toward others will help husbands to overcome some of the emotional deprivation they feel when they are separated from their spouses. Thus, even if time does not permit couples to cultivate a wide circle of friends and relatives, husbands can still learn to feel comfortable with a few people outside their immediate families. Counselors can perhaps help husbands to become more expressive and to identify the sources of their frustrations and resentments when they are separated from their wives.

Wives (and husbands) who are close to their parents and friends may often feel guilty that they are unable to devote sufficient time to them. Feelings of guilt will be compounded if a parent is ill and needs physical and emotional comfort. Here the dual-career member feels a duty to take on the role of support-

ive child but, because of energy and time constraints, is unable
to do so. When prolonged, such situations can wear out the couple and have adverse consequences on behavior. Counselors can
help the couple to be realistic in facing such situations and not
let feelings of guilt and sorrow affect their relationship.

Dilemmas Caused by Environmental Sanctions. The normative or environmental sanction dilemma arises when there is
incongruence between traditionally imposed values and the actual behaviors necessary for pursuing a nontraditional life-style.
Spouses who have a strong internal locus of control (that is,
those who feel they can shape their own destinies) do not experience as much stress from these incongruencies as those who
have a strong external locus of control (those who feel their actions are governed by others). Traditional norms of behavior are
governed by gender-based roles that stipulate that the wife take
on the responsibility for homemaking and child rearing and subordinate her career ambitions to those of her husband. Traditional norms also prescribe that the husband concentrate on
career success, be the head of the house, and be the main provider for the family. When these norms are transgressed by the
couple, the wife is blamed (for not being a good homemaker or
mother), held in contempt, or completely ignored in social
interactions. The husband is ridiculed as "spineless" or "hen-
pecked" and is not shown the respect due to him as an individual.

Wives especially are sensitive to other people's reactions
and fear rejection, because they rely on the moral and physical
support of others to maintain their self-esteem and family well-
being. If there is a big gap between societal expectations and
their own preferred modes of behaviors, fears of being rejected
loom large for them. This, added to their identity dilemmas,
keeps most wives shackled to role behaviors that may be inappropriate for achieving both career progress and family satisfaction. One of the primary areas of concern to them is child
rearing. Holding themselves personally responsible for their children's proper upbringing, mothers personalize the failure if their
children do not live up to their expectations.

Normative dilemmas create other kinds of problems as

well. Societal norms dictate that the husband should be more successful in his career than his wife in hers. Hence, if the wife surpasses her husband in this regard, she feels guilty and tries to avoid future success and promotions. Husbands either deny or rationalize their competitive feelings (Johnson and Johnson, 1977; Rapoport and Rapoport, 1971b; Sekaran, 1982b). Such coping behaviors lead to feelings of repression, denial, blaming, and so on. Normative dilemmas also pose problems in the world of work. What responsibilities should be given to dual-career wives, how people should interact with each other, and who gets connected to whom in a mentor-protégé relationship all become problematic issues because of traditional norms and environmental prescriptions.

To sum up, the major problems and dilemmas experienced by couples stem from their inability to cope with perceived incongruencies among tradition-bound norms, required functional behaviors, and the actual role behaviors enacted by them. Spouses who are traditional or are incompatible in their value orientations, as well as those who are insensitive to each other, have difficulty managing their time, setting priorities, and engaging in joint problem solving and decision making. Those who have an external locus of control feel the dilemmas and tensions more acutely than those who have an internal locus of control.

How Counselors Can Help

Couples can learn how to deal with the various problematic issues just discussed when those in helping relationships take a systemic view of the undercurrents in dual-career families. By understanding the range of ambivalences, conflicting norms, required behaviors, and tensions experienced by couples, counselors can deal with the causes of conflict rather than merely the symptoms that manifest themselves during therapy sessions. Counselors have opportunities to work with dual-career couples in at least seven basic areas: defining self-concept and self-identity, exploring value orientations and developing functional values, equalizing power distribution and role sharing in the family, defining success, managing stress, establishing new functional behaviors, and developing appropriate skills to ensure a good quality of dual-career life.

Defining Self-Concept and Self-Identity. By developing a strong sense of the self and anchoring self-identity in both career and family, husband and wife can together transcend their narrower roles and become caring individuals supportive of each other. Couples will then be able to meet life's challenges better, handle failures with less stress, and develop greater tolerance for ambiguity.

Schwartz and Waetjen (1976) emphasize the importance of self-concept in handling failures and tolerating ambiguity. When wives incorporate into their self-concept and identity a strong egalitarian power base and a success orientation, rid of the fear that they will lose their femininity and become cut off from male support, much of the ambivalence they experience will get sorted out. My research (Sekaran, 1985b) indicated that wives, irrespective of their level of competence, felt uncomfortable when they spent more of their time on career activities than on family ones. They seemed to be constantly in the throes of a dilemma as to whether careers could or should be given the same attention and priority as the family.

In fact, however, wives can learn to see themselves as both careerists and family persons—that is, as capable and strong individuals who, given proper structural support inside and outside the family, can operate effectively in the many facets of their lives. Husbands, likewise, can be helped to establish their self-concept and identity as egalitarian partners in the marital relationship who take equal responsibility for housework, child care, and all other family activities as caring individuals. Counselors can help spouses to feel comfortable in establishing such identities and self-concepts.

Exploring Value Orientations and Developing Functional Values. Couples can learn how to explore and understand their gender-role identity—masculine, feminine, or androgynous. They can also examine their central life interests to determine whether the family or the career has assumed primacy. When tensions are experienced by one or both partners and they grow dissatisfied with their work or family lives or both, counselors can identify the reasons for the tensions. The couple can then be made aware of the fact that unless they adopt androgynous values and behaviors or have complementary values, they will continue to experience frustrations. Keith and Schafer (1980) also point out that the more traditional the dual-career spouses are, the greater will be the threat to their mental health. Counselors should emphasize how important it is for spouses to accept the attitudes toward role transition and to make the necessary shifts in their values and behaviors. In other words, husbands need to feel comfortable doing household work and wives need to feel comfortable letting their spouses take equal charge of the home so that they can devote more time to their careers. The more both spouses become androgynous in their values and behaviors, the greater will be their marital and career satisfaction.

Equalizing Power Distribution and Role Sharing in the Family. Nonegalitarian role sharing stems from felt status inequalities between the spouses in terms of education, income, and occupational status. Traditional beliefs that wives are responsible for homemaking also contribute to unequal role sharing. Family power constellations result from the status ascribed to the two partners. However, power also has some less discernible sources. Safilios-Rothschild (1976) describes nine sources of family power, which include some of French and Raven's (1962) six bases of social power: legitimate power, decision-making power, influence power, resource power, expert power, affective power, dominance power, tension-management power, and moral power (setting norms of fairness and justice).

Power can be exercised in covert and overt ways. The wife who in very gentle and subtle ways exercises her tension-management and influence powers may be unaware of her own strengths, and both spouses may not realize that the happiness and well-being of the entire family rest on how she positions herself on critical issues. How power is exercised or recognized in the family is a function of the needs, motives, self-concepts, and ideologies of the spouses (Safilios-Rothschild, 1976). By enhancing the self-concepts of partners, redefining value bases, and analyzing family dynamics, it becomes possible to equalize power in a family so that neither partner feels like a pawn on a chessboard. Counselors can help family members become aware of the bases of power and reformulate their self-concepts and ideologies. When status and occupational inequalities are de-emphasized, power equalization is recognized at the conscious level and androgynous behaviors are practiced, role sharing becomes equitable, and both partners find themselves able to pursue a career and to enjoy family life.

Defining Success. Having established their values, identities, and roles, spouses can learn to define what success means to them individually and jointly. Counselors can help the couples to come to an understanding of what each wants and then negotiate any conflicts on differences. For example, counselors can point out any incongruencies in the couple's definition of success, their gender-based values, and their preferred role behaviors and then specify what changes the couple must make to achieve its goals.

Managing Stress. There is no doubt that both spouses will experience some physical stress when sharing housework after a full day at their workplaces. But several structural and process-oriented measures and techniques can relieve these stresses considerably. Structural interventions include such support systems as hired help, the use of time management techniques, and setting priorities so that work gets done efficiently. Process interventions would consist of using relaxation techniques, easing the transition from work to home, and trying to anticipate the nature, intensity, and frequency of unexpected contingencies so that structures can be created to take care of or minimize them.

Feelings of guilt also create stress. Guilt is experienced by couples when their behaviors do not fit their values and norms. Wives feel guilty about neglecting their children, not maintaining their houses as well as they should, or surpassing their spouses in career. Husbands feel guilty when they are unable to provide the emotional support that they know their wives need from them, when they entertain competitive or jealous feelings, or when they see their wives shouldering the entire burden of homemaking. When both spouses finally realize the benefits of becoming a truly egalitarian pair, however, they can considerably reduce their feelings of guilt and channel the released emotions into more fulfilling endeavors.

Establishing New Functional Behaviors. Any value changes that occur must also be reflected in behavioral changes. Androgynous role making instead of traditional role taking, flexibility in adjusting to new roles, a tolerance for inadequacies and imperfection as new roles are learned and being practiced, and being appreciative and encouraging of each other can all become a part of each spouse's repertoire of behaviors. Counselors can help couples to establish and monitor the desired behaviors.

Developing Appropriate Skills. To achieve their newly formulated goals, the couple has to develop several skills, including communication skills, listening skills, role-making skills, joint problem-solving and decision-making skills, time-management skills, and conflict resolution skills. Taken together, these are termed "survival skills." Learning and using these skills can be both challenging and exciting. Through counseling, couples can discover how to develop self-awareness and sensitivity toward each other and ultimately to act as mutual consultants whenever behavioral or value changes are called for. Spouses can also learn to identify situations that call for dependent, independent, and interdependent behaviors and to understand each other's need to engage in all three modes in their daily lives.

Humphrey (1983) describes the therapist as a catalyst, counselor, mediator, and educator. He stresses that in the modern family system, where egalitarian values are more emphasized, couples need to learn bargaining skills so that they can negotiate goals, philosophies, and behaviors. Walsh (1980) explains that "the dual goal of the family therapist is to enhance the effectiveness of the total family system but at the same time to try to enhance the growth, development, and individuation of each family member as well" (p. 121). Thus, counselors play a vital role in assisting dual-career couples. Couples can minimize most of their emotional, physical, mental, sexual, attitudinal, and behavioral malresponses if they are taught to deal with the dilemmas they face in a comprehensive way.

Strategies for Bringing About Change

Rice (1979) and Humphrey (1983), among others, recommend joint counseling sessions with marital partners rather than individual clinical sessions so that a therapeutic alliance is promoted for collaborative problem solving between the couple. Rice also recommends that there be an agenda detailing the items that need to be worked on—for example, building an effective relationship, decision making, or financial management. Therapists can use such different techniques as behavioral contracts, behavioral exchange models, videotaping of therapy sessions, group therapy, seminars for raising awareness, workshops for young career couples, and subliminal tapes.

Behavioral Contracts. Knox (1973) discusses behavior-based contracts in marriage counseling. Behavior modification is the approach taken in developing these contracts. The assumption is that attitudes and feelings are based on behavior and that behavior, being learned, can be changed. Taking the unit of treatment as behavior and not the individual per se, Knox states that therapy can proceed to enhance desirable behaviors through behavioral contracts that reinforce positive behaviors. A behavioral contract is a negotiated agreement in writing that states the conditions under which one person will do something for another. For instance, if one spouse usually spends a great deal of time at work and very little time with the family during weekdays and the other spouse spends the weekends visiting parents, they might arrive at the following negotiated agreement (in writing): If the former comes home before 5:30 P.M. for four consecutive days in the week, the latter will not be away from the house that weekend; instead, they will spend the weekend together.

Such structured mechanisms to establish and monitor behaviors can be used with regard to role making, time management, setting priorities, developing a team spirit, practicing equity, and increasing flexibility and tolerance. A chief advantage of behavioral contracts is that role expectations of family members are clearly applied to observable behavior (Eisler and Hersen, 1975). This reduces unproductive verbal exchanges when individuals do not carry out their prescribed roles.

Behavioral Exchange Models. Rappaport and Harrel (1975) suggest the behavioral exchange model to eliminate undesirable behavior, to teach skills for reciprocal exchange between the partners, and to foster self-reliance in them. Stressing the principles of social exchange and reciprocity, the authors suggest that the couple prepare a hierarchy of undesirable behaviors in each other and, beginning with the least difficult target behaviors, try to bring about changes in their life-style. Implementation of this model involves five steps—exposing the spouses to the principles of reciprocal exchange and behavior modification, labeling undesirable behaviors, labeling positive or desirable behaviors, implementing the contract, and renegotiating the contract. This technique might help couples to more quickly practice androgynous behaviors. By constantly making, implementing, monitoring, and renegotiating contracts that reduce undesirable behaviors and enhance desirable behaviors, couples will be motivated to change more easily and quickly.

Liberman (1975) stressed that the behavioral approach when consistently applied is more effective and faster than most other change models. He also stated that a behavioral and learning approach in the context of family therapy enables the counselors to define their role as an educator in collaboration with the family.

Videotaping of Therapy Sessions. Couple interactions and behavior can be videotaped during regular therapy sessions. This allows partners to process and interpret their own behaviors, body language, and interactions through instant replays. Couples can also view the tape in their own homes at leisure. By seeing themselves acting in particular ways, partners are able to review and understand their behavioral responses to each other and to become sensitive to verbal and nonverbal maladaptive behaviors.

Eisler and Hersen (1975) describe a case in which spouses watched a replay of a typical conflict situation in their family. The counselors then focused the attention of the couple on a series of aversive behaviors that escalated the conflict. The wife was shown her coercive attempts to obtain cooperation from her husband, and the husband was shown his passivity to his wife's anger. Since such behaviors did not seem likely to solve the problem, the therapist then modeled more functional behaviors that the couple tried to emulate. The authors report that a follow-up three months after the conclusion of ten sessions indicated that the couple had developed problem-solving skills that were sufficiently reinforcing to all family members as to be self-sustaining.

Group Therapy. Gray (1980), among others, recommends a group approach to therapy since couples learn from each other what kinds of problems they face and how they can be resolved. This helps younger couples to anticipate and to be prepared to tackle problems, and it helps older couples to learn from each other alternative approaches for resolving issues. Group therapy also makes couples aware that they are not alone in dealing with issues and that there are others who have managed their life-styles well despite periodic frustrations.

Seminars for Raising Awareness. Culbert and Renshaw (1972) recommend adopting a seminar format for establishing individual differences between spouses, developing awareness of one's position, and using force-field analysis to recognize the forces that foster and hinder a couple's marriage. They recommend using the feelings of the spouses as data points for counseling. The seminar is basically meant to enhance understanding and empathy between the partners.

Workshops for Young Career Couples. Amatea and Cross (1983) have developed a six-phase format for young couples to (1) enable them to become aware of their family and career roles, (2) encourage collaborative efforts between the couple, (3) introduce them to coping mechanisms, (4) clarify personal values, (5) develop communication and joint problem-solving skills, and (6) foster mutual support and counseling. The workshop enables couples to examine their present life-style with regard to decision making, managing conflicts, and understanding personality predispositions. It also helps couples to understand the pitfalls in communication, such as trying to read one another's minds, fuzzy signaling, and jumping to conclusions.

Subliminal Tapes. One of the potentially promising methods for bringing about change in dual-career families is subliminal and self-hypnotic tapes. Havens (1982) describes the advent of hypnotic tapes in business boardrooms to increase awareness of hidden abilities, to improve the functioning of personnel, and to reduce burnout. He states that in one company hypnosis has shown considerable promise as a technique for management training. Subliminal and self-hypnotic tapes are now being developed and effectively used for a variety of purposes. Among other things, they are used to transcend pain, anger, anguish, and allergies, to enhance public speaking effectiveness, and to improve memory. (Potentials Unlimited of Grand Rapids, Michigan, has developed such tapes.) It is possible to develop similar tapes to enhance spouses' sensitivity to each other, to increase problem-solving and decision-making skills, to stimulate egalitarian behaviors, to inculcate androgynous values and behaviors, and to reduce stresses experienced in the dual-career context. The potential for changing attitudes, values, and behaviors in couples so as to enhance the quality of their experienced life seems almost infinite. Subliminal messages could well become an important medium for helping dual-career couples in the future.

A Note of Caution

One of the concerns of some researchers—see, for example, Rice (1979)—is that practitioners themselves be neutral in the role of counselors and not have biases against either dual-career families in general or the wives (or husbands) in such families in particular. Haring, Beyard-Tyler, and Gray (1983) found that the male counselors in their sample were biased against women who pursued nontraditional careers and even more prejudiced against men in nontraditional careers. The authors emphasized the need to improve the attitudes of these members. Practitioners' own attitudes and values are important because they have a great deal of influence on their clients. When they maintain a neutral attitude, counselors can coach their clients to modify their actions to become effective dual-career couples. Judicious counseling and reinforcement (Aldous, 1974) help therapists to achieve their goals. Rice (1979) discussed the important role of co-therapists who can model the egalitarian behaviors that they advocate to their clients. Rice also suggests the use of psychodynamic, intrapsychic, behavioral, and gestalt techniques in therapy. He points out that there could be dyadic resistance of the couple to therapy and that couples therefore should be first made to establish a therapeutic alliance.

Members from dual-career families are likely to seek counseling at various stages of their lives when they find it difficult to handle problematic issues by themselves. Counselors can play a key role in helping couples to examine their values, interests, and goals and to define what they mean by a good quality of life. Counselors can help couples to understand and resolve the intricacies and dilemmas inherent in the dual-career life-style that result in feelings of guilt, anxiety, competition, anger, resentment, lowered self-esteem, and depression. Counselors can guide spouses to set goals, clarify roles, negotiate with each other in an ongoing fashion, and balance the several aspects of their life in keeping with the way the spouses define success at various stages of their lives. But counselors can beneficially serve dual-career couples only if they have clarified their own value systems and are able to offer counsel without entertaining feelings of prejudice toward their clients, whatever those clients' life-styles may be.

TEN

Dual-Career Families, Organizations, and Society: Future Trends

There has been a phenomenal increase in the number of dual-career families in the United States over the last two decades. In 1983 the number of dual-career spouses was estimated at 3.3 million as compared to 900 thousand in 1960 (Conference Board, 1985). Because more and more young men and women are entering professional programs in our universities, we can expect the rate of increase in dual-career families to be even greater in the future. The growing number of dual-career families will have an impact on many aspects of our everyday lives. As more and more career women postpone their marriages until they are relatively well entrenched in their careers (Doudna, 1985), the likelihood of their marrying other professional men will increase, thus adding to the number of dual-career families in society. This increase will influence the economic, governmental, educational, and social and cultural trends in our society.

Opportunities for Entrepreneurs

To begin with, we can anticipate that not only will there be an expansion of existing facilities, but new industries and services will come into operation to ease the lives of busy couples. We can expect the restaurant industry, the day-care facilities, infant health care services, kindergarten schools, and such home services as catering, housecleaning, gardening, and baby-sitting to experience a tremendous boom. Referral agencies that connect families with needed services will grow in numbers in cities big and small. These phenomena, in turn, will call for an increase in professional education and training of members operating the industries and services in areas such as costing, budgeting, scheduling, and the legal aspects of the business, in addition to developing specialized technical expertise. For example, individuals who operate day-care centers or health care units for sick children could face law suits if they are not conversant with appropriate and acceptable ways of conducting their business and dealing with children. Thus, these individuals will have to be professionally trained, not only in the technical aspects of day care or health care, but also in the economic, social, cultural, and legal aspects of their business.

It is not only dual-career families that will create a demand for various types of goods and services. The increasing number of dual-earner and single-parent families will also be instrumental in creating new demands. Thus, there is virtually unlimited scope for entrepreneurs to start new industries and services to cater to the needs of these growing segments of the working population. We can expect many innovative establishments to spring up and begin to offer family-oriented group activities. The possible future impact of dual-career and dual-earner families on recreational and educational activities is enormous. Consider the opportunities in family-based meditation and yoga centers, exercise gymnasiums, recreational vacation spots, and high-tech educational centers that would teach computer skills to young and old alike.

A Government Responsibility?

Beyond their economic and business implications, dual-career and other nontraditional life-styles are bound to have a great impact on government policies. Sooner or later, the federal government will have to formulate a family policy or, as an alternative, will have to develop some kind of infrastructure—such as tax credits or subsidies for day care, insurance, and the like—to preserve the family as an integral part of our society. Many people have bemoaned the fact that among the advanced countries, the United States is the only nation that does not have a family policy to ensure that the children of working parents are well cared for (see, for instance, Immerwahr, 1984). The contradictory viewpoints that exist regarding government responsibility for child care are that (1) quality child care is expensive and it is government's responsibility to help parents pay the cost of this kind of care and (2) the ultimate responsibility for ensuring that children get quality care belongs to parents and a federally funded structure for child-care facilities is therefore unnecessary.

Again, the views of Representative Patricia Schroeder, who introduced a bill that would require employers to provide four months of parenting leave to either the father or mother of a newborn infant or a sick child, and those of James A. Klein, manager of pension and employee benefits at the United States Chamber of Commerce, who feels that parenting leave is no concern of the government, reflect the fact that there is little agreement in the debate on this national issue. This in itself is a compelling reason for the government to seriously examine its various options with regard to parenting and child-care policies. Government has the choice of (1) producing a virtually childless society in the future, (2) force many members of society to revert to an impoverished single-earner family life-style, or (3) formulate national policies on parenting leave and child care that will allow dual-career members to enjoy their family lives while also making contributions at work.

With continued increases in the cost-of-living index, numerous families have been forced to become two-earner couples. However, if these persons are not productive at the workplace because of role overload, the gross national product will decline—a result that the government would scarcely find desirable. Thus, sooner or later, the government will have to enunciate a carefully considered and clearly articulated policy on child care.

Educational Trends

The impact of dual-career families on our future educational curriculum will also be significant. Already, in some schools, young children of both sexes are given training in looking after infants, feeding them, and changing their diapers so that they will develop androgynous behaviors and co-parenting will be second nature to them in their future life. As noted elsewhere, at Harvard and other universities, the implications of dual careers, family, and other personal demands on life have been made part of the curriculum. Many professors at various universities are deliberately introducing the topic of dual-career family life into their organizational behavior, management, finance, marketing, and accounting courses. Time-management courses will now have to expand their content to include the question of how best to allocate personal, couple, and family time.

Thus, students will increasingly pursue a curriculum that includes workshops, experiential exercises, role playing, and case studies relevant to two-career couples in organizational and family contexts. In fact, as mentioned in Chapter Four, Catalyst, a nonprofit institution that works with both organizations and individuals, recently started a project aimed at sensitizing young students to issues regarding the integration of career and family life. This experimental research project is being conducted at such universities as California State University at Chico, Duke University, Florida State University, and Southern Illinois University at Edwardsville.

The media have played no small part in awakening society to the issue of dual-career families. On February 6, 1986, for example, ABC's "20/20" portrayed the lives of three dual-career families in a program entitled "When Mom Has to Work," which highlighted the themes of child care, the guilt felt by mothers who work, and the strains that this places on marriages. Anchor person Barbara Walters voiced the need for a national policy on child care and the priority that should be given to such issues as (1) a national policy on guaranteed paid maternity leave, (2) good day-care facilities offered by organizations, and (3) more flexible employment policies in organizations. Hardly a day goes by without some information on dual-career families appearing in some newspaper, journal, or magazine. More television and radio coverage will expedite the dissemination of knowledge concerning two careers.

Several other efforts are also being made to come to grips with the stresses caused by work-family overlaps. For instance, efforts are in progress to form a commission on work and family under the auspices of the National Vocational Guidance Association. To put work and family in perspective, organizations such as San Francisco's Superwomen Anonymous, which subscribes to the motto "Not only can you not have it all, but you don't want it all," are being established to reduce the pressure on working women (Leighty, 1986). Men are also developing their own support systems to examine and legitimize a new male identity. There are newsletters circulated and conferences held for men under auspices of the National Organization for Changing Men. Gilbert (1985) states: "The emphasis of the women's movement in the 1980s has been on restructuring family obligations and forging new concepts of equity. In the light of the pressure being exerted by interested groups of men, the 1990s are likely to witness a new wave of changes, one that gives men the right to father with nurturance and expressivity and to be an intimate member of the family; the courage to share anxieties, sorrows, and joys; and the strength to evolve beyond the traditional male role" (p. 158).

Society and the Emerging Work Force

Societal attitudes and values, which have already changed substantially in regard to nontraditional families over the past decade, will become even more supportive of the dual-career concept in the future. A primary reason for this is that Americans place a high value on the family as a social structure. Not surprisingly, the growth in the divorce rate in this country since the late 1970s has caused much concern. However, there is also some encouraging evidence; the divorce rate actually declined in 1982 and again in 1983 (*Britannica Book of the Year*, 1985). Moreover, the Monthly Vital Statistics Report (1985) indicates that the divorce rate leveled off in 1985 and is currently 4.9 per 1,000 population. One could speculate that this lowering in divorces from 5.3 per 1,000 population in 1981 is at least partly attributable to the fact that organizations are beginning to help working families more, that dual-career and dual-earner couples are learning to deal with their work and nonwork tensions better, and that society is starting to create structures that support dual-career couples. The future will bring more innovative changes in social structures that will foster a better quality of life for non-traditional families. A large part of these social changes will be brought about by the media. Educational television, newspaper articles, magazines, thought-provoking publications, and realistic documentaries will highlight problems, explore the causes, offer alternative solutions, and recommend the best courses of action from the individual, family, social, educational, organizational, and governmental perspectives. As George Miller, U.S. congressman and chairman of the House Select Committee on Children, Youths, and Families, stated at the Catalyst Round-Table Conference in 1984, the two-gender work force is here to stay and will have profound effects on the restructuring of American society. No doubt this work force will contribute much to society (such as capitalizing on the best talent available) just as it will raise some serious concerns (such as who looks after children). Social changes of great magnitude always produce stresses and strains, but this society has always resolved problematic situations by developing carefully thought-out solutions. Thus, we can be optimistic about resolving the tensions that the dual-career phenomenon produces through the combined efforts of organizations, society, and the government.

Hunt and Hunt (1977, 1982) have very forcefully discussed the widening economic gap between childless households (two-career families) and families with children (traditional families) and foresee the emergence of a "child-free" society as a function of the dual-career family phenomenon.

But given the importance attached to the family as a social unit, not to mention the desire of most men and women to become parents, the probability of childless families on a large scale in the future is small. With society (organizations, private industry, and government) facilitating quality child care, with organizations becoming more flexible, and with individuals becoming more discriminating in the way they allocate time to various activities, the family as a social unit will not only thrive but will become even more dynamic. As couples become more egalitarian and learn to enjoy co-parenting experiences, family members will come to interact with each other in a more intimate way. Some of the children who are growing up today are already being trained to operate as effective dual-career family members. Taking all this into consideration, we can predict that the quality of life in society as a whole will be better in the future. Certainly a new group of service institutions and individuals will arise to facilitate the life of dual-career and single-parent families. Rather than viewing these individuals as second-class citizens catering to the needs of an elite group, as some may argue, they should be viewed as valuable members of society who are making their contributions to the nation's gross national product and benefitting themselves in the process.

Another emerging concern relates to the growing number of elderly people who need care. Dual-career couples already find it difficult to balance the roles of career person, spouse, and parent, yet they may be faced with taking care of their elderly parents who may need both physical and emotional support. Not only will the stress of this added role increase their tensions, but the additional feelings of guilt when they are unable to satisfactorily discharge this obligation may impose additional stresses and strains on the marriage and the family, and these may carry over to the workplace. Hull (1985) believes that the conflict between careers and caretaking for women is likely to intensify as the population of elderly people grows. The number of people over 65 has doubled in the last thirty years and will double again by the year 2020. In the future, dual-earner families in general, and dual-career families in particular, will not be able to devote as much time to taking care of their elderly parents. As a society we need to evolve better structures and mechanisms for caring for older people who need personal care and attention. Providing quality care at affordable prices is an issue that society, including government, will need to confront.

Organizations, for their part, have already started to respond to the changing needs of the work force. Some organizations are beginning to create dynamic and supportive work environments that facilitate the best use of employee talent. Such organizations offer rewards based on merit and create opportunities for employees to be innovative. In the lead here are such institutions as AT&T, Control Data, the Equitable Life Insurance Society, Hewlett-Packard, Honeywell, and IBM (Scholl, 1983). There is already some evidence that sex discrimination is diminishing and that executive women are advancing faster than their predecessors (Rogan, 1984a).

Like all changes that transform society, the dual-career family system has already produced some traumas and will produce more before it becomes a viable and satisfying social reality. Some adverse interim effects of the phenomenon will be alcohol and drug abuse resulting from the abnormal stresses and strains experienced by spouses. During the transitional period, until the necessary structures have evolved to facilitate the dual-career lifestyle, the physical and mental health of members may suffer, the dilemmas of child care will increase, and divorces due to competition and other marital and organizational tensions will continue to occur. Cooper and Davidson (1982) state that the ratio of female to male alcoholics, which was one to five in 1962, became one to two in the 1970s, perhaps because of the increase in dual-career families and society's neglect of their dilemmas. Davidson and Cooper (1980) predict that career wives will resort to Type A behavior as they face the multiple pressures of family and work obligations and discrimination at the workplace, thus raising the incidence of heart disease among women. But as we become increasingly aware of, and better comprehend, the complex dynamics operating in dual-career families, we will be able to create more facilitating and supportive structures for dual-career families.

We can identify the trends that will shift the values operating in families, organizations, and society in the future. The West Coast will probably be the pacesetter inasmuch as most changes originate in that part of the United States and are more pronounced there. These changes will spread to other parts of the country—swiftly in some cases and rather slowly in others. Large companies employing women professionals in great numbers and high-tech organizations will be the innovators from the organizational perspective. We already know that some organizations along the East and West coasts have started designing creative structures to accommodate their dual-career members. Societal infrastructures will also be modified so that dual-career couples, dual-earner families, and single-parent families can comfortably function in their dual roles of professionals and homemakers. The day-care centers and facilities for sick children that are slowly coming into existence in various parts of the country are only the beginning.

Not all changes will take place with the same speed and at the same time, but changes in organizational policies will speed up changes in the family system. As organizations and families change, society will also increase its support for dual-career families.

Shifts in Family Values

Changes in family values and norms will primarily occur in the areas of division of household labor, parenting, sensitivity of both spouses to both family and career issues, androgynous behavior, authenticity, concern for overall quality of life, and a more proactive problem-solving style. In other words, spouses will move away from traditional role patterns in handling household responsibilities toward more equitable role sharing. Current concerns and preoccupations with equality will, in time, yield to a concern for equity. Equity denotes fairness and justice to both members and involves a step beyond equality, since, as we have seen in earlier chapters, sharing a burden equally may not necessarily be equitable. The dilemmas of role cycling will yield to carefully made decisions regarding family size and timing. Maternal overprotection of children and guilt feelings will be replaced by intimate and meaningful co-parenting relationships within the family where both partners will be sensitive to each other and to the family's needs. Such sensitivity and understanding will mean that predetermined role behaviors and role performance will be replaced by androgynous role behaviors and creative role making. In such families, healthy and supportive interactions that enable both husbands and wives to reach their potential will have taken the place of competitiveness. Power ploys and gamesmanship will yield to authenticity and open channels of communication. Over-emphasis on career progress will slowly decline, and spouses will pay greater attention to the overall quality of their lives. These developments will be facilitated by more support groups for members of dual-career families. Instead of silently accepting all demands, couples will articulate their concerns and work together to solve the problems that they confront.

Shifts in Organizations

Changes in organizations will involve the issues of the equity, flexibility, and quality of family life as well as work-related concerns. For instance, organizations will move away from discrimination toward equitable hiring and promotion practices, from building "old-boy" networks to establishing networks that enhance human potential, from promoting upward mobility for a select few to developing multiple-career paths to accommodate all, and from inflexible policies and constricting work environments toward policies that promote productivity and provide nourishing environments. These changes will gradually transform organizational culture into an egalitarian human management system where tokenism is devalued. This egalitarianism will spread from the organization to the family system as discussed earlier in the book, thus facilitating the contributions of both spouses to their careers and to the family.

Shifts in Society's Roles and Values

Society will become more accepting of androgynous role sharing in dual-career families. The legal, organizational, social, and religious sectors will develop policies encouraging co-parenting (see for instance, Lamb and Sagi, 1983). Society will also provide support structures, such as excellent child-care facilities, that will help dual-career members to experience a good quality of life. Educational institutions and the media will create an awareness and offer practical skills to enable younger generations to successfully manage their future lives as dual-career members. Government will also slowly develop family policies that will foster the growth of the gross national product as well as of the nation's most valued resource—future generations. In effect, society will move away from having reservations about the dual-career life-style to accepting it with enthusiasm, from normative sanctions against androgynous role behaviors to encouraging such behaviors, from patriarchy to egalitarianism, from benign neglect of dual-career families to active support for such families, from providing questionable child care to offering nurturing, professional facilities for children and dependents who need help, from concern about governmental interference to healthy family policies, and from educational institutions that impart only job-based knowledge and skills to those that offer holistic life knowledge and skills.

Research Agenda

The last twenty years of research on dual-career families, which started with the work of the Rapoports, has greatly increased our understanding of the dynamics that operate in the dual-career family setting. But what researchers have neglected thus far is the actual performance of dual-career members at the workplace. An empirical base of findings will help us to understand what combinations of factors—including the types of dual-career couples (coordinated, complementary, divergent), the nature of their occupations, their work patterns and styles, the kinds of organizational facilities and benefits they enjoy, their personal predispositions, and their family backgrounds and environments—will serve to enhance the productivity of couples. Such research will require enormous time and effort since different but comparable performance and productivity measures will have to be developed for various occupations. Tracing the multitude of work and nonwork variables that affect performance and productivity will also be an intimidating assignment for researchers. But the next stage in our research on dual-career families must encompass these difficult tasks if we are to fully understand the concept of dual careers. We have, hitherto, devoted most of our research efforts to the family side of couples' lives, and it is now time to turn to the career and organizational side of their lives.

This becomes particularly imperative in the context of the present generation of dual-career members, who for the most part enter organizations after professional academic training. Thus, the organizations make heavy investments in them from the day they join the organization. Furthermore, it is important for organizations to know whether all their enabling structures (such as child care and extended vacations for parenting) are actually paying off for them. Thus, preperformance and postperformance data should be obtained for each change process initiated in organizations so that the effectiveness of the changes for both the organization and its members can be evaluated. Organizations can aid the development of such research designs by allowing qualified researchers to gather data from organizational members on company time. The investigators can then help organizations benefit from the results of their research. The results of the analysis of the data would indicate which changes offer more benefits to the organization in terms of increased productivity of organizational members and what other types of changes will be beneficial to employees and organizations alike. Thus, organizations will get good factual data on how their investments in making the changes are paying off.

Another focus for future research is the progress of children in dual-career families. Preliminary research has indicated that children of dual-career parents are well-adjusted and resourceful (Nadelson and Nadelson, 1980) and that day-care facilities help children to acquire verbal skills and at the same time further their overall emotional adjustment (McCartney and others, 1982). But we need to conduct methodologically sound longitudinal research to assess the long-term effects of having parents who are professionals. The physical, emotional, intellectual, attitudinal, behavioral, and developmental effects of various types of child care and schooling on the offspring of dual-career family members also need to be investigated.

It will be beneficial to conduct longitudinal studies on the quality of life in dual-career families according to the model proposed in Chapters Two and Three, even if it is only with a small number of families. Researchers could begin studying these families at the time of their formation and evaluate their progress periodically. The work-family overlaps can be expected to increase as technological advances create new vistas as yet unexplored. These new vistas will offer other fruitful areas for future research.

Counselors who provide therapy for dual-career members can contribute significantly to our understanding of the variables that enhance the quality of life in dual-career families by maintaining records of the types of concerns they are approached for, what techniques were used to resolve problems, and with what results.

Conclusion

In this book I have tried to consolidate the research findings on dual-career families so as to examine the practical implications of this emerging phenomenon for organizations, counselors, and society. I have made numerous suggestions for structural and procedural changes that should allow organizations to capitalize on the contributions of dual-career members. I have also outlined a framework for those in helping relationships that should facilitate their taking a systemic view of the dynamics of dual-career family members, and I have also pointed out directions for significant future research.

Dual careers are here to stay, and all sectors of society have the responsibility to ensure that the emerging phenomenon contributes to the economic, social, and cultural well-being of our society. Moreover, the concept of dual careers is a worldwide phenomenon. By making it a viable concept here, we can perhaps show other countries how to benefit from it. While recognizing that there are many obstacles to face and difficult problems to resolve, I have propounded an optimistic view of the future of dual-career families throughout this book. Indeed, as long as we continue to cherish the family and children as our most important national resources, we have no option but to work toward enhancing the quality of life for dual-career couples.

Appendixes

Research on
Dual-Career Families

A. Questionnaire Survey
B. Interviews with Couples

A. Questionnaire Survey

As stated in Chapter Three, the aims of my research were to understand as much as possible about the dynamics operating in dual-career families, the attitudinal and behavioral responses to work and work organizations of the members of such families, and their experienced quality of life.

Sample

A representative sample of organizations in a metropolitan area and a small town in the Midwest and a metropolitan area and a small town on the West Coast was chosen for the study. A total of ten business and service organizations, four hospitals, and two universities were approached, and all agreed to participate in the study. A brief note about the survey and how it would help dual-career families was posted on the bulletin boards of these institutions. The personnel manager in each organization then sent out a memo asking for volunteers who were members of dual-career families and would be willing to participate in the survey. An added stipulation was that the spouse should also be willing to respond to a questionnaire survey. The personnel manager in each organization then made available to the researcher a list of volunteers and their addresses.

A total of 179 couples participated in the survey. However, because of incomplete data, only 166 couples' responses could be used for final data analyses. Of these, 127 couples were from the Midwest and 39 from the West Coast. The mean age of the husbands in these 166 families was thirty-eight and that of the wives was thirty-five. The majority of the couples were in their first marriage, although a few were in their second or third marriages. At the time of the survey in 1980, the spouses had been married to each other for an average of twelve years. There were two children on the average in each family. Thirty-one percent of the husbands and 15 percent of the wives had careers in business; those in the field of medicine numbered 4 percent and 14 percent, respectively. Nine percent of the husbands and 12 percent of the wives were in the field of higher education. Others were in different professions, and some had jobs rather than careers. Of the 166 couples, 82 were members of dual-career families. In 38 households, the husband pursued a career and the wife held a job; in 18 families, the wife was a professional and the husband was a nonprofessional; and in 28 families neither the husband nor the wife was a professional.

The Survey Instrument

A two-part questionnaire was designed to assess demographic and background information, personality predispositions, involvement in various facets of life, experienced outcomes, and organizational characteristics. Variables included for each of these are:

Demographic and Background Factors	*Personality Predispositions*
Age	Need for dominance
Gender	Tolerance for ambiguity
Educational level	Self-esteem
Academic training	Career salience
Occupation	Enabling (facilitating) pro-
Job level	cesses in the family
Tenure	Experienced level of role
Career length	stresses

Demographic and
Background Factors, Cont'd.

Length of marriage
Number of times divorced
Number of children below six-
teen years of age
Number of children over six-
teen years of age
Mother's employment history
Whether planned for dual-
career life
Number of hours per week on
an average spent on work
beyond work hours at the
workplace
Number of hours per week on
an average spent on work
at home beyond work
hours
Whether utilizing hired help
Income
Family income

Personality
Predispositions, Cont'd.

Extent of integration of work
and family

Involvements In

Community
Leisure activities
Family activities
Cultural activities
Union activities
Social activities
Personal growth

Organizational Factors

Type
Size
Type of facilities expected
from the organization

Experienced Outcomes

Job involvement
Sense of competence
Self-esteem from the job
Satisfaction with
• Work itself
• Supervision
• Co-workers
• Pay
• Promotion
General overall satisfaction
Life satisfaction
Mental health
Satisfaction with facilities pro-
vided by the organization

Measures Used

All demographic and background information, members' involvement in various facets of life, and the types and sizes of organizations were tapped through single items in the questionnaire. Measures for career salience, role stresses (multiple role stress), integration of work and family, enabling or facilitating processes, expectations of members that the organization would facilitate dual careers, and the extent to which members were satisfied with the actual facilities provided were developed specifically for this research. The items tapping these variables and the scales are as follows:

Exhibit 1. Items Measuring Career Salience.

Strongly Disagree 1	Disagree 2	Slightly Disagree 3	Neutral 4	Slightly Agree 5	Agree 6	Strongly Agree 7

1. My career choice is a good occupational decision for me. _____
2. My career enables me to make significant contributions to society. _____
3. The career I am in fits me and reflects my personality. _____
4. My education and training are not tailored for this career. _____
5. I don't intend changing careers. _____
6. All the planning and thought I gave for pursuing this career are a waste. _____
7. My career is an integral part of my life. _____

Note: Items 4 and 6 are to be reversed.

Exhibit 2. Items Measuring Multiple-Role Stresses.

Some common pressures and concerns of families pursuing careers are identified below. Please indicate the extent to which you personally experience *stress* in respect of each, by *circling* the appropriate number on the scale, which specifies:

Very Little 1	Some 2	A Moderate Amount 3	Quite a Bit 4	Very Much 5

1. Child care. 1 2 3 4 5
2. Getting household help. 1 2 3 4 5
3. Managing illness. 1 2 3 4 5

(continued on next page)

Exhibit 2. Items Measuring Multiple-Role Stresses, Cont'd.

| Very Little | Some | A Moderate Amount | Quite a Bit | Very Much |
| 1 | 2 | 3 | 4 | 5 |

4. Care of older family members.	1	2	3	4	5
5. Helping children in their activities.	1	2	3	4	5
6. Commuting distances.	1	2	3	4	5
7. Shortage of time spent with family.	1	2	3	4	5
8. Shortage of couple time.	1	2	3	4	5
9. Shortage of personal time.	1	2	3	4	5
10. Career pressures.	1	2	3	4	5
11. Handling unforeseen or new situations.	1	2	3	4	5
12. Being pulled in different directions.	1	2	3	4	5
13. Establishing priorities.	1	2	3	4	5
14. Constantly shifting roles.	1	2	3	4	5
15. Not knowing how much of outside activities and responsibilities you should take on.	1	2	3	4	5
16. Having limited time for friends and social activities.	1	2	3	4	5
17. Not being able to put more time and energy into your career.	1	2	3	4	5
18. Restricted interactions with family members.	1	2	3	4	5
19. Just not being able to be yourself.	1	2	3	4	5
20. Being a parent, spouse, career person (and other roles to different people) all at the same time.	1	2	3	4	5

Exhibit 3. Items Measuring Integration Versus Segregation.

Here are some questions that tap the "integration" versus "separation" of family and work life. Both styles are effectively adopted by two-career families. Please circle the most appropriate response for you. The scale is indicated below.

| Strongly Agree | Agree | Neither Agree nor Disagree | Disagree | Strongly Disagree |
| 1 | 2 | 3 | 4 | 5 |

1. I am interested in things that happen in my spouse's workplace.	1	2	3	4	5
2. I often discuss things that happen in my workplace with my spouse.	1	2	3	4	5
3. I make it a policy to leave work problems at work and not let them disturb my peace at home.	1	2	3	4	5
4. I feel that work and family are distinct aspects of my life and should be segregated as such.	1	2	3	4	5
5. My spouse and I discuss our career and family goals and expectations.	1	2	3	4	5
6. I think my spouse feels that family life should be segregated and kept distinct from work life.	1	2	3	4	5

Exhibit 4. Items Measuring Enabling Processes.

Again, to what extent do you agree with the following statements? Please *circle* the appropriate response.

Strongly Agree 1	Agree 2	Neither Agree nor Disagree 3	Disagree 4	Strongly Disagree 5

1. Emotional battles and stresses are a little too much in my house because we are a two-career family.	1	2	3	4	5
2. The principle of "give-and-take" is the golden rule we follow in my house.	1	2	3	4	5
3. Being a two-career home has posed no problems for the family.	1	2	3	4	5
4. If my spouse were a little more understanding and supportive, my life would be much easier to handle.	1	2	3	4	5
5. A good deal of the credit for what I have achieved in life is due to my spouse.	1	2	3	4	5
6. I often wish that my spouse did not pursue a career.	1	2	3	4	5
7. I seem to be taking on far more responsibility for home and family obligations than my spouse does.	1	2	3	4	5
8. My spouse and I have incompatible goals, objectives, and philosophies.	1	2	3	4	5

Note: Items 2, 3, and 5 are to be reversed.

Exhibit 5. Items Measuring Facilities Expected from the Organization.

Institutions can help dual-career families by offering various services. Please indicate the extent to which you are inclined to agree with the following statements by *circling* the appropriate number on the scale.

Strongly Agree 1	Agree 2	Somewhat Agree 3	Neither Agree nor Disagree 4	Somewhat Disagree 5	Disagree 6	Strongly Disagree 7

1. If I could leave my children in a good day-care center, it would be a big help.	1	2	3	4	5	6	7
2. It would be nice to have an arrangement where all I have to do is to call up an agency and get domestic help whenever I need it.	1	2	3	4	5	6	7
3. How wonderful it would be to have a "dial-a-baby-sitter" service!	1	2	3	4	5	6	7

(continued on next page)

Exhibit 5. Items Measuring Facilities Expected from the Organization,
Cont'd.

Strongly Agree 1	Agree 2	Somewhat Agree 3	Neither Agree nor Disagree 4	Somewhat Disagree 5	Disagree 6	Strongly Disagree 7
4. I would like to see my work organization take a more active role in establishing referral systems for the three types of services above.				1 2 3 4 5 6 7		
5. Work organizations should introduce flexible work hours so that employees could better manage their personal and work lives.				1 2 3 4 5 6 7		
6. I would appreciate some good career counseling from my organization.				1 2 3 4 5 6 7		
7. More systematic training and development in my organization would have helped me personally in my career.				1 2 3 4 5 6 7		
8. With the increasing pressures of modern society, organizations should offer psychological and health counseling for their members.				1 2 3 4 5 6 7		
9. With dual-career families on the increase, organizations should provide family emergency days off, unpaid leave of absence, etc.				1 2 3 4 5 6 7		
10. Organizations should gear their transfer and travel policies to the needs and convenience of two-career families.				1 2 3 4 5 6 7		

Exhibit 6. Items Measuring Satisfaction with Organizational Facilities.

To what extent are you *satisfied* with the following facilities provided by
your organization now? Please circle the appropriate response, as per the
scale indicated below.

Very Dissatisfied 1	Somewhat Dissatisfied 2	Neither Satisfied nor Dissatisfied 3	Rather Satisfied 4	Very Satisfied 5
11. Vacations provided			1 2 3 4 5	
12. Time off for emergencies			1 2 3 4 5	
13. Flexible working hours			1 2 3 4 5	
14. Special career counseling			1 2 3 4 5	
15. Training for career mobility			1 2 3 4 5	
16. Transfer policies			1 2 3 4 5	

Exhibit 6. Items Measuring Satisfaction with Organizational Facilities, Cont'd.

Very Dissatisfied 1	Somewhat Dissatisfied 2	Neither Satisfied nor Dissatisfied 3	Rather Satisfied 4	Very Satisfied 5				
17. Travel policies			1	2	3	4	5
18. Day-care centers			1	2	3	4	5

19. Briefly list some of the ways in which your organization can facilitate your being a more effective dual-career family member.

Sources for the Other Measures

Need for dominance	Steers and Braunstein (1976)
Tolerance for ambiguity	Lorsch and Morse (1974)
Self-esteem	Rosenberg (1965)
Job involvement	Lodahl and Kejner (1965)
Sense of competence	Wagner and Morse (1975)
Self-esteem from the job	Quinn and Shepard (1974)
Satisfaction facets	Smith, Kendall, and Hulin (1969)
Satisfaction with job in general	Kunin (1955)
Life satisfaction	Kornhauser (1965)
Mental health	Kornhauser (1965)

Data Collection

The volunteers from each organization were personally contacted by the survey team, which consisted of the researcher and two graduate assistants. Each volunteer received two sets of differently colored questionnaires with envelopes, one set to be completed by the individual and the other by his or her spouse. Confidentiality of responses was assured verbally as well as in the questionnaire, and both written and verbal instructions were given to the spouses to complete the questionnaires individually, without consulting each other or having discussions about the questionnaire. After ten days—which gave the respondents two weekends to respond—the graduate assistants collected the completed questionnaires from the spouses either at the workplace or in their homes. Similar procedures were followed on the West Coast; but, instead of graduate assistants, two other members of the team assisted in the data collection.

Data Analysis

After coding, the data were first subjected to factor analysis to ensure that the items used to measure the concepts were, in fact, perceived to be relevant by the respondents. Further data analyses to test various hypotheses included correlations, *t* tests, multiple-regression analysis, discriminant analysis, and higher-order factor analysis. The results of these can be found in Sekaran (1982a, 1983a, 1983b, 1985a, 1985b).

B. Interviews with Couples

The purpose of the interview was to understand the phenomenology of the dynamics operating in dual-career families. In-depth interviews were conducted. Spouses were asked questions regarding their commitment to career and family, the demands, choices, and constraints they had in their work and nonwork lives, the extent of work-family overlaps, and what it took to run a two-career family successfully.

Sample

A selected subsample of the original members who had responded to the questionnaire was chosen at random from the two metropolitan areas. Forty members from the Midwest and twenty-four from the West Coast were interviewed during 1981. In the Midwest, the interviews, which were conducted at the workplace of the interviewees, lasted between forty-five and ninety minutes, depending on the amount of time the respondent could spare and how insightful and articulate he or she was. On the West Coast, the interviews were held at the residence of the interviewee at a time convenient to the individual. These interviews were more relaxed and on the average lasted about seventy-five minutes. Almost all the interviewees responded enthusiastically to the questions asked and did not object to our taping the conversations. Four interviewees in the Midwest, however, did not want tape recorders to be used during their interviews.

Of the total of sixty-four persons interviewed, forty were husband and wife pairs who were interviewed separately. Of the remaining twenty-four, six were women professionals, ten were male professionals, and eight were women nonprofessionals.

Interview Protocol

Although every interview followed a structured format as in the questions below, many questions not in the schedule were also asked and answered. These questions involved issues brought up by the interviewee during the open-ended responses. The interview was thus semistructured.

Interview Schedule

Name	How long married
Organization	Number of children at home
Tenure	Number of children not at home
Job position	Estimated age of respondent

About Work Life

1. There are demands on every job, apart from the technical aspects, that people must do. The demands could include such things as traveling to meet clients, late evenings, and the like. What kinds of demands do you face in your job? (Professors, for instance, have to meet with students outside of class and attend conferences that they might consider demands.)

2. What are some of the factors that limit or constrain you from achieving the things that you would like to accomplish in your job? For example, a professor may be able to attend no more than one conference per year due to limitations of university resources, and this might adversely affect the individual's visibility.

3. What are some of the choices you can exercise at work? For instance, a professor can do research on any topic and in any organization.

4. What are your career goals and aspirations?

5. Do you have a mentor here or elsewhere who takes an in-

terest in your career? Who is it and how does the person help?

Nonwork and Work Life Connections

6. What are the demands, constraints, and choices for you in your nonwork life that have a direct impact on your career?
7. Do you ever feel that your spouse and you compete with each other?
8. Between your commitment to your family and your career, which would gain precedence for you?
9. What does it take to manage a two-career family? (Many further questions were invariably asked of the respondents following their answers to this question.)
10. Working couples are steadily on the increase, and this trend will continue in the future. What do you think are the implications of this for organizations?
11. How do your satisfactions and dissatisfactions at work impact on your home life, and vice versa?
12. Do you have any thoughts on what else we should be looking into while researching dual-career families?

Thank you!

Data Analysis

The tapes and notes taken during the interviews were transcribed for greater clarity and were then content analyzed. Much of what was learned from these interviews is discussed in Chapters Two and Three of this book.

References

Albrecht, S. L. "Informal Interaction Patterns of Professional Women." In J. R. Garden (ed.), *A Diagnostic Approach to Organizational Behavior.* Newton, Mass.: Allyn & Bacon, 1983.

Aldous, J. "The Making of Family Roles and Family Change." *The Family Coordinator,* 1974, *23* (3), 231-235.

Allen, S. M., and Kalish, R. A. "Professional Women and Marriage." *Journal of Marriage and the Family,* 1984, *46* (2), 375-382.

Amatea, E. S., and Cross, E. G. "Coupling and Careers: A Workshop for Dual-Career Couples at the Launching Stage." *Personnel and Guidance Journal,* 1983, *62* (1), 48-51.

"America's New Immobile Society." *Business Week,* July 27, 1981, pp. 58-62.

Bailyn, L. "Career and Family Orientations of Husbands and Wives in Relation to Marital Happiness." *Human Relations,* 1970, *23* (2), 97-113.

Bailyn, L. "Family Constraints on Women's Work." *Annals of the New York Academy of Science,* 1973, *208,* 82-90.

Bailyn, L. "The 'Slow Burn' Way to the Top: Implications of Changes in the Relation Between Work and Family for Models of Organizational Careers." *Career Development Bulletin,* 1979, *1* (1), 15.

Bailyn, L. "Issues of Work and Family in Organizations: Responding to Social Diversity." *Working with Careers,* Columbia School of Business, 1984.

Barnett, R. C., Baruch, G. K., and Rivers, C. "The Secret of Self-Esteem." *Ladies Home Journal,* 1985, *102* (2), 54-62.

Bartolomé, F. "The Work Alibi: When It's Harder to Go Home." *Harvard Business Review,* 1983, *61* (2), 67-74.

Bartolomé, F., and Evans, L. P. A. "Must Success Cost So Much?" *Harvard Business Review,* 1980, *58* (2), 137-148.

Battaile, J. "Debate on Nepotism Rules Grows with a Rise in Working Couples." *New York Times,* May 9, 1978, p. 30.

Bebbington, A. C. "The Function of Stress in the Establishment of the Dual-Career Family." *Journal of Marriage and the Family,* 1973, *35* (3), 530-538.

Beck, D. *Marriage and the Family Under Challenge.* New York: Family Service Association of America, 1976.

Beer, M., and others. "Managing Human Assets." *Personnel Administrator,* 1985, *30*, 60-67.

Bem, S. L. "The Measurement of Psychological Androgyny." *Journal of Consulting and Clinical Psychology,* 1974, *42* (2), 155-162.

Bem, S. L., and Lenney, E. "Sex Typing and the Avoidance of Cross-Sex Behavior." *Journal of Personality and Social Psychology,* 1976, *33* (1), 48-54.

Benningson, L. A. "Managing Corporate Cultures." *Management Review,* 1985, *74* (2), 31-32.

Berger, M., Foster, M., Wallston, B. S., and Wright, L. "You and Me Against the World: Dual-Career Couples and Joint Job Seeking." *Journal of Research and Development in Education,* 1977, *10* (4), 30-37.

Berman, E., Sacks, S., and Lief, H. "The Two-Professional Marriage: A New Conflict Syndrome." *Journal of Sex and Marital Therapy,* 1975, *1*, 242-253.

Berry, P. "Mentors for Women Managers—Fast Track to Corporate Success." *Supervisory Management,* 1983, *28* (8), 36-40.

Berryman, F. C. "Optimal Training for Opposite-Sex Managers." *Training and Development Journal,* 1985, *39* (2), 26-29.

Bird, G. W., Bird, G. A., and Scruggs, M. "Determinants of Family Task Sharing: A Study of Husbands and Wives." *Journal of Marriage and the Family,* 1984, *46* (2), 345-355.

Birnbaum, J. "Life Patterns and Self-Esteem in Family-Oriented and Career-Committed Women." In M. Mednick and others (eds.), *Women and Achievement: Social and Motivational Analysis.* New York: Wiley, 1975.

Blitzer, C. G. "Couples with Two Careers Have Special Benefit Needs." *Business Insurance,* 1982, *30,* 38.

"BNA's Job Absence and Turnover Report—3rd Quarter 1980." *Bulletin to Management.* Washington, D.C.: Bureau of National Affairs, Dec. 11, 1980.

Booth, A. "Wife's Employment and Husband's Stress: A Replication and Refutation." *Journal of Marriage and the Family,* 1977, *39* (4), 645-650.

Brass, D. J. "Men's and Women's Networks: A Study of Interaction Patterns and Influence in an Organization." *Academy of Management Journal,* 1985, *28* (2), 327-341.

Brazelton, B. *Toddlers and Parents: A Declaration of Independence.* New York: Dell, 1976.

Britannica Book of the Year. Chicago: Encyclopedia Britannica, University of Chicago, 1985.

Broderick, C. B. "The New Improved 1983 Model Husband: Is He for Real?" *Working Mother,* 1983, *6* (10), 80, 96.

Bryson, J. B., and Bryson, R. B. "Salary and Job Performance Differences in Dual-Career Couples." In F. Pepitone-Rockwell (ed.), *Dual-Career Couples.* Beverly Hills, Calif.: Sage, 1980.

Bryson, R. B., Bryson, J. B., and Johnson, M. F. "Family Size, Satisfaction, and Productivity in Dual-Career Couples." *Psychology of Women Quarterly,* 1978, *3* (1), 67-77.

Bryson, R. B., Bryson, J. B., Licht, M. H., and Licht, B. G. "The Professional Pair—Husband and Wife Psychologists." *American Psychologist,* 1976, *31* (1), 10-16.

Burke, R. J., and Weir, T. "Relationship of Wives' Employment Status to Husband, Wife, and Pair Satisfaction." *Journal of Marriage and the Family,* 1976a, *38* (2), 279-287.

Burke, R. J., and Weir, T. "Some Personality Differences Between Members of One-Career and Two-Career Families." *Journal of Marriage and the Family,* 1976b, *38* (3), 453-459.

Butler, M., and Paisley, W. "Coordinated-Career Couples: Convergence and Divergence." In F. Pepitone-Rockwell (ed.), *Dual-Career Couples.* Beverly Hills, Calif.: Sage, 1980.

Carlson, B. E. "Preschoolers' Sex-Role Identity, Father-Role

Perceptions, and Paternal Family Participation." In J. Aldous (ed.), *Two Paychecks: Life in Dual-Earner Families.* Beverly Hills, Calif.: Sage, 1980.

Cascio, W. F. *Costing Human Resources: The Financial Impact of Behavior in Organizations.* Boston: Kent, 1982.

Castro, J. "More and More, She's the Boss." *Time,* Dec. 2, 1985, pp. 64–66.

Catalyst. *Corporations and Two-Career Families.* New York: Catalyst, 1981.

Catalyst. *The Two-Gender Work Force and Corporate Policy.* New York: Catalyst, 1984.

Challenger, J. E. "Moving Two Careers." *Management World,* 1985, *14,* 38–39.

Changing Roles of Women in Industrial Societies: A Bellagio Conference. New York: Rockefeller Foundation Working Papers, 1977.

"Child Care: Where Companies Still Fear to Tread." *Management Review,* 1984, *73* (4), 6.

Chusmir, L. H. "Characteristics and Predictive Dimensions of Women Who Make Nontraditional Vocational Choices." *Personnel and Guidance Journal,* 1983, *61,* 43–47.

Clawson, J. G., and Kram, K. E. "Managing Cross-Gender Mentoring." *Business Horizons,* 1984, *27* (3), 22–31.

Clinton, L. H. "After the Baby: The Wild and Wonderful First Six Months." *Working Mother,* Oct. 1983, pp. 82–83, 134, 136, 138.

Cockrum, R. B. "Has the Time Come for Employee Cafeteria Plans?" *Personnel Administrator,* July 1982, *27,* 66–72.

Collins, G. "M.B.A.'s Learn Value of Home Life." *New York Times,* Oct. 16, 1985, pp. 19–20.

Conference Board. *Corporations and Families: Changing Practices and Perspectives.* Report no. 868. New York: Conference Board, 1985.

Cooke, R. A., and Rousseau, D. M. "Stress and Strain from Family Roles and Work-Role Expectations." *Journal of Applied Psychology,* 1984, *69* (2), 252–260.

Cooper, C. L., and Davidson, M. J. "The High Cost of Stress on Women Managers." *Organizational Dynamics,* Spring 1982, *10,* 44–53.

Coopersmith, S. *The Antecedents of Self-Esteem.* New York: W. H. Freeman, 1967.

Crouter, A. C. "Spillover from Family to Work: The Neglected Side of the Work-Family Interface." *Human Relations,* 1984, *37* (6), 425-442.

Culbert, S. A., and Renshaw, J. R. "Coping with the Stresses of Travel as an Opportunity for Improving the Quality of Work and Family Life." *Family Process,* 1972, *11* (3), 321-327.

Cunningham, M. "Corporate Culture Determines Productivity." *Industry Week,* May 4, 1981, pp. 82-86.

Darley, S. A. "Big-Time Careers for the Little Woman: A Dual-Role Dilemma." *Journal of Social Issues,* 1976, *32* (3), 85-98.

Davidson, M., and Cooper, C. L. "The Extra Pressures on Women Executives." *Personnel Management,* 1980, *12,* 48-55.

Davis, L. E., and Cherns, A. B. *The Quality of Working Life.* Vol. 1. New York: Free Press, 1975.

Davis, M. R. *Families in a Working World: The Impact of Organizations on Domestic Life.* New York: Praeger, 1982.

Deal, T. E., and Kennedy, A. A. *Corporate Cultures: The Rites and Rituals of Corporate Life.* Reading, Mass.: Addison-Wesley, 1982.

Doudna, C. "Competition Between Couples: The Dark Side of Success." *Glamour,* 1985, *83* (3), 298, 299, 354, 356-359, 363, 365.

Douvan, E., and Pleck, J. "Separation as Support." In R. Rapoport and R. N. Rapoport (eds.), *Working Couples.* New York: Harper & Row, 1978.

Dubno, P. "Attitudes Toward Women Executives: A Longitudinal Approach." *Academy of Management Journal,* 1985, *28* (1), 235-239.

Duncan, O. D. "Comment on Family Investment in Human Capital: Earnings of Women." *Journal of Political Economy,* 1974, *82,* 109-110.

Edgell, S. *Middle-Class Couples: A Study of Segregation, Domination, and Inequality in Marriage.* London: Allen & Unwin, 1980.

Eisler, R. M., and Hersen, M. "Behavioral Crisis Intervention Techniques." In A. S. Gurman and D. G. Rice (eds.), *Couples in Conflict.* New York: Aronson, 1975.

Eiswirth-Neems, N. A., and Handal, P. J. "Spouse's Attitudes Toward Maternal Occupational Status and Effects on Family Climate." *Journal of Community Psychology,* 1978, *6* (2), 168-172.

Epstein, C. F. *Women's Place: Options and Limits on Professional Careers.* Berkeley: University of California Press, 1970.

Epstein, C. F. "Law Partners and Marital Partners." *Human Relations,* 1971, *24* (6), 549-564.

Ferrara, J. V. "Fairchild's QWL Program Improves Performance." *Personnel Administrator,* July 1983, *28,* 64-69.

Flamholtz, E. G. "Toward a Theory of Human Resource Value in Formal Organizations." *Accounting Review,* 1972, *47* (2), 666-678.

French, J. R. P., and Raven, B. "The Bases of Social Power." In D. Cartwright (ed.), *Group Dynamics: Research and Theory.* New York: Harper & Row, 1962.

Galloway, P. "The Woes of Yuppie Love and Marriage." *Chicago Tribune,* May 26, 1985, sec. 2, pp. 1-4.

Gappa, J. M., O'Barr, J. F., and St. John-Parsons, D. "The Dual-Career Couple and Academe: Can Both Prosper?" *AAHE Bulletin,* 1980.

Gerstel, N. R. "The Feasibility of Commuter Marriage." In P. Stein, J. Richman, and N. Hannon (eds.), *The Family: Functions and Conflicts and Symbols.* Reading, Mass.: Addison-Wesley, 1977.

Gifford, D. "The Status of Flexible Compensation." *Personnel Administrator,* May 1984, *29,* 19-25.

Gilbert, L. A. *Men in Dual-Career Families: Current Realities and Future Prospects.* Hillsdale, N.J.: Erlbaum, 1985.

Gilmore, C. B., and Fannin, W. R. "The Dual-Career Couple: A Challenge to Personnel in the Eighties." *Business Horizon,* 1982, *25* (3), 36-74.

Goddard, R. W. "Building Careers for Your Employees." *Management World,* 1985, *14* (6), 12-14.

Good, J., Kirkland, F. R., and Grissom, G. R. *Working Relationships Between Men and Women: Effects of Sex and Hierarchical Position on Perceptions of Self and Others in a Work Setting.* Philadelphia: University Science Center, 1979.

Gordon, T. *Parent Effectiveness Training.* New York: McKay, 1970.

Gove, W. R., and Geerken, M. R. "The Effect of Children and Employment on the Mental Health of Married Men and Women." *Social Forces,* 1977, *56* (1), 66–76.

Gray, T. D. "Counseling Women Who Want Both a Profession and a Family." *Personnel and Guidance Journal,* 1980, *59* (1), 43–46.

Greenhaus, J. H., and Beutell, N. J. "Sources of Conflict Between Work and Family Roles." *Academy of Management Review,* 1985, *10* (1), 76–88.

Groh, K. F. "Counseling Centers Ease Adjustment to a New City." *Personnel Journal,* 1984, *63* (6), 88–90.

Gross, H. E. "Dual-Career Couples Who Live Apart: Two Types." *Journal of Marriage and the Family,* 1980, *42* (3), 567–576.

Gutek, B. A. *Sex and the Workplace: The Impact of Sexual Behavior and Harassment on Women, Men, and Organizations.* San Francisco: Jossey-Bass, 1985.

Gutzer, B., and Maher, B. "Six Steps to Contemporary Career Development." *Training,* 1982, *19* (12), 48.

Gysbers, N. C., and Associates. *Designing Careers: Counseling to Enhance Education, Work, and Leisure.* San Francisco: Jossey-Bass, 1984.

Haitch, R. "Paternity Battle." *New York Times,* Dec. 12, 1982, p. 57.

Hall, D. T. "A Model of Coping with Role Conflict: The Role Behavior of College-Educated Women." *Administrative Science Quarterly,* 1972, *17* (4), 471–489.

Hall, D. T., and Gordon, F. E. "Career Choices of Married Women: Effects on Conflict, Role Behavior, and Satisfaction." *Journal of Applied Psychology,* 1973, *58* (1), 42–48.

Hall, D. T., and Rabinowitz, S. R. "Caught up in Work." *Wharton Magazine,* 1977, *2* (1), 19–25.

Hall, D. T., and Richter, J. "The Baby Boom in Midcareer." *Career Center Bulletin,* 1984, *4* (3), 15–16.

Hall, F. S., and Hall, D. T. *The Two Career Couple.* Reading, Mass.: Addison-Wesley, 1979.

Haring, M., Beyard-Tyler, K., and Gray, J. "Sex-Biased Attitudes of Counselors: The Special Case of Nontraditional Careers." *Counseling and Values,* July 1983, *27,* 242-247.

Havens, R. A. "The Mind Uncaged: Hypnosis and the Manager." *Management World,* June 1982, *11,* 26-34.

Hawkes, G. R., Nicola, J., and Fish, M. "Young Marrieds: Wives' Employment and Family Role Structure." In F. Pepitone-Rockwell (ed.), *Dual-Career Couples.* Beverly Hills, Calif.: Sage, 1980.

Hawkins, J. L., Weisberg, C., and Ray, D. W. "Spouse Differences in Communication Style: Preference, Perception, and Behavior." *Journal of Marriage and the Family,* 1980, *42* (3), 585-593.

Heckman, N. A., Bryson, R., and Bryson, J. B. "Problems of Professional Couples: A Content Analysis." *Journal of Marriage and the Family,* 1977, *39* (2), 323-330.

Heinen, J. S., McGlauchlin, D., Legeros, C., and Freeman, J. "Developing the Woman Manager." *Personnel Journal,* 1975, *54* (5), 282-286.

Hiller, D. V., and Philliber, W. W. "Predicting Marital and Career Success Among Dual-Worker Couples." *Journal of Marriage and the Family,* 1982, *44* (1), 53-62.

Holahan, C. K., and Gilbert, L. A. "Conflict Between Major Life Roles: Women and Men in Dual-Career Couples." *Human Relations,* 1979a, *32* (6), 451-467.

Holahan, C. K., and Gilbert, L. A. "Interrole Conflict for Working Women: Career Versus Jobs." *Journal of Applied Psychology,* 1979b, *64* (1), 86-90.

Holmstrom, L. L. *The Two-Career Family.* Cambridge, Mass.: Schenkman, 1972.

Hopkins, J., and White, P. "The Dual-Career Couple: Constraints and Supports." *Family Coordinator,* 1978, *27* (3), 253-259.

Hornung, C. A., and McCullough, B. C. "Status Relationships in Dual-Employment Marriages: Consequences for Psychological Well-Being." *Journal of Marriage and the Family,* 1981, *43* (2), 125-141.

Houseknecht, S. K., and Spanier, G. B. "Marital Disruption and Higher Education Among Women in the United States." *Sociological Quarterly,* 1980, *21* (3), 375-389.

Houseknecht, S. K., Vaughan, S., and Macke, A. S. "Marital Disruption and Professional Women: The Timing of Career and Family Events." *Social Problems,* 1984, *31* (3), 273-284.

Huber, J., and Spitze, G. "Wives' Employment, Household Behaviors, and Sex-Role Attitudes." *Social Forces,* 1981, *60* (1), 150-169.

Hull, J. B. "Women Find Parents Need Them Just When Careers Are Resuming." *Wall Street Journal,* Sept. 9, 1985, p. 21.

Humphrey, F. G. *Marital Therapy.* Englewood Cliffs, N.J.: Prentice-Hall, 1983.

Hunt, J. G., and Hunt, L. L. "Dilemmas and Contradictions of Status: The Case of the Dual-Career Family." *Social Problems,* 1977, *24* (4), 407-416.

Hunt, J. G., and Hunt, L. L. "The Dualities of Careers and Families: New Integrations or New Polarizations?" *Social Problems,* 1982, *29* (5), 499-510.

Huser, W. R., and Grant, C. W. "A Study of Husbands and Wives from Dual-Career and Traditional-Career Families." *Psychology of Women Quarterly,* 1978, *3* (1), 78-89.

Immerwahr, J. "Building a Consensus on the Child-Care Problem." *Personnel Administrator,* Feb. 1984, *29,* 31-37.

Jablin, F. M. "Use of Discriminatory Questions in Screening Interviews." *Personnel Administrator,* Mar. 1982, *27,* 41-44.

Jamison, K. "Managing Sexual Attraction in the Workplace." *Personnel Administrator,* Aug. 1983, *28,* 45-51.

Johnson, C. L., and Johnson, F. A. "Attitudes Toward Parenting in Dual-Career Families." *American Journal of Psychiatry,* 1977, *134* (4), 391-395.

Johnson, C. L., and Johnson, F. A. "Parenthood, Marriage, and Careers: Situational Constraints and Role Strain." In F. Pepitone-Rockwell (ed.), *Dual-Career Couples.* Beverly Hills, Calif.: Sage, 1980.

Jones, W. A., and Jones, R. A. *Two Careers—One Marriage.* New York: AMACOM, 1980.

Josefowitz, N. "Sexual Relationships at Work: Attraction, Transference, Coercion, or Strategy." *Personnel Administrator,* Mar. 1982, *27,* 91-96.

Kaley, M. M. "Attitude Toward the Dual Role of the Married

Professional Woman." *American Psychologist,* 1971, *26* (3), 301–306.

Kanter, R. M. *Men and Women of the Corporation.* New York: Basic Books, 1977.

Kantrowitz, B., Weathers, D., Doherty, S., and Atkins, S. "Changes in the Workplace: Child Care Is Now an Item on the National Agenda." *Newsweek,* Mar. 31, 1986, p. 57.

Kantrowitz, B., and others. "Love on the Run: When Two Careers Means Two Homes, Couples Pay the Price." *Newsweek,* Nov. 18, 1985, pp. 111–113.

Kassner, M. L. "Will Both Spouses Have Careers? Predictors of Preferred Traditional or Egalitarian Marriages Among University Students." *Journal of Vocational Behavior,* 1981, *18* (3), 340–355.

Kaye, B. L. *Up is Not the Only Way.* Englewood Cliffs, N.J.: Prentice-Hall, 1982.

Keith, P. M., and Schafer, R. B. "Role Strain and Depression in Two-Job Families." *Family Relations,* 1980, *29,* 483–488.

Kessler-Harris, A. "It's Still a Man's World." *New York Times Book Review,* Aug. 4, 1985, p. 12.

Knox, D. "Behavior Contracts in Marriage Counseling." *Journal of Family Counseling,* 1973, *1,* 22–28.

Kopelman, R. E., Rosensweig, L., and Lally, L. H. "Dual-Career Couples: The Organizational Response." *Personnel Administrator,* Sept. 1982, *27,* 73–78.

Kornhauser, A. *Mental Health of the Industrial Worker.* New York: Wiley, 1965.

Kram, K. E. "Phases of Mentor Relationship." *Academy of Management Journal,* 1983, *26* (4), 608–625.

Kram, K. E. *Mentoring at Work: Developmental Relationships in Organizational Life.* Glenview, Ill.: Scott, Foresman, 1985.

Kram, K. E., and Isabella, L. A. "Mentoring Alternatives: The Role of Peer Relationships in Career Development." *Academy of Management Journal,* 1985, *28* (1), 110–132.

Krett, K. "Maternity, Paternity, and Child-Care Policies." *Personnel Administrator,* 1985, *30* (6), 125–136, 218.

Kunin, T. "The Construction of a New Type of Attitude Measure." *Personnel Psychology,* Spring 1955, *8,* 65–78.

LaMarre, S. E., and Thompson, K. "Industry-Sponsored Day Care." *Personnel Administrator,* Feb. 1984, *29,* 53-65.

Lamb, M. E. (ed.) *Nontraditional Families: Parenting and Child Development.* Hillsdale, N.J.: Erlbaum, 1982.

Lamb, M. E., and Sagi, A. *Fatherhood and Family Policy.* Hillsdale, N.J.: Erlbaum, 1983.

Layman, P. L. "Employee Relocation Plans Expanding." *Chemical and Engineering News,* 1982, *60* (27), 10-12.

Lehrman, K. "Firms Can't Afford to Neglect Employee Child Care." *Wall Street Journal,* Dec. 19, 1985, p. 17.

Leighty, J. M. "Supermom Shedding Their Caped Crusades." *St. Louis Post Dispatch,* Jan. 16, 1986, p. 4F.

Le Louarn, J., and DeCotiis, T. A. "The Effect of Working Couple Status on the Decision to Offer Geographic Transfer." *Human Relations,* 1983, *36* (11), 1031-1044.

Liberman, R. P. "Behavioral Principles in Family and Couple Therapy." In A. S. Gurman and D. G. Rice (eds.), *Couples in Conflict.* New York: Aronson, 1975.

Lodahl, T. N., and Kejner, M. "The Definition and Measurement of Job Involvement." *Journal of Applied Psychology,* 1965, *49* (1), 24-33.

London, M., and Poplanski, J. R. "Effects of Information on Stereotype Development in Performance Appraisal and Inter-view Contexts." *Journal of Applied Psychology,* 1976, *61* (2), 199-205.

Lopata, H. Z., Barnewolt, D., and Norr, K. "Spouses' Contribution to Each Other's Roles." In F. Pepitone-Rockwell (ed.), *Dual-Career Couples.* Beverly Hills, Calif.: Sage, 1980.

Lorsch, J. W., and Morse, J. J. *Organizations and Their Members: A Contingency Approach.* New York: Harper & Row, 1974.

Lublin, J. "Juggling Job and Junior." *Wall Street Journal,* Mar. 21, 1980, p. 24.

Lyles, M. A. "Strategies for Helping Women Managers or Anyone." *Personnel,* 1983, *60* (1), 67-77.

McCartney, K., and others. "Environmental Differences Among Day-Care Centers and Their Effects on Children's Development." In E. F. Zigler and E. W. Gordon (eds.), *Day Care:*

Scientific and Social Policy Issues. Boston: Auburn House, 1982.

McClelland, D. C. "Toward a Theory of Motive Acquisition." *American Psychologist,* 1965, *20* (5), 321-333.

McClelland, D. C. *Assessing Human Motivation.* New York: General Learning Press, 1971.

McDaniels, C. "Work and Leisure in the Career Span." In N. C. Gysbers and Associates (eds.), *Designing Careers: Counseling to Enhance Education, Work, and Leisure.* San Francisco: Jossey-Bass, 1984.

McKendrick, J. E. (ed.). "The Generalist: People Management— New Ideas, Challenges." *Management World,* Nov. 1982, *11,* 21-24.

McKendrick, J. E. "Ways to Find Excellence." *Management Review,* 1985a, *73* (7), 25.

McKendrick, J. E. "What a Difference Day Care Made." *Management World,* Mar. 1985b, *14,* 24.

Mackoff, B. "Shifting Gears from Job to Home." *McCalls,* 1985, *112* (9), 26.

Mall, J. "About Women: Victims of Myths and Paradox." *Los Angeles Times,* Dec. 16, 1979, p. 10.

Maret, E., and Finlay, F. "The Distribution of Household Labor A· ong Women in Dual-Earner Families." *Journal of Marriage and the Family,* 1984, *46* (2), 357-364.

Martin, T. W., Berry, K. J., and Jacobsen, R. B. "The Impact of Dual Career Marriages on Female Professional Careers: An Empirical Test of a Parsonian Hypothesis." *Journal of Marriage and the Family,* 1975, *37* (4), 734-742.

Mathews, J. R., and Mathews, L. H. "Going Shopping: The Professional Couple in the Job Market." In F. Pepitone-Rockwell (ed.), *Dual-Career Couples.* Beverly Hills, Calif.: Sage, 1980.

Mathews, P. A. "The Changing Work Force: Dual-Career Couples and Relocation." *Personnel Administrator,* Apr. 1984, *29,* 56-62.

Maynard, C. E., and Zawacki, R. A. "Mobility and the Dual-Career Couple." *Personnel Journal,* 1979, *58* (7), 468-472.

Meier, G. S. *Job Sharing: A New Pattern for Quality of Work and Life.* Kalamazoo, Mich.: W. E. Upjohn Institute for Employment Research, 1978.

Meyers, W. "Child Care Finds a Champion in the Corporation."
New York Times, Aug. 4, 1985, sec. 3, pp. 1, 6.

Miller, C. S. "Dual Careers: Impact on Individuals, Families, Organizations." In V. Jean Ramsey (ed.), *Preparing Professional Women for the Future.* Ann Arbor: Division of Research, Graduate School of Business Administration, University of Michigan, 1985.

Minor, A. "An Overview of Relocation Services." *Personnel Administrator,* Apr. 1984, *29,* 64-68.

Moen, P. "The Two-Provider Family: Problems and Potentials." In M. E. Lamb (ed.), *Nontraditional Families: Parenting and Child Development.* Hillsdale, N.J.: Erlbaum, 1982.

Monthly Vital Statistics Report. *Provisional Data from the National Center for Health Statistics.* DHHS Pub. No. (PHS) 84-1120. Hyattsville, Md.: Public Health Service, Apr. 26, 1985.

"Most Firms' Policies Outdated: Psychologist." *Business Insurance,* Sept. 27, 1982, p. 39.

Murray, H. A. *Explorations in Personality.* New York: Oxford University Press, 1938.

Nadelson, C. C., and Nadelson, T. "Dual-Career Marriage: Benefits and Costs." In F. Pepitone-Rockwell (ed.), *Dual-Career Couples.* Beverly Hills, Calif.: Sage, 1980.

Naisbitt, J. *Megatrends: Ten New Directions Transforming Our Lives.* New York: Warner Books, 1982.

Nelson, D. L., and Quick, J. C. "Professional Women: Are Distress and Disease Inevitable?" *Academy of Management Review,* 1985, *10* (2), 206-218.

Newgren, K. E., and Gardner, W. L. "Professional Couples: Their Impact on American Institutions and How to Predict a Company's Policies." *Southern Management Association Proceedings,* 1980, pp. 61-63.

Newgren, K. E., Kellogg, C. E., and Gardner, W. L. "Corporate Responses to Dual-Career Couples: A Decade of Social Transformation, 1980-1990." Paper presented at 45th annual meeting of the Academy of Management, San Diego, Aug. 1985.

Norman, N., and Tedeschi, J. T. "Paternity Leave: The Unpopular Benefit Option." *Personnel Administrator,* Feb. 1984, *29,* 39-43.

Odiorne, G. S. "Mentoring—An American Management Innovation." *Personnel Administrator,* May 1985, *30,* 63-68.

"One-on-One Child Care: How to Find It, What It Costs."
Working Mother, Aug. 1985, pp. 35-45.

Orden, S. R., and Bradburn, N. M. "Working Wives and Marriage Happiness." *American Journal of Sociology,* 1968, *74*
(4), 392-407.

Ornati, O., and Buckham, C. "Day Care: Still Waiting Its Turn
as a Standard Benefit." *Management Review,* 1983, *72* (5),
57-61.

O'Toole, J. *Making America Work: Productivity and Responsibility.* New York: Continuum, 1981.

Parker, M., Peltier, S., and Wolleat, P. "Understanding Dual-
Career Couples—Overview of Literature and Dysfunctional
Coping Strategies." *Personnel and Guidance Journal,* 1981,
60 (1), 14-18.

Parson, T. *Essays in Sociological Theory.* New York: Free Press,
1954.

Pave, I. "Move Me, Move My Spouse: Relocating the Corporate
Couple." *Business Week,* Dec. 16, 1985, p. 57.

Peters, T. J., and Waterman, R. H., Jr. *In Search of Excellence.*
New York: Harper & Row, 1982.

Pines, A., and Kafry, D. "The Experience of Tedium in Three
Generations of Professional Women." *Sex Roles,* 1981, 7 (2),
117-134.

Pingree, S., Butler, M., Paisley, W., and Hawkins, R. "Antinepotism's Ghost: Attitudes of Administrators Toward Hiring
Professional Couples." *Psychology of Women Quarterly,*
1978, *3* (1), 22-29.

Pleck, J. H. "The Work-Family Role System." *Social Problems,*
1977, *24* (4), 417-425.

Pleck, J. H., and Staines, G. L. "Work Schedules and Work-Family Conflicts in Two-Earner Couples." In J. Aldous (ed.), *Two
Paychecks.* Beverly Hills, Calif.: Sage, 1982.

Poloma, M. M. "Role Conflict and the Married Professional
Woman." In C. Safilios-Rothschild (ed.), *Toward a Sociology
of Women.* Lexington, Mass.: Xerox, 1972.

Quinn, R. P., and Shepard, L. J. *The Quality of Employment
Survey.* Ann Arbor, Mich.: Survey Research Center, 1974.

Raelin, J. A. *The Salaried Professional—How to Make the Most of Your Career.* New York: Praeger, 1984.

Rapoport, R., and Rapoport, R. N. "Work and Family in Contemporary Society." *American Sociological Review,* 1965, *30* (3), 381–394.

Rapoport, R., and Rapoport, R. N. "The Dual-Career Family: A Variant Pattern and Social Change." *Human Relations,* 1969, *22* (1), 3–30.

Rapoport, R., and Rapoport, R. N. *Dual Career Families.* Middlesex, England: Penguin Books, 1971a.

Rapoport, R., and Rapoport, R. N. "Further Considerations on the Dual-Career Family." *Human Relations,* 1971b, *24* (6), 519–533.

Rapoport, R., and Rapoport, R. N. *Dual-Career Families Reexamined—New Integrations of Work and Family.* New York: Harper & Row, 1976.

Rappaport, A. F., and Harrel, J. E. "A Behavioral Exchange Model for Marital Counseling." In A. S. Gurman and D. G. Rice (eds.), *Couples in Conflict.* New York: Aronson, 1975.

Reich, M. H. "Executive Views from Both Sides of Mentoring." *Personnel,* 1985, *62* (3), 42–46.

Reif, W. E., Newstrom, J. W., and Monczka, R. M. "Exploding Some Myths About Women Managers." *California Management Review,* 1975, *17* (4), 72–79.

Report of the Committee on Human Resource Accounting. In H. R. Anton, P. A. Firmin, and H. D. Grove (eds.), *Contemporary Issues in Cost and Managerial Accounting.* (3rd ed.) Boston: Houghton Mifflin, 1978.

Rice, D. G. *Dual-Career Marriage, Conflict, and Treatment.* New York: Macmillan, 1979.

Richter, J. "Switching Gears Between the Office and the Living Room." Paper presented at the 45th annual meeting of the Academy of Management, San Diego, Aug. 1985.

Ritchie, R. J., and Moses, T. L. "Assessment Center Correlates of Women's Advancement into Middle Management: A Four-Year Longitudinal Analysis." *Journal of Applied Psychology,* 1983, *68* (2), 227–231.

Rodriguez, R. A. "How to Judge Your Day-Care Options." *Personnel Administrator,* Aug. 1983, *28,* 41–44.

Rogan, H. "Young Executive Women Advance Farther, Faster Than Predecessors." *Wall Street Journal,* Oct. 26, 1984a, pp. 33, 36.

Rogan, H. "Women Executives Feel That Men Both Aid and Hinder Their Careers." *Wall Street Journal,* Oct. 29, 1984b, p. 35.

Rogan, H. "Executive Women Find It Difficult to Balance Demands of Job, Home." *Wall Street Journal,* Oct. 30, 1984c, p. 31.

Rose, G. L., and Andiappan, R. "Sex Effects on Managerial Hiring Decisions." *Academy of Management Journal,* 1978, *21* (1), 104-112.

Rosen, B., and Jerdee, T. H. "Sex Stereotypes in the Executive Suite." *Harvard Business Review,* Mar.-Apr. 1974, *52,* 45-48.

Rosen, B., Jerdee, T. H., and Prestwich, T. L. "Dual-Career Marital Adjustment: Potential Effects of Discriminatory Managerial Attitudes." *Journal of Marriage and the Family,* 1975, *37* (3), 565-572.

Rosen, J. L., and Palmer, M. B. "Retirement Adaptations and Self-Concept in Professional Women." Paper presented at the 90th annual meeting of the American Psychological Association, Washington, D.C., Aug. 1982.

Rosen, M. D. "Marriage is Back In Style . . . with a Difference." *Ladies Home Journal,* June 1985, pp. C11, 6, 98-102, 159, 161.

Rosenberg, M. *Society and the Adolescent Self-Image.* Princeton, N.J.: Princeton University Press, 1965.

Rueschemeyer, M. *Professional Work and Marriage.* London: Macmillan, 1981.

Safilios-Rothschild, C. "The Dimensions of Power Distribution in the Family." In H. Grunebaum and J. Christ (eds.), *Contemporary Marriage: Structure, Dynamics, and Therapy.* Boston: Little, Brown, 1976.

Sandell, S. H., and Shapiro, D. "The Theory of Human Capital and the Earnings of Women: A Reexamination of the Evidence." *Journal of Human Resources,* 1978, *8,* 102-117.

Scanzoni, J., and Fox, G. L. "Sex Roles, Family, and Society: The Seventies and Beyond." *Journal of Marriage and the Family,* 1980, *42,* 743-756.

Scanzoni, J., and Szinovacz, M. *Family Decision Making.* Beverly Hills, Calif.: Sage, 1980.

Schein, E. H. *Career Dynamics: Matching Individual and Organizational Needs.* Reading, Mass.: Addison-Wesley, 1978.

Scholl, J. "Corporations of the Year." *Savvy,* June 1983, pp. 30–37.

Schwartz, E. B., and MacKenzie, A. "Time Management Strategy for Dual-Career Women." *Business Quarterly,* 1977, *42* (3), 32–41.

Schwartz, E. B., and Waetjen, W. B. "Improving the Self-Concept of Women Managers." *Business Quarterly,* 1976, *41* (4), 20–27.

Sears, S. "A Definition of Career Guidance Terms: A National Vocational Guidance Association Perspective." *Vocational Guidance Quarterly,* 1982, *31* (2), 137–143.

Sekaran, U. "An Investigation of the Career Salience of Men and Women in Dual-Career Families." *Journal of Vocational Behavior,* 1982a, *20* (1), 111–119.

Sekaran, U. "Prospects for Enhancing the Quality of Life in Dual-Career Families." Working Paper, Southern Illinois University, Carbondale, 1982b.

Sekaran, U. "Factors Influencing the Quality of Life in Dual-Career Families." *Journal of Occupational Psychology,* 1983a, *56* (2), 161–174.

Sekaran, U. "How Husbands and Wives in Dual-Career Families Perceive Their Family and Work Worlds." *Journal of Vocational Behavior,* 1983b, *23* (3), 288–302.

Sekaran, U. "Paths to Mental Health: An Exploratory Study of Husbands and Wives in Dual-Career Families." *Journal of Occupational Psychology,* 1985a, *58* (2), 129–137.

Sekaran, U. "Understanding the Dynamics of Self-Concept of Members in Dual-Career Families." Paper presented at the 45th annual meeting of the National Academy of Management, San Diego, Aug. 1985b.

Sekaran, U., and Snodgrass, C. R. "Organizational Effectiveness: A Cultural Perspective." Working Paper, Southern Illinois University, Carbondale, 1985.

Sekas, M. H. "Dual-Career Couples—A Corporate Challenge." *Personnel Administrator,* Apr. 1984, *29,* 37–45.

Shuman, E., and Shuman, C. "Battling the Ax." *Savvy,* June 1983, pp. 17-20.

Skinner, D. A. "Dual-Career Family Stress and Coping: A Literature Review." *Family Relations,* 1980, *29,* 473-481.

Smith, P. E., Kendall, L. M., and Hulin, C. L. *The Measurement of Satisfaction in Work and Retirement.* Skokie, Ill.: Rand McNally, 1969.

Smith, W. J. "Review of Comparable Worth." *Management World,* July-Aug. 1985a, *14,* 13-14.

Smith, W. J. "What You Should Know About Comparable Worth." *Management World,* July–Aug. 1985b, *14,* 12-14.

Sorensen, J., and Winters, C. J. "Parental Influences on Women's Career Development." In S. H. Osipow (ed.), *Emerging Woman: Career Analysis and Outlook.* Westerville, Ohio: Merrill, 1975.

Staines, G. L., and Pleck, J. H. "Nonstandard Work Schedules and Family Life." *Journal of Applied Psychology,* 1984, *69* (3), 515-523.

Staines, G. L., Pleck, J. H., Shepard, L. J., and O'Connor, P. "Wives' Employment Status and Marital Adjustment: Yet Another Look." *Psychology of Women Quarterly,* 1978, *3* (1), 90-120.

Stake, J. E. "Women's Self-Estimates of Competence and the Resolution of the Career/Home Conflict." *Journal of Vocational Behavior,* 1979, *14* (1), 33-42.

Steers, R. M., and Braunstein, D. N. "A Behaviorally Based Measure of Manifest Needs in Work Settings." *Journal of Vocational Behavior,* 1976, *9* (2), 251-266.

Stewart, A. J., and Winter, D. G. "Self-Definition and Social Definition in Women." *Journal of Personality,* 1974, *42* (2), 238-259.

Streib, Y., and Beck, R. W. "Older Families: A Decade Review." *Journal of Marriage and the Family,* 1980, *42* (4), 937-956.

Stringer-Moore, D. M. "Impact of Dual-Career Couples on Employers: Problems and Solutions." *Public Personnel Management,* 1981, *10* (4), 393-401.

Sullivan, A. *The Father's Almanac.* New York: Doubleday, 1980.

Sundal-Hansen, L. S. "Interrelationship of Gender and Career." In N. C. Gysbers and Associates (eds.), *Designing Careers: Counseling to Enhance Education, Work, and Leisure.* San Francisco: Jossey-Bass, 1984.

Super, D. E. "Perspectives on the Meaning and Value of Work." In N. C. Gysbers and Associates (eds.), *Designing Careers: Counseling to Enhance Education, Work, and Leisure.* San Francisco: Jossey-Bass, 1984.

Thomas, E. G. "Update on Alternate Work Methods." *Management World,* Jan. 1982, *11,* 30-32.

Thomas, K. "Conflict and Conflict Management." In M. D. Dunnette (ed.), *Handbook of Industrial and Organizational Psychology.* Skokie, Ill.: Rand McNally, 1976.

Thomas, S., and others. "Determinants of Marital Quality in Dual-Career Couples." Paper presented at the 90th annual meeting of the American Psychological Association, Washington, D.C., Aug. 1982.

Thompson, P., Keele, R., and Couch, V. "What Managers Can Learn from Their Subordinates." *Management Review,* July 1985, pp. 28-32.

Toufexis, A. "The Perils of Dual Careers: Married Couples Who Work Are Crowding Therapists' Offices." *Time,* May 13, 1985a, p. 67.

Toufexis, A. "Giving Goodies to the Good." *Time,* Nov. 18, 1985b, p. 98.

Unger, R. K. *Female and Male.* New York: Harper & Row, 1979.

Wagner, F. R., and Morse, J. T. "A Measure of Individual Sense of Competence." *Psychological Reports,* 1975, *36* (2), 451-459.

Walker, E. J. " 'Til Business Us Do Part?" *Harvard Business Review,* Jan.-Feb. 1976, *54,* 94-101.

Walker, J. W., and Gutteridge, T. J. *Career Planning Practices.* New York: AMACOM, 1979.

Wallston, B., Foster, M. A., and Berger, M. "I Will Follow Him: Myth, Reality, or Forced Choice: Job-Seeking Experiences of Dual-Career Couples." *Psychology of Women Quarterly,* 1978, *3* (1), 9-22.

Walsh, W. M. *A Primer in Family Therapy.* Springfield, Ill.: Thomas, 1980.

Wanous, J. P. *Organizational Entry: Recruitment, Selection, and Socialization of Newcomers.* Reading, Mass.: Addison-Wesley, 1980.

Watkin, E. "Career and Family: The Juggling Act of the '80s." *Today's Office,* Aug. 1983, pp. 42-52.

Watkins, L. "Executive Fathers Start Preparing Their Daughters for Corporate Life." *Wall Street Journal,* Oct. 25, 1985, p. 21.

Weingarten, K. "The Employment Pattern of Professional Couples and Their Distribution of Involvement in the Family." *Psychology of Women Quarterly,* 1978a, *3* (1), 43-52.

Weingarten, K. "Interdependence." In R. Rapoport and R. N. Rapoport (eds.), *Working Couples.* New York: Harper & Row, 1978b.

Wessel, D. "Working Fathers Feel New Pressure Arising from Child-Rearing Duties." *Wall Street Journal,* Sept. 7, 1984, pp. 29, 45.

"What's New in Career Development." *Career Development Bulletin.* Vol. 1, no. 1. New York: Columbia University, 1979.

"When Career Couples Have Conflicts of Interest." *Business Week,* Dec. 13, 1976, pp. 86-90.

White, C. M., Crino, D. M., and DeSanctis, G. L. "A Critical Review of Female Performance, Performance Training, and Organizational Initiatives Designed to Aid Women in the Work-Role Environment." *Personnel Psychology,* 1981, *34* (4), 227-248.

Williams, S. W., and McCullers, J. C. "Personal Factors Related to Typicalness of Career and Success in Active Professional Women." *Psychology of Women Quarterly,* 1983, 7 (4), 343-357.

Winter, D. G., Stewart, A. J., and McClelland, D. C. "Husband's Motive and Wife's Career Level." *Journal of Personality and Social Psychology,* 1977, *35* (3), 159-166.

Yankelovich, D., and Lefkowitz, B. "American Ambivalence and the Psychology of Growth." *National Forum,* 1982a, *62* (3), 12-15.

Yankelovich, D., and Lefkowitz, B. "Work and American Expectations." *National Forum,* 1982b, *62* (2), 3-5.

Yogev, S. "Do Professional Women Have Egalitarian Marital Relationships?" *Journal of Marriage and the Family,* 1981, *43* (4), 865-871.

Young, J. "The Traditional American Family." Paper presented at annual convention of the American Personnel and Guidance Association, Atlanta, Ga., Mar. 1980.

Young, M., and Willmott, P. *The Symmetrical Family—A Study of Work and Leisure in the London Region.* Boston: Routledge & Kegan Paul, 1973.

Youngblood, S. A., and Chambers-Cook, K. "Child-Care Assistance Can Improve Employee Attitudes and Behavior." *Personnel Administrator,* Feb. 1984, *29,* 45-95.

Zigler, E. F., and Gordon, E. W. (eds.) *Day Care: Scientific and Social Policy Issues.* Boston: Auburn House, 1982.

Zuckerman, D. "Self-Esteem, Personal Traits, and College Women's Life Goals." *Journal of Vocational Behavior,* 1980, *17* (3), 310-319.

Zweig, C. "The Eleventh Megatrend." *Esquire,* May 1983, *99,* 138.

Name Index

Subject Index